Changing Schools places educational and social aims at the centre of a discussion of educational change. It draws on 14 case studies to explore school change which is oriented towards social justice and democracy.

In an age of global mobility, economic polarization and unprecedented environmental and cultural challenges, the education of all children and young people to higher levels has become a key issue of international policy. Educational reform in such a context requires a serious rethinking and reworking of school and classroom practices. Social justice is integral to the challenge of raising standards, since this requires removing the ongoing influence of poverty on school success.

This thoughtful book presents new thinking and practice for bringing about school change, drawn from diverse contexts around the world. It distils and compares the experiences and theories-in-action of engaged teachers, school principals and academics. It seeks to challenge the dominance that human capital theories of school improvement currently hold on policy making. The authors draw on contemporary innovations in practice and theory and also long-standing traditions of alternative thinking and practice. Linking together and articulating other ways of conceiving of and implementing school change, it bases its findings on values of equality and global citizenship. It shows how schools can work to make different languages, knowledge, narratives and truths integral to the mainstream curriculum, everyday pedagogy, assessment and general culture of the school.

*Changing School*s is directed at all who are concerned with progressive school change and the promotion of democratic citizenship and social justice. It will prove an invaluable source of inspiration for all involved in schools, including teachers, headteachers, policy makers and those currently studying for school leadership positions.

Terry Wrigley is Visiting Professor of Education at Leeds Metropolitan University, UK.

Pat Thomson is Professor of Education in the School of Education at the University of Nottingham, UK.

Bob Lingard is Professor in the School of Education at the University of Queensland, Australia.

Changing Schools

Alternative ways to make a world of difference

Edited by Terry Wrigley,
Pat Thomson and Bob Lingard

Routledge
Taylor & Francis Group

LONDON AND NEW YORK

First published 2012
by Routledge
2 Park Square, Milton Park, Abingdon, Oxon OX14 4RN

Simultaneously published in the USA and Canada
by Routledge
711 Third Avenue, New York, NY 10017

Routledge is an imprint of the Taylor & Francis Group, an informa business

British Library Cataloguing in Publication Data
A catalogue record for this book is available from the British Library

Library of Congress Cataloging in Publication Data
Changing schools : alternative approaches to make a world of
difference / [edited by] Robert Lingard, Pat Thomson, Terry Wrigley.
– 1st ed.
       p. cm.
   Includes bibliographical references and index.
   1. School improvement programs – Cross-cultural studies.
   2. Critical pedagogy. I. Lingard, Bob. II. Thomson, Pat, 1948-
   III. Wrigley, Terry.
   LB2822.8.C525 2011
   371.2′07–dc22   2011004647

ISBN: 978-0-415-55859-4 (hbk)
ISBN: 978-0-415-55860-0 (pbk)
ISBN: 978-0-203-81820-6 (ebk)

Typeset in Galliard and Gills Sans
by HWA Text and Data Management, London
Printed and bound in Great Britain by
CPI Antony Rowe, Chippenham, Wiltshire

Contents

Illustrations

Figures

Table

Contributors

Leonie Arthur is a senior lecturer in early childhood education and the Head of the Early Childhood Program at the University of Western Sydney. Leonie's recent work in Australia and Chile focuses on curriculum that is responsive to social and cultural contexts and builds capacity. She was a member of the consortium that was awarded the tender to write *Belonging, Being and Becoming: The Early Years Learning Framework for Australia*. Recent publications include *The Early Years Learning Framework: Building Confident Learners* (2010) and *Stars are Made of Glass: Children as Competent and Creative Communicators* (2010) with Felicity McArdle and Marina Papic and *Programming and Planning in Early Childhood Settings* (2007, 4th edition), with Bronwyn Beecher, Elizabeth Death, Sue Docket and Sue Farmer.

Lori Beckett is the Winifred Mercier Professor of Teacher Education, Faculty of Education, Leeds Metropolitan University. A long-term advocate and academic partner in disadvantaged schools in Australia and in England, her research currently focuses on practitioner research; school–university partnerships; and policy aspects of the equity agenda. She works as an academic partner to a network of schools in Leeds, and nationally, as well as with academic colleagues to realize progressive educational policies and practices. Her forthcoming publications include 'Professional learning in community: academics and teachers working together to improve the education provision for disadvantaged students in schooling and higher education' (*Australian Educational Researcher*) and 'Engaging democratic educational politics against school closure' (*International Handbook of Urban Education*).

Bjørn Bolstad is headteacher of Ringstabekk School in southern Norway, a 'youth school' for 13- to 16-year-olds. He worked at the school previously as a teacher and deputy head, and has also taught at various other schools. His educational career began in youth work in downtown Oslo. He studied school leadership at the Norwegian School of Management and the University of Oslo. He edited and was co-author of the book *Moderne Pedagogikk*, a presentation of theory and pedagogical practice at Ringstabekk.

Roseli Salete Caldart was awarded her doctorate in education at the Federal University of Rio Grande do Sul, Brazil in 1999 for her studies of the Landless Workers Movement. She is pedagogical adviser to the Technical Institute for Education and Research on Agrarian Reform (ITERRA) based in Veranopolis, and coordinator for teacher qualification courses for education in rural areas (a partnership between ITERRA, the University of Brasilia and the Ministry of Education). Her experience includes philosophy of education, social movements in the countryside, school education and pedagogy of social movements.

Ola Erstad is Professor at the Institute for Educational Research, University of Oslo, Norway. He has been working both within the fields of media and educational research. He has published on issues of technology and education, especially on 'media literacy' and 'digital competence'. He is leader of a research group at the Faculty of Education, Oslo, called 'TransAction – learning, knowing and identity in the information society' and is leading a research project called 'Local literacies and community spaces – investigating transitions and transfers in the "learning lives" of Groruddalen', funded by the Norwegian Research Council. Recent publications are an article on 'Trajectories of remixing: digital literacies, media production and schooling' in *Digital Literacies* edited by C. Lankshear and M. Knobel (2008), and two articles in *Digital Storytelling, Mediatized Stories: Self-Representations in New Media* edited by K. Lundby (2008).

Susan Groundwater-Smith is Honorary Professor of Education in the Faculty of Education and Social Work at the University of Sydney. She has a long-term commitment to practitioner research, with a particular emphasis upon giving students an active voice in school-based enquiries. She has published widely in the area of teacher professional learning including: *Teachers' Professional Learning in an Age of Compliance* (with Nicole Mockler, 2009) *Connecting Inquiry and Professional Learning in Education* (edited with Anne Campbell, published by Routledge) and most recently, a three volume set, *Action Research and Professional Learning in Schools* (also edited with Anne Campbell, 2010).

Eric 'Rico' Gutstein teaches mathematics education at the University of Illinois – Chicago. His work includes teaching mathematics for social justice, Freirean approaches to teaching and learning, critical and culturally relevant urban education, and mathematics education policy. He has taught middle and high school mathematics in Chicago public schools, is author of *Reading and Writing the World with Mathematics: Toward a Pedagogy for Social Justice* (2006) and is co-editor of *Rethinking Mathematics: Teaching Social Justice by the Numbers* (2005). Rico is also a founding member of Teachers for Social Justice (Chicago) and is active in social movements against education privatization.

Margery Hertzberg is a lecturer in the School of Education at the University of Western Sydney and immediate past President of e:lit – The Primary English Teaching Association. She lectures in ESL, Drama and Literacy across pre-service and postgraduate programs. Her research investigates how educational drama methodology enhances children's language and literacy development, particularly children learning English as an Additional Language. Most of Margery's research is conducted in low SES schools in South Western Sydney.

Lynne Hinton is Adjunct Professor in the Faculty of Education at Queensland University of Technology, Brisbane, Australia, where she teaches the pedagogies of philosophical inquiry to pre-service and postgraduate students. She also works as an educational consultant. Lynne was principal of Buranda State Primary School in inner-city Brisbane for 14 years.

Bob Lingard is a professor in the School of Education at The University of Queensland and has previously been professor at the Universities of Sheffield and Edinburgh and Chair of the Queensland Studies Authority. His research deals with globalization and education policy, with a focus on social justice, inequality and gender. His most recent books include: *Globalizing Education Policy* (2010) with Fazal Rizvi, *Educational Research by Association* (2010) with Trevor Gale, *Boys and Schooling* (2009) with Wayne Martino and Martin Mills and *Transforming Learning in Schools and Communities* (2008) with Jon Nixon and Stewart Ranson.

Glenda McGregor is an early career academic at Griffith University, Queensland Australia. She teaches in the School of Education and Professional Studies and convenes the Graduate Diploma of Education (Secondary) Program. Her research interests include sociology of youth, social justice and education and educational reform. Recent articles include 'Engaging Gen Y in schooling: the need for an egalitarian ethos of education', (*Pedagogy, Culture and Society*, in press), 'Moving beyond "Y": the children of new times' (*Discourse: Studies in the Cultural Politics of Education*, 2010) and 'Educating for (whose) success? Schooling in an age of neoliberalism' (*British Journal of Sociology of Education*, 2009).

Martin Mills is a professor at the University of Queensland in the School of Education, where he is Director of Research and Graduate Studies. His research interests include gender, pedagogy, school reform and social justice issues in education. Recent books include *Boys and Schooling: Contexts, Issues and Practices* (2009) with Bob Lingard and Wayne Martino and *Troubling Gender in Education* (2009) with Jo-Anne Dillabough and Julie McLeod. He is also an editor of the international journal, *Discourse: Studies in the Cultural Politics of Education*.

Nicole Mockler is a lecturer in the School of Education at the University of Newcastle in Australia. She is a former teacher and school leader, and over the past decade has worked as an academic partner with a wide variety of schools and school systems. The current focus of her research and writing is teacher professional identity, teacher professional learning and practitioner inquiry, and her most recent books are *Teacher Professional Learning in an Age of Compliance: Mind the Gap* (with Susan Groundwater-Smith, 2009) and *Rethinking Educational Practice Through Reflexive Inquiry* (edited with Judyth Sachs, 2010).

Geoff Munns, associate professor at the University of Western Sydney, principally researches into ways to improve social and academic outcomes for educationally disadvantaged students, including those from Indigenous backgrounds. He has had active research and professional development involvement in educationally disadvantaged schools over a ten-year period. Before working at the University of Western Sydney, he had 25 years experience in schools serving poor communities as a classroom teacher, school executive and principal. As a university researcher his research has continued this strongly focused commitment to making schools and classrooms more productive for poor students.

Peter Renshaw is Head of the School of Education at the University of Queensland. His research has centred on reforming classroom practices based on sociocultural approaches to pedagogy. He has had a long commitment to social justice in education and offers courses for beginning teachers on how to provide quality educational opportunities for diverse student groups. With other colleagues he is engaged in a number of research projects investigating how to engage adolescents from marginalised social groups in learning at school and how to ensure their access to further education and employment. In recent years he has been inspired by teachers, such as Dr Ron Tooth, who have developed powerful and innovative pedagogies across many years of committed engagement with other teachers. This kind of collaboration has created a sense of hope and optimism for the transformative possibilities of high quality education open to all.

Lorna Rose is an artist and facilitator-researcher working in early years settings. She graduated from the Royal College of Art with an MA in mixed media textiles in 2000 and since 2004 has been part of Creative Partnerships (Culture, Creativity and Education) teaching and learning programme. She has taken part in a range of study tours within Europe to investigate how creativity can be used most effectively in early years development, including visits to Reggio Emilia in Italy, Denmark's forest schools and Sweden's pre-school provision. She is currently resident artist and Vice-Chair of Governors at Lillian de Lissa Nursery School, a *School of Creativity* based in Birmingham, and has written for E.Y.E magazine (*'Strength in Diversity'*, May 2009) and a chapter for *Turning Pupils Onto Learning* (2011), edited by Rob Elkington.

Chris Sarra, an Indigenous Australian, completed a Diploma of Teaching, a Bachelor of Education, a Master of Education and a PhD in Psychology. Chris experienced first-hand many of the issues faced by Indigenous students in his own schooling. After being a teacher, in the late 1990s Chris took on the challenges of Indigenous education as the Principal of Cherbourg State School in southeast Queensland. Chris is now the Executive Director of the Stronger Smarter Institute, which is making an impact in Indigenous education through engagement with principals, teachers, community leaders and Government. He has a book, *Strong and Smart* (2011).

Wayne Sawyer is an associate professor and Head of Research in the School of Education and a member of the Centre for Educational Research at the University of Western Sydney. He is a past Chair of the New South Wales Board of Studies English Curriculum Committee and an Honorary Life Member of both state and national English Teaching Associations. He currently researches in the areas of secondary English curriculum, curriculum history, effective teaching, literacy policy and pedagogy in low SES schools. Wayne has most recently edited *Charged with Meaning* (with Sue Gannon and Mark Howie, 2009) and *Imagination, Innovation, Creativity* (with Paul Brock, Don Carter and Jacqueline Manuel, 2009) and *Only Connect* (with Brenton Doecke and Mark Howie, 2006).

Gregory Smith is a professor in the Graduate School of Education and Counseling at Lewis and Clark College in Portland, Oregon, USA. He has been writing about environmental and place- and community-based education for the past 20 years and is the author or editor of the following books: *Reducing the Risk: Schools as Communities of Support* (with Gary Wehlage, Robert Rutter, Nancy Lesko and Ricardo Fernandez, 1989); *Education and the Environment: Learning to Live With Limits* (1991); *Public Schools That Work: Creating Community* (1993); *Ecological Education in Action* (with Dilafruz Williams, 1999); *Place-based Education in the Global Age: Local Diversity* (with David Gruenewald, 2008); and *Place- and Community-based Education in Schools* (with David Sobel, 2010).

Pat Thomson is Professor of Education in the School of Education at the University of Nottingham. A former school principal of disadvantaged schools, her research currently focuses on: the arts and creativity and school and community change; doctoral and research education; and the work of school leaders. She works as a consultant to the national Schools of Creativity programme. Her most recent books are *School Leadership: Heads on the Block?* (2009), *The Routledge Doctoral Students Companion* and *The Routledge Doctoral Supervisor's Companion* (with Melanie Walker, 2010) and *Researching Creative Learning: Issues and Methods* (with Julian Sefton-Green, 2010).

Susanne Thurn has been headteacher of the Laborschule (Laboratory School) at the University of Bielefeld, Germany, since 1990. She is also Honorary Professor of school education at the Martin-Luther-University, Halle-Wittenberg. Like all the teachers of the Laborschule she is an action researcher herself, and supervises much of the research done at the school. Her main areas of interest are heterogeneity in education, school development, inclusive schools, early foreign language teaching, mirroring results and performance of students and the teaching of history. Numerous writings have been published in German.

Ron Tooth is the founding Principal of the Pullenvale Environmental Education Centre and an applied educational researcher and leader in environmental education. Ron is the architect of Storythread pedagogy, which he initially researched in his doctorate, and has an extended history of professional engagement with teachers and students through the Pullenvale Environmental Education Centre and the Storythread approach, as well as through his scholarly inquiry into the forms of narrative and place-based pedagogy that emerged from this prolonged professional engagement. He is an adjunct professor in the School of Education at the University of Queensland.

Jill Wood is the headteacher of a challenging inner-city primary school in the north of England which has made transformational changes over the last five years. The school supports a culturally diverse community in an economically challenging area and is committed to improving outcomes for children and their families. She is the chair of the Local Family of Schools (16 primary and three secondary), chair of the Extended Services Joint Consultative Committee and sits on many strategic steering groups within the education authority.

Terry Wrigley is now a Visiting Professor of Education at Leeds Metropolitan University, having recently retired from the University of Edinburgh. His work centres particularly on issues of school change, with a focus on pedagogy and curriculum, democratic citizenship and social justice. He is editor of the journal *Improving Schools*. His books are: *The Power to Learn* (2000), *Schools of Hope* (2003) and *Another School is Possible* (2006).

Katina Zammit is a lecturer in the School of Education at the University of Western Sydney. She has previously worked on national and state literacy projects for the NSW Department of Education and as a primary literacy consultant. Her research deals with literacy pedagogy focusing on the integration of information and communication technologies (ICT). Her most recent work on the new learning environments curriculum and pedagogy framework has been published in journal articles and a book chapter. Her other research and publications focus on the teaching and learning of multiliteracies and new literacies.

Acknowledgements

We thank Anna Clarkson and Phillip Mudd at Routledge for their support of this book through proposal stage to reconceptualisation to this final edited collection. Their forbearance is very much appreciated.

We would also most sincerely thank Aspa Baroutsis, an experienced teacher and a PhD student at the University of Queensland, for her great work in getting the manuscript ready for submission to the publisher. Aspa: many, many thanks; your commitment to exactness and detail is very much appreciated.

Thanks as well go to all of the contributors who have met their deadlines and responded to editorial changes we have offered.

We are grateful to the Brazilian publisher Expressão Popular for allowing us to re-use and summarize extracts from Roseli Caldart's book *Pedagogia do Movimento Sem Terra*. We also thank Roseli for her agreement to this.

We thank one another for the contributions of each to this collection, from our first conversations through to the completion of the concluding essay, and for the stimulating debate that has arisen between us. This has been productive work and writing.

Bob thanks Carolynn Lingard for her support for all of his academic work over a very long period of time. He also thanks colleagues at the University of Queensland and those at the University of Edinburgh, where the three of us conceived this project. Pat thanks Randy Barber, without whose cups of tea and exhortations to stop work and go outside she would certainly be much less productive. She also wants to put on record the importance of the network of colleagues involved in the arts and creativity agenda to her continued optimism about schooling – even in troubled times. Terry thanks Kathy Wrigley for her support over many years and her tolerance on discovering that retirement from a full-time university post has done little to diminish his enthusiasm.

We thank Ron Tooth and Peter Renshaw, who provided the photos used in their chapter and gave permissions for their usage in this book. We also thank Lillian de Lissa Nursery and Belgravia Children's Centre's Lorna Rose for the photos included in Lorna Rose's chapter with Pat Thomson.

We all thank the many wonderful teachers who are acknowledged throughout this book and who have inspired us to edit and write this book, and all those who are active in campaigning for education and a better world.

Terry Wrigley, Pat Thomson and Bob Lingard

Chapter 1

Reimagining school change
The necessity and reasons for hope

Pat Thomson, Bob Lingard and Terry Wrigley

Introduction

Changing schools. This phrase can be read in two ways. The first is a description of schools being in a continual state of flux driven by social, cultural and economic shifts, and policy agendas. We are using it in a second and more positive sense to talk about changing schools for educative, democratic and socially just purposes. Of course, talking about changing schools immediately raises issues about who is driving change, for what ends, and in whose interests. And today, the idea of change inevitably draws our attention to the increasingly global contexts in which schools are located and the ways in which a range of technologies mediate who knows what and who is able to know about what.

Our collective research and experience strongly suggest that one of the key attributes of schools that change in educative ways is that, more or less explicitly, they work with deep funds of professional knowledge and theory. They mobilise and extend intellectual resources well beyond what is available in much current policy. They are not eclectic in their approach but are focused, pulling together a coherent mix of philosophies, commitments, practices, material resources and people. Together, these position their activities, events, programmes, stories and rewards and allow them to do what is required – and much more besides.

The purpose of this book is to make such intellectual resources and practices more broadly available. We offer these not as technical solutions but rather as contributions to the development of a more generous and generative imaginary of schools and what they can do. In doing so, we also hope to contribute to an alternative lexicon of change useful for teachers in their reflection and dialogue about the practices and purposes of their everyday work in classrooms and schools. We aim to provide some intellectual resources for continued hope, in a spirit of 'non-stupid optimism', as our colleague Erica McWilliam (2005) often puts it.

We worry that, as an institution, mass schooling still bears too many of the residues of its origins in an industrial age. This can be seen in

- the design of school buildings – where some classrooms still have raised platforms for teachers; the majority of schools are designed on the basis of one teacher–one class and, in secondary schools, where one child per desk remains the norm;
- curriculum assumptions – that knowledge emanates from the teacher and textbooks, that it comes in discrete units called subjects, and that children acquire it in an ordered, linear and timetabled fashion;
- the way that knowledge itself is conceived – namely, as a thing that can simply be transferred or delivered from the one who knows to the ignorant.

The weight of international research clearly shows that knowledge is a social construction, which is built collectively in often unpredictable interactions among teachers, children and young people, texts, family members, media and objects, and through events and experiences. It is ironic that, even though teachers understand that children learn in multiple ways and at different rates, the curriculum is built on the assumption of linear transmission, and official policy in some countries says the only way to deal with these differences is by tracking and setting. Teachers also recognise that, with the digitised world that young people live in, they have multiple sources of knowledge and modes of expertise, often unrecognised by the official curriculum. It is increasingly difficult to maintain the view that schools are enclosures cut off not only from their local community but also from the wider world. How this affects the role of teaching and the policies and practices of schools is debated too infrequently (Crook et al. 2010; Lankshear et al. 1997).

Too often, we believe, schools underestimate children and young people and focus, as Gonzales, Moll and Amanti (2005) suggest, on what children cannot do rather than what they can. This is because children are seen as empty vessels and not already possessed of knowledge, experiences, interests, concerns, languages, skills, competences and values. The educational challenge is how to construct a common set of learnings that respectfully accommodate the myriad cultural experiences of most student populations today. Unfortunately, this goal comes starkly up against the standardising imperatives of contemporary policy and accountability frameworks. This denial of difference is evident both in traditional forms of summative assessment, such as essay-driven examinations, and in contemporary forms of high-stakes testing. Designing curriculum as small measurable bites frames students as homogenous units, resulting in a pedagogy of the same, rather than pedagogies of and for difference (Lingard 2007).

The logical conclusion to these concerns is not a blind opposition to educational accountability but rather a recognition that we need richer and more intelligent genres. One of the hallmarks of an alternative accountability approach would be respect for teachers' professional judgement and a demand for sophisticated assessment literacy in all teachers – and also in education systems, with accountability working in multiple directions. Further, such accountability would work with communities and respect their funds of knowledge and aspirations for schools.

Whose change, whose schools?

Teaching is often seen as a craft-based occupation that some people are innately positioned to undertake rather than as a research-informed and research-informing profession (Lingard and Renshaw 2009). In some locations, it is almost impossible to suggest that teachers are knowledgeable and are capable of building a professional knowledge base. Because of the lack of trust in the profession – an attitude endemic in much contemporary policy even if denied by policy makers – it is assumed that directions for change need to come from elsewhere and be teacher-proof.

It seems to us that, with some notable exceptions, much international reform policy, as it floats between nation states in deeply de-contextualised ways, misrecognises specificity and professional expertise and therefore fails to deliver what it promises. In addition, the orthodox school reform literatures – often because of their narrow research base – have easily been co-opted into technical recipes for change (Thrupp and Wilmott 2003). Despite paying lip service to context, in reality much of this work overstates what it is that schools can achieve. When it does take account of social and economic context, it generally focuses on health and welfare needs alone, rather than acknowledging local cultural assets and strengths. There is also a widespread failure to acknowledge the need to redress wider structural inequalities. Though much of this school reform literature has either overlooked context or dealt with it in a narrow way, some earlier sociology of education emphatically denied all possibility of schools and school systems confronting inequality and underachievement. We disagree with both these positions: though there is irrefutable evidence that structural inequalities are reproduced from generation to generation, partly through schooling, there is also evidence that schools can make a significant difference. Just because schools can't do everything doesn't mean that they cannot achieve something; schools can make *a* difference but not *all the* difference.

We start from an understanding that individual schools and their communities can and do change for educative, democratic and socially just purposes. Such schools

- understand that though some communities have acute needs and troubling problems, they also have valuable assets in the form of histories, expertise, experience and networks;
- see differences as valuable resources, not only as bridges to the mandated curriculum but as valuable knowledges in and of themselves;

- see their school community as a polis, with citizenship rights for students, parents, community members and teachers;
- are committed to developing, extending and challenging students, refusing to accept that they are incapable of achieving the highest levels of learning;
- understand that the production and reproduction of privilege are complex processes that require clear thinking and considerable effort to redress;
- intervene in formal curriculum, pedagogy and assessment practices to allow students to demonstrate what they have learned;
- produce detailed interrogation of school structures, cultures and default settings;
- work within the mandated frameworks when and as they must but also seek to do much more;
- reflect upon, debate, and have dialogue about what they do, why they do what they do, and its individual and collective effects.

Such schools work within and against the grain of policy simultaneously. They do not simply acquiesce, unquestioningly adapt, or mutinously rebel. They strategically work out how to 'feed the bureaucracy' (Haberman 1999) while also doing what they as a school collectively have agreed is right and worthwhile. These schools take up and create opportunities to work together to oppose and change uneducative, regressive policies. Research, theory and professional experience are intellectual resources used by such schools to challenge these policies and also to justify and protect their own policies and practices. The focus of such schools is on learning – learning for teachers and community and for young people. It is also on serving rather than the provision of services. These schools enact education as a public good.

We are interested in how the intellectual resources – or the know-what and know-how – that are organically developed in these schools might be able to have a positive influence across broader systemic and policy settings: what some policy makers and policy commentators call 'capacity building' and 'scaling up'. The processes of making meaning and changing professional practice are more complex than are allowed for in such terms, which seem to imply that it is possible to locate two or three key 'levers' or 'recipes' through which change can be rolled out. Educational change involves negotiating a tangle of taken-for-granted ideas, practices, identities, histories and deeply held 'truths'. Bringing about change in systems that have evolved over long periods of time, and in which there are powerful vested interests committed to the status quo, is not an easy matter but requires hard intellectual and emotional work against the odds and, often, prevailing policy trends.

There are undeniably policy makers who simply wish to borrow or transfer what apparently 'works' in specific schools and 'roll it out' to every school, even across national educational systems. We reject this kind of one-best-blueprint approach, delivered top-down via websites, glossy publications and high-priced consultants. In rejecting this approach, we acknowledge the specificity, or this-ness, of each and every school (Thomson 2002) but also see the absolute necessity for systemic reform and policy learning. This would be systemic reform of a vastly different kind. Such a school system would work top-down, bottom-up and inside-outside. Most often in contemporary schooling systems, policies are developed at the top and ushered into schools, which are expected to simply implement them. Opposition to this often takes the form of arguing the reverse: that all policy should come from the grass roots of schools and communities – the bottom-up approach. By contrast, we see that both of these directions are essential and mutually informing: that is, we take a view that policy and the change it produces should be both top-down and bottom-up. Similarly, in opposing externally imposed change, some people want to argue that all developments should be entirely internally designed by a stand-alone school, perhaps in concert with a handful of like-minded others. We believe that external ideas can be helpful to a school, raise challenges, and provide new perspectives. Furthermore, localism cannot provide the kinds of common learnings to which all children and young people can lay claim as an entitlement of citizenship – and as an international human right. Finally, a commitment to equity and social justice demands that there be a system with a centralised capacity to redistribute the necessary resources to ensure that all young people have access to high-quality schooling and associated life chances.

The schooling system we envisage would be characterised by reciprocal relationships and richer mutual forms of accountability, where the giving of account works in multiple directions simultaneously. A significant step in this direction would be the development of 'opportunity-to-learn' standards where systems are held to account for what they provide to schools to ensure more equitable outcomes (Darling Hammond 2010). Another step would be to immediately remove draconian, punishment-driven regimes of naming, shaming, blaming, sacking and closing. No person or institution can undertake sustainable and productive change under threat. The accountability system we envisage would work with and enable schools to pursue a broad array of social, cultural and educative purposes, purposes well beyond those implicit in many contemporary accountability regimes that reduce educational accountability to test results. Such an approach would uncouple the relationship between the kinds of information needed by school systems to determine equity and develop capacity, and the sorts of formative and summative assessment that students require to learn. In our view, the current conflation of these is educationally destructive and often denies students the systematic feedback they need in order to make genuine progress.

In times when fragmentation (of institutions, communities and individuals) seems to be the order of the day, we are concerned with how the very idea of a schooling system might be rethought. At a broad level, such rethinking requires debating what kinds of nation states we want and, therefore, what kinds of education systems are not only desirable but possible.

Our wider concern is that nations should recognise difference and redistribute public 'wealth' and resources in ways that are fair. We want states that are democratically governed not by spin-dominated elites but by informed citizens who can respect and trust bureaucracies and professions, at the same time as they are respected and trusted by them. This demands a vibrant civic society and a vibrant state, and places demands on schooling to produce generations of educated local-global citizens.

Our conception of desirable educational change sits in stark contrast with the model of change that has dominated in the last 20 years, particularly in the most powerful Anglophone countries. This model of change has also been promoted by many international organisations and has steered change discourses in many countries across the globe. The model is directed toward greater efficiency of designated outputs through top-down, centralised change, and it requires comparability of student and school performance measured through international and national tests. This approach does generate data to judge whether schools and systems are equitable in terms of gender, ethnicity, or class (or something approximating it) and how much headway they are making to redress historical patterns of inequitable outcomes. Conversely, the system itself (re)produces the patterns it proposes to measure in part through the use of measures that conflate the needs of systems and schools, and also by using the data to produce competitive markets of school choice.

Tests focusing on limited aspects of basic literacy and numeracy have led to a narrowing of curriculum. Where testing becomes high-stakes, the requirement to meet targets can result in cheating at all levels, from selecting potentially high-achieving students, removing those who fail to produce the desired results, conducting educational triage on those who might fall just below the desired 'line', intensive teaching and leading to the test, substituting easier qualifications and curricula, and even to official bodies lowering pass marks and grade criteria. The fear of failure, experienced by students, teachers, and schools and school systems alike, leads to a pedagogical impoverishment where anxious teachers shift toward transmission pedagogies tightly orientated toward test items. These are the pedagogies of under-attainment (Lingard 2011; Luke 2010; Thomson et al. 2010) produced from the obsessive pursuit of short-term attainment targets and indicators of alleged effectiveness, which have undermined deeper-level and longer-term learning and achievement. Such high-pressure systems have generally failed to bring about greater equity of outcomes or educational experience; even where the average level of attainment has been raised, the gap between the highest- and lowest-achieving students has widened.

The socio-political rationale underlying the dominant reform policies has a business orientation, leading to the contractualisation and privatisation of administrative and educational system functions, the introduction of managerial practices into organisations, the introduction of markets into schooling via choice policies, and the promotion of entrepreneurialism at all levels of education. Children are often seen as 'human capital', curriculum relevance is justified solely in terms of vocational preparation, and teachers are delivery agents of predetermined services. What is often referred to as neoliberal discourse has reconstructed educational practices and ways of thinking (Rizvi and Lingard 2010).

The enlightened emphasis in much school improvement literature on engaging teachers emotionally and intellectually in the change process is in sharp contrast with centralised control over curriculum, teaching and school organisation. Often school leadership, whether seen as transactional or transformational, solo or distributed, has been reduced to drawing on systems and personal charisma to bring about the compliance of teachers into the top-down agenda. In Helen Gunter's words:

> The neo-liberal version of the performing school requires teachers and students to be followers, but to feel good about it... The problems of education have been laid at the door of teachers while their capacity for finding solutions has been taken away. The rhetoric has been of empowerment, participation and teams, but the reality is that teachers have had to continue to do what they have always done – be empowered to do what they have been told to do.
>
> (2001:122, 144)

In addition, in many systems, centralised control operates variably; schools that are seen to perform have more freedom to innovate, whereas schools that struggle against the odds, those that have the most urgent needs and need the most support to do things differently, are subject to greater scrutiny and 'stick and carrot' regimes (Hargreaves 2003; Hursh 2008; Lingard 2010; Lipman 2004; Taubman 2009; Thomson and Sanders 2009).

Our combined experience of schools that have risen to the challenge of preparing young people for democratic citizenship and improving the life chances of marginalised students shows the tensions involved in manoeuvering in a tightly controlled system and policy environment, but also the possibilities. In order to do more than survive and manage to get by, schools need to draw on other forms of knowledge – pedagogical, curricular, political – than that which is provided through official channels. The biggest challenge facing school systems, schools and teachers today, in all parts of the world, is how to wind back the stark differences in achievement that are borne out of race and ethnicity, disability, gender and class. These differences are amenable to change, but interventions that will effect some redress must occur at multiple levels and across multiple locations. Furthermore, they must operate across multiple dimensions. We mean here that state policy agendas must be both *redistributive* – that is, put resources where they are most needed rather than where they have traditionally been placed and where they advantage those who are already advantaged – and *recognitive* – that is, see, hear and work with the individual and collective identities that comprise our complex multicultural societies. Here we are drawing on Nancy Fraser's (1997) argument that social justice requires both a politics of redistribution focused on reducing structural inequalities, and a politics of recognition that focuses on valuing and working with differences.

In schooling, redistribution and recognition are enacted through change agendas that

- do not see educational change as being the job of education systems alone. Changes in housing, health and transport policy, for example, and those concerned with employment and the labour markets, income support and welfare benefits all profoundly affect the everyday lives and life chances of children and young people.
- do not see change in schooling as a matter only for school policy; educational provision for adults/parents, not about parenting, but which is both general and vocational, plays out in a greater range of cultural resources available in the home; the initial and continuing education of teachers is, of course critical to the education that is available to children and young people.
- work from understandings that schools in the most challenging contexts have to do more with less; they need additional material resources, staffing procedures that support them to get the right staff and keep them, integrated health and welfare services to support troubled and troublesome children and young people, and the permission and resources to carry on the hard intellectual work of making a difference.

School systems also need to work hand in hand with schools to change hard-to-shift historical patterns of inequity and injustice. The schools in this book are examples – but not exemplars or blueprints that can simply be copied – of ways of working that hold promise for renewed educational possibilities.

The difficulties of talking across cultures and internationationally

The chapters in this book use a varied terminology to refer to four key issues: young people in schools, teachers, pedagogy and change. Though we have encouraged authors to use the terms that are current in their own contexts, be they national or a particular type of school, we need to make our interpretation of these concepts clear. Indeed, we think such clarification is significantly linked to considerations of educative school change in the twenty-first century.

Though we have restricted our discussion to only four terms, we also know that all educators are faced with language that continually shifts and that part of the process of school-based change is the development of local definitions and meaning-making practices.

Young people in schools

Those to whom schools are meant to offer life chances and access to powerful knowledges are variously called children and young people, students, pupils and learners. These are English terms and, of course, others exist in other languages with no straightforward translations available and with connotations that don't align. These nomenclatures variously reflect, among other things, the age of the school cohort, the object of their engagement in schooling, historical lineage, cultural positioning, philosophical traditions and different professional discourses. We suggest that making language problematic is part of the process of making strange what is familiar about education, thus precipitating insight and debate. Our preferred term is *children and young people*, which allows for life beyond the school gates, sees each individual in a holistic way, and leaves indeterminate and available for local decision making the age at which children become young people. Interestingly, our research in England and Australia in both primary and secondary schools has suggested that *student* is now a preferred descriptor in both places.

Who is a teacher?

Vygotsky argues that the desire to teach is central to the definition of being human (Daniels 2001: 3). This recognition of the intergenerational task of social and cultural (re)production is often obscured by the equation of schooling and education and actually ignores not only the kinds of learning that occur outside school, but also what Bernstein (2001) has called 'the totally pedagogised society'. More pragmatically, we use *teacher* in this text to refer to educators located across all levels of education, including universities and including formal and informal leaders. An educative schooling system would, therefore, be one saturated in pedagogies. For us, the focus of a good schooling system is one that has learning as the centre of all of its activities. We are also troubled by a teaching/learning binary that assumes that children and young people cannot teach but must only learn, and that the adults who work with them are not themselves also learners. As we show in this book, teachers increasingly draw upon knowledges located outside the institution in real and virtual communities and neighbourhoods, and help children and young people to do the same.

What is pedagogy?

Is *pedagogy* just another pretentious academic word for teaching? We think not. It is perhaps helpful for us to say first what pedagogy is not. It is not just method or instruction. It is not equivalent to curriculum or assessment, but is rather the need for alignment between knowledge, curriculum, assessment, institutional mores and social context framed by understandings about the nature of knowledge, of reality and human society, of human capacity for learning and growth and of aspirations for a better future. The European origins of the term lie in an Enlightenment belief in the intrinsic worth of all human beings and the potential for personal and social improvement through education. We think that foregrounding this construction of pedagogy, rather than using a reductive technical definition, is important for placing the entire child and young person, and children and young people collectively, at the centre of schooling rather than subjects, classes, lessons, learning objectives, data, testing regimes and school reputation. It also foregrounds the nature of teachers' work and demonstrates its cultural and social significance; it supports a practice of teacher education rather than a narrow training; and requires a policy agenda that would involve teachers centrally in both policy production and practice.

Change, improvement and reform?

It seems these days that any change is an improvement and any reform is a good development. These words have become hollowed out, able to become containers for whatever governments or systems or lobby groups desire, however inequitable, undemocratic or irrational. Educational change is often reduced to alleged economic gains, and narrow constructions of efficiency and effectiveness dominate the educational policy agendas of many countries. Equity is reduced to the distribution of test results against population categories that purport to stand for deep social divisions of class, gender, race, religion and ethnicity. There is no new lexicon that we can find, and thus, in this book, we have used the term *change*, but always co-located with considerations of the broader purposes of schooling in a digitised, globalised and profoundly unjust world facing serious ecological challenges.

What is on offer in this book

This book is focused on the intellectual resources that schools use and might use to think through and accomplish the work of change. As we have already intimated, our research (Thomson 2002, 2009) suggests strongly that those schools that undertake the most innovative change draw on a range of 'thinking tools'. These are drawn from a wide range of sources: academic disciplines, historical and contemporary examples, social movements and political engagements, in addition to their own practices and those of other schools.

We see that all practice is embedded in theory, whether explicit or not, and that all theory has an imagined practice. Our basic premise is that there is nothing as practical as good theory. We reject the notion that the best ideas and innovations come either from outside schools or inside them. We see that both occur. For us, it is not a question of either/or but how educational knowledges constructed in many places are debated and realised in the micropolitics of schools and classrooms and in dialogue with school communities. In this book, we have sought to show ideas generated within individual schools or networks of schools, and ideas developed by academics working with schools, with various directions of flow of theory and practice.

The case studies in this book show the various purposes/philosophies taken up by some inspirational schools and groups of schools in a variety of locations around the world. Despite their particularities and differences, there are some trends apparent across these schools. Common to all of them are active experiential approaches to learning, attempts to shift traditional divisions of knowledge and what counts as valuable knowledge and how it might be evaluated and assessed. All of the schools demonstrate that it is possible to differentiate – that is, tailor-make the curriculum for the specific interests, concerns, languages, needs, identities and knowledges of particular individuals and groups of children and young people – without this becoming a means of creating hierarchies of 'ability'. There are various ways to group students that do not involve tracking and setting, and in this book they include new structures of collaborative learning, breaking the age-grade nexus, and using structures that keep groups of children and teachers together over longer periods of time. Indeed, the innovative use of space/time is a hallmark of much of this innovation, as is the recognition that deep and productive learning takes time. The schools reported here also share a commitment to putting identities and places at the centre of the curriculum to maximize relevance and connection and to work with and show respect for differences, as with Fraser's concept of 'recognition'. These changes are made possible through concerted efforts to share leadership across teachers and students and through meaningful, substantive conversations and rich partnerships with communities, other schools and universities. However, change in some of the cases has had to be managed within the frames of unsympathetic policy regimes, and it can be clearly seen that these schools are adept not only at managing the difficulties in their particular contexts, but at managing, tactically and strategically, the political tensions that arise in their particular national/provincial schooling systems.

The book also sets out to elaborate ideas. These are exemplified in many chapters, whereas in others they provide perspectives from which to critique current mainstream practices. Deconstruction of the problems with contemporary practice is always the starting point for generating new approaches, if not the end point. In our view, it is not productive to reject critique for its abstractions and distance from the everyday world of schools. Rather, the task is to look for what follows from the insights gained from critique and ascertain how they might help us think and do otherwise. Such critique is usually grounded in the specificities and materialities of a given schooling system. We suggest the need for wariness, then, in borrowing from these ideas grounded in such specificities and stress the importance of recontextualizing the ideas to the specific context of a particular schooling system or school. Good school leaders and good schools are always willing to learn, but through the lens of the needs of their particular location and institution.

Concluding comment

This book is offered, then, as a resource for optimism regarding contemporary school change. We think the practices and ideas reported here proffer some real grounds for hope. We are critical of many policies and developments in schooling systems around the globe and have contributed to critiques of them (e.g. Lingard 2007, 2010, 2011; Rizvi and Lingard 2010; Thomson 2002, 2009; Thomson et al. 2010; Wrigley 2000, 2003, 2006). The future we desire requires a rethought social imaginary, one stretching well beyond the failed reductivism and inequitable effects of the neoliberal project. It seems to us that despite the fallout from the global financial crisis, the neoliberal project remains the default setting for contemporary social and educational policy. We offer this collection as evidence of small narratives of progressive school change, and as thinking towards a reimagined future, which would result in reworked schooling systems and different policy frames, as part of a new social democratic social imaginary. Our future depends upon good schools, good school leaders and good teachers producing critical thinkers and local-global citizens, as well as challenging the intransigent nexus between student social class background, school learning and achievement. Our collection is thus offered in the spirit of Raymond Williams' (1983) insightful observation that progressive politics is always about making hope practical, rather than despair convincing. This is not stupid optimism: the chapters here provide good reasons for hope, and recognize the necessity of hope as we struggle toward a better future.

References

Bernstein, B. (2001) 'From pedagogies to knowledge.' In A. Marais et al. (eds) *Towards a Sociology of Pedagogy: The Contribution of Basil Bernstein to Research*. New York: Peter Lang.

Crook, C., Harrison, C., Farrington-Flint, L., Tomas, C., and Underwood, J. (2010) *The Impact of Technology: Value-Added Practice. Final Report*. London: BECTA.

Daniels, H. (2001) *Vygotsky and Pedagogy*. London: Routledge.

Darling Hammond, L. (2010) *The Flat World and Education: How America's Commitment to Equity Will Determine Our Future*. New York: Teachers College Press.

Fraser, N. (1997) *Justice Interruptus: Critical Reflections on the 'Postsocialist' Condition*. London: Routledge.

Gonzales, M., Moll, L., and Amanti, C. (2005) *Funds of Knowledge*. Mahwah, NJ: Lawrence Erlbaum.

Gunter, H. (2001) *Leaders and Leadership in Education*. London: Paul Chapman.

Haberman, M. (1999) *Star Principals: Serving Children in Poverty*. Indianapolis, IN: Kappa Delta Pi.

Hargreaves, A. (2003) *Teaching in the Knowledge Society: Education in the Age of Insecurity*. New York: Teachers College Press.

Hursh, D. (2008) *High-Stakes Testing and the Decline of Teaching and Learning: The Real Crisis in Education*. Lanham, MD: Rowman and Littlefield.

Lankshear, C., Bigum, C., Durrant, C., Green, B., Morgan, W., Murray, J., Snyder, I. and Wild, M. (1997) *Digital Rhetorics. Literacies and Technologies in Education – Current Practices and Future Directions*, vols. 1–3. Canberra: DEETYA.

Lingard, B. (2007) 'Pedagogies of indifference.' *International Journal of Inclusive Education, 11*(3), 245–266.

Lingard, B. (2010) 'Policy borrowing, policy learning: testing times in Australian schooling.' *Critical Studies in Education, 51*(2), 129–147.

Lingard, B. (2011) 'Changing teachers' work in Australia.' In J.Sachs and N. Mockler (eds) *Rethinking Educational Practice through Reflexive Research: Essays in Honour of Susan Groundwater-Smith*. Dordrecht: Springer.

Lingard, B., and Renshaw, P. (2009) 'Teaching as a research-informed and research-informing profession.' In A. Campbell and S. Groundwater-Smith (eds) *Connecting Inquiry and Professional Learning in Education International Perspectives and Practical Solutions* (pp. 26–39). London: Routledge.

Lipman, P. (2004) *High Stakes Education: Inequality, Globalization and Urban School Reform*. New York: Routledge.

Luke, A. (2010) 'Documenting reproduction and inequality: revisiting Jean Anyon's "social class and school knowledge."' *Curriculum Inquiry, 40*(1), 167–182.

McWilliam, E. (2005) 'Schooling the yuk/wow generation.' APC Monographs. Available online. http://research.acer.edu.au/apc_monographs/17 (Accessed 24 November 2010).

Rizvi, F., and Lingard, B. (2010) *Globalizing Education Policy*. London: Routledge.

Taubman, P. (2009) *Teaching by Numbers: Deconstructing the Discourse of Standards and Accountability in Education*. New York: Routledge.

Thomson, P. (2002) *Schooling the Rustbelt Kids: Making the Difference in Changing Times*. Crows Nest: Allen and Unwin.

Thomson, P. (2009) *School Leadership: Heads on the Block?* London: Routledge.

Thomson, P., and Sanders, E. (2009) 'Creativity and whole school change: an investigation of English headteachers' practices.' *Journal of Educational Change,* *11*(1), 63–83.

Thomson, P., Hall, C., and Jones, K. (2010) 'Maggie's day: a small scale analysis of English education policy.' *Journal of Education Policy, 25*(5), 639–656.

Thrupp, M., and Wilmott, R. (2003) *Educational Management in Managerialist Times: Beyond the Textual Apologists.* Buckingham: Open University Press.

Williams, R. (1983) *Towards 2000.* Harmondsworth: Penguin.

Wrigley, T. (2000) *The Power to Learn: Stories of Success in the Education of Asian and Other Bilingual Pupils.* Stoke-on-Trent: Trentham.

Wrigley, T. (2003) *Schools of Hope: A New Agenda for School Improvement.* Stoke-on-Trent: Trentham.

Wrigley, T. (2006) *Another School Is Possible.* London: Bookmarks.

Chapter 2

Making a difference through philosophy

Australia

Lynne Hinton

> In the space between the railway line and the creek not far from the city centre, nestle the old buildings and small grounds of [Buranda] State School. Outside, one of the multi-age classes is studying the local ecology; they have walked past the permaculture garden and the chicken coop... onto the banks of the creek. Inside, another group sits in a circle, focused and concentrating as they discuss 'what is fair?' in a philosophy class. Minds stretch... [Buranda] is a place where learning comes first.
>
> (Lingard et al. 2003: 80)

Introduction

Once, this was a vision – a dream in the imaginations of a principal, a group of teachers, children and parents. Now it is a reality. Buranda State School in inner-city Brisbane, Australia, is indeed a place where learning comes first.

This chapter runs from the appointment of a new principal until her leaving 14 years later. It describes the undertaking by the principal and teachers of serious pedagogical reform and the 'far-reaching and extraordinary' changes that occurred as a result (Department of Education, Science and Training [DEST] 2003: 8).

Context for change

Buranda caters to children in their first eight years of formal education. The neighbourhood is officially identified as low socio-economic and high migrant. It is also an area of high crime.

When the new teaching principal was appointed, enrolments had declined from several hundred to just 48. There were only two other teachers.

Buildings and grounds were in disrepair; there was very little parent involvement or, for various reasons, concern about student safety. The school offered no extracurricular activities such as instrumental music or interschool sport, and few computers were available.

Of greatest concern were the students, who showed no joy, and little interest, in learning. School simply had to be endured. Not surprisingly, academic results were poor, with the children unable to apply their skills to real situations. Student learning needed to be brought to the forefront unequivocally.

The following sections describe this process and the extraordinary outcomes achieved.

Creating the vision

The process of reinventing the school began with the big question: Why do schools exist? The principal, teachers, support staff, parents and a visiting educational adviser agreed that schools exist to help children to become as good as they can be in everything they do. Every single one of them. The Melbourne Declaration, echoing sentiments from previous Declarations, states that 'schools play a vital role in promoting the intellectual, physical, social, emotional, moral, spiritual and aesthetic development and wellbeing of young Australians' to build a 'democratic, equitable and just society' (MCEETYA 2008: 4). That's the core business of schools, and it's huge. The moral purpose of education is equity and excellence. *Every single child, as good as they can be.*

The focus then moved to an environmental scan of the school itself. With a spirit of openness and honesty, participants identified things that were being done well and things that could be done better. The teachers were asked, 'What do you believe about children and learning? What would you like to see happening in this school? What would your ideal school look like?' They questioned their personal teaching philosophies, reflected on their own practice, and discussed educational issues. Individual beliefs, talents and passions were identified. It quickly became clear that this was a small group of highly competent, talented, dedicated educators with very clear ideas on what they believed about teaching and learning (Hinton 2003: 49). Out of the process came a shared vision for Buranda. Participants found they shared the belief that fundamental to children's achieving great things academically is the need for them to be happy and to feel safe, respected and valued at school – a sense of well-being. So they wanted their school to be supportive of all participants and with strong community involvement. Believing that a good environment lays the foundation for success in learning, they wanted a school where the values and beliefs of the students are openly respected.

Participants agreed that the key to academic success, once student well-being is established, is to engage the children intellectually – to acknowledge that children are clever, to expect great things of them, and to provide challenging and interesting experiences. They wanted their school to be a place where learning is creative, fun, joyful, exciting, surprising and challenging.

They wanted a school where children take their learning seriously, where they talk, accept mistakes as a normal part of learning, work hard and succeed beyond their expectations.

The resulting beliefs on which to rebuild the school can be described thus:

Wellbeing + Intellectual Engagement = Achievement

In addition, each of the three teachers was passionate about something in particular to do with educating children – multi-age classes, real-life learning and philosophy – and each accepted responsibility to promote this across the school.

Unpacking the vision

Well-being

Well-being + Intellectual Engagement = Achievement

Sizer (1992: 128) talks about good schools being thoughtful places where everyone is known. No one is ridiculed, no one is the servant of another, the work is shared. He describes an environment of 'common sense and civility'. It is a school that is 'compassionate, respectful and efficient' (Sizer 1992: 45).

Well-being of all would be centred on the development of a community of learners based on fairness and respect. Children (and adults) would always be given a fair hearing, everyone would strive to see the other's point of view and disagreements would be explored reasonably and respectfully. The personhood of each child and adult would be respected and appreciated. Time would be taken to find the 'goodness' in others.

The first step was to communicate to the children that they were a vital part of the changes taking place. That what they thought mattered.

As Warner (2006: 47) points out, '[T]here must be a commitment from the leadership and staff of a school to completely refocus from an environment that values adult knowledge and authority to one that shares knowledge creation and authority with young people'.

Students were asked, 'What makes a good school?' and 'How do you want your school to be?' and their responses, along with the values and beliefs of the wider school community, formed the basis for the Supportive School Environment Plan. At each stage of the process, the draft was taken back to the students for their input, a responsibility they took very seriously. As a result, management of behaviour at Buranda rests on the values and beliefs of the children. The children are aware of this.

The emphasis in managing behaviour is not on 'crime and punishment' but on dealing with issues as they arise, listening carefully and talking calmly to one another, finding acceptable ways to deal with anger, and discussing ways of redressing wrongs and avoiding further occurrences. Children will seek adult help when needed and often choose to deal with playground problems in the forum of a class meeting. This is encouraged. Teachers will always take time to prevent or address playground problems, however minor they appear.

The student population was and remains diverse – academically, culturally, socio-economically and behaviourally. Currently, there are students who are seriously gifted academically and a large number who require one-to-one support to achieve some degree of success. There is a small group of children with extremely high needs. Upward of 8 per cent of the student population speaks English as a second language – fewer than was the case in previous years. This includes several refugee families from the Horn of Africa. A wide range of family and socio-economic structures is represented, and the current ratio of boys to girls is 4:3. For several years, Buranda has accepted students who may not be succeeding at other schools. These students, mainly boys, usually have a history of suspension or exclusion. To date, all these children have eventually responded to the trusting environment at Buranda, becoming productive and settled.

For such an interesting and diverse group, the notion of equity takes on great importance. Pedagogies reflective of and conducive to allowing each learner to progress at his or her own pace become crucial to success. One means by which this is accomplished is through mixed-age classes. The original environmental scan indicated that one teacher believed passionately in engaging pedagogies, such as a multi-age structure, to focus on individual needs, thus allowing each child to work to her or his potential. Inherent in that structure is the need for children to become independent, self-directed learners, to take a share of the responsibility for their learning and to become aware of their own capacities. Inherent, too, is the positive contribution to be made by cooperative group learning, ensuring students learn to negotiate, collaborate and solve problems amicably and productively together.

Multi-age structures had been part of the school through necessity, because of the small enrolments. Cooperative learning was being done well by that teacher in her own classroom. The decision was made to commit to a multi-age structure even when it was no longer needed. The decision was made also that all teachers would learn about and implement cooperative group learning strategies in their classrooms (Hinton 2003).

This focus on the well-being of all who learn at Buranda has justifiably earned a 'reputation of respect for all' (Lingard et al. 2003: 81).

Intellectual engagement

Well-being + *Intellectual Engagement* = Achievement

Feeling happy and safe at school is necessary but not sufficient: students must also feel challenged. There should be a sharp, clear focus on the academic program (Sizer 1996). Opportunities must be provided for children to ask questions, follow leads, puzzle over paradoxes, hypothesize, try out ideas and discover new learnings for themselves and with others. This was to be a school where children take their learning seriously, where they talk, make mistakes, work hard and succeed beyond their expectations. As Lipman et al. (1980: 13) explain, '(Children) will not acquire meaning by learning the contents of adult knowledge. They must be taught to think, and in particular, to think for themselves'. Aristotle argued that what sets people apart from other living things is their capacity to think and acquire wisdom. He says we are the most human when we think, and we are best when we think well and attain wisdom.

At Buranda, a culture of thinking would be established. Thinking and learning would be enjoyable and fun, with the expectation that this would engender in the children a disposition toward being successful learners (Warner 2006). Children would be given frequent opportunities to engage in open-ended and collaborative problem solving, to explore the big issues of life and to undertake relevant and meaningful tasks: real-life learning.

A prime example is using the outdoor environment. The previous principal had built a permaculture garden and a rainforest area, but they were not being used to the best advantage for learning. These days the students take responsibility for the chickens, the frog-breeding program and the worms. Students grow and pick, weigh, cook and eat vegetables. The garden is often so productive that the students sell vegetables to the school community. This involves discussing marketing strategies, designing and making posters, developing rosters, deciding on costing and running the stall. Each week a junior class uses the chickens eggs and lettuce from the garden to make egg and lettuce sandwiches to sell to the teachers. The students appointed a class accountant (who had to write an application for the job) and earned enough money to buy construction materials and reading books for their classroom (Hinton 2003).

At the creek, the students have undertaken wildlife surveys and graphed the results, they have tested the water for turbidity and pH levels and they have written scientific reports related to their results. They have worked with the council to revegetate the banks of the creek.

Some of the older students noticed a lot of dead fish in the creek. They wrote to the local councillor, the Brisbane daily newspaper, the local paper, the Department of the Environment and their member of state parliament. They had a response from the council, made the front page of the local paper, and had a visit from a Department of the Environment officer, who explained what had been done and what had been found and who thanked the children for alerting the department to the problem. They were also visited by the local member of state parliament, to whom they presented a petition. This was subsequently tabled in parliament (Hinton 2003).

The intellectual engagement and real-life learning implicit in such activities are obvious.

Philosophy

Well-being + Intellectual Engagement = Achievement

The third teacher, who was also the principal, imagined a school where children could think clearly and have confidence in their own ideas. Where they were reflective and thoughtful, and listened to and respected one another's ideas. She imagined a place where the insatiable curiosity and excitement for discovery that children bring with them when they come to school stays with them throughout the school day and, ideally, throughout their school lives.

Plato said, 'Philosophy begins in wonder'. Small children wonder about everything, so philosophy at primary school seemed like a place to begin. Would it be possible to build on the insatiable curiosity of childhood, the perpetual awe and wonderment of children? It was worth a try.

Philosophy would be taught to all children at the school. Philosophy for Children was begun by Mathew Lipman in the early 1970s. Like Dewey before him and others, Lipman emphasized the central place in school education of learning to think (Dewey 1966, 1997; Lipman 2003; Sizer 1992). Both Dewey and Lipman emphasized learning in community (i.e. with others) and learning through inquiry. This gives rise to the notion of a 'community of inquiry' – simply a community of learners inquiring together, albeit through rigorous ordered discussion (see Peirce 1955). When the focus of the inquiry is philosophical, it becomes a 'philosophical community of inquiry'.

Through philosophy, teachers at Buranda State School set about teaching the children to think. They were encouraged to wonder, imagine, question, puzzle, reflect and talk. They were taught to think about things on their own and to think about things together. They thought about things such as justice, freedom, truth, existence and fairness.

The teachers asked questions such as 'Is progress always a good thing?' and 'Where do your thoughts go when you have finished with them?' and the children asked questions such as, 'Do things only exist if someone is thinking about them?' 'Do we actually respect stronger people or are we just afraid?' and 'If you seek vengeance do you lose your freedom and become a slave?'

The manner in which the philosophical topic is discussed is ordered and rigorous, with children being expected to utilize the intellectual and inquiry skills they have been explicitly taught, such as giving examples and counter-examples, recognising mistakes in reasoning, making distinctions and building appropriate analogies. Children are also given many opportunities to reflect on their own progress and the progress of the group.

Philosophy was expected to improve academic results. This certainly happened, as is shown through much quantitative and qualitative data. As it turned out, the other critical element – well-being – was also addressed. In philosophy, through a classroom community of inquiry, both respect and reason are practised. By actively listening to one another, building on one another's ideas, exploring disagreements respectfully and accepting that there may be more than one correct answer, children are practising being respectful. They learn to be fair and open-minded, intellectually cooperative, and mutually respectful. By reflecting on prevailing beliefs, critically examining issues and ideas, exploring possible alternatives and giving and accepting reasons, children learn to be reflective, sensitive to meaning, divergent and reasonable. Children become thoughtful, reasonable citizens, able to make reasoned judgements. As Sizer (1996: 155) suggests, 'Philosophy... is an enabling subject'.

Achievement

Well-being + Intellectual Engagement = *Achievement*

The Hon. Dean Wells, speaking to the Queensland parliament on 9 February, 2010, described Buranda State School children as having learned

> the philosopher's skills: the ability to sort the relevant from the irrelevant [and] the ability to recognize when an argument leads to absurdity or self-contradiction.

and also

> the philosopher's virtues: the willingness to follow the argument where it leads, even if it does not go where you want it to; the understanding that there are two sides to an argument; and the strength to contemplate that you might be wrong.
>
> (Queensland Parliament 2006: 106)

The teaching of philosophy is now firmly entrenched at Buranda State School. It underpins and integrates all curriculum offerings. It has led to an improvement in social skills and in the engagement and happiness of students.

These are children who now demonstrate critical, creative and caring thinking well beyond what would normally be expected. These are children who are wonderful problem solvers, who can devise ingenious and creative solutions. These are children who seek out new ways of doing things and who have an insatiable curiosity about life and learning.

Buranda students had performed below the state average in year 6 tests. Qualitative changes began to appear within six months of the introduction of philosophy, with students becoming more reflective. There was also an unexpected 'settling' in the playground. (A visiting researcher at the time commented, 'Your children don't fight, they negotiate.')

About 18 months after the introduction of philosophy, results improved markedly and have been maintained or improved upon since that time. For the last ten years of the state testing program, Buranda students scored above or well above the state average.

This is not because Buranda 'gets all the good kids'. Indeed, up to 2007, its year 2 children achieved below average in state screening tests, yet in years 3, 5 and 7 they achieved above average.

From 48 students, the school now has up to 214. No more than this can be accommodated within the current facilities. Students from the identified catchment area are the only ones who are assured of a place at the school, with some families moving into the area to ensure enrolment for their children.

Buildings and grounds continue to be improved, extracurricular offerings are many and varied, and there is a high level of parental involvement and support. Systemic School Opinion Surveys indicate that parents are extremely satisfied with the education their children are receiving, the fair treatment of their child, student behaviour and child safety. In 2008, 97 per cent of parents at Buranda State School nominated this as 'a good school' (see Buranda Annual Report 2008).

Reflections on leadership

The core business of any school is teaching and learning for all students – excellence and equity. The central purpose of school leadership is, therefore, 'the maximization of students' academic and social outcomes' (Lingard et al. 2003: 19). Everything the school leader does must be directed toward successful student learning.

There are common threads that a school leader must attend to: vision, purpose and goals; a focus on curriculum, pedagogy and assessment; capacity building; dispersal of leadership; and social relations within the school. These can be recognized in the change process at Buranda. Two other considerations are particularly relevant: 'a bias for reflective action' and 'persistence and flexibility in staying the course' (Fullan 2006: 8).

Vision, purpose and goals

Using the beliefs, values and passions of the teachers and parents at the time, a common purpose and direction were developed, owned and acknowledged by all. One parent commented that parents were 'thrilled with this innovative, teacher-driven response to increasing the academic and personal skills of our children'.

A focus on curriculum, pedagogy and assessment

Many change theories are flawed because they lack a focus on changing pedagogy (Fullan 2006: 5). At Buranda, the changes were fundamentally linked to pedagogy – to improving the ways in which teachers practised their craft and thus engaged learners. This was done through multi-age groupings, real-life learning and the development of a thinking culture by teaching all students philosophy.

Capacity building

A professional learning community developed as the teachers sought to become experts in teaching philosophy. The improved learning outcomes of the students led to a huge amount of interest being shown in philosophy across Australia. The school is now held in high esteem within Australia and around the world; it has received many awards for the teaching of philosophy and was even featured at the United Nations Educational, Scientific and Cultural Organization (UNESCO, Paris, France) on World Philosophy Day in 2005.

All permanent teachers at the school, through university-based training, are now qualified to lead professional development activities in philosophy. They have trained more than 400 teachers in all states of Australia, including remote communities, and overseas.

From being part of a school that no one seemed to want to go to, the staff now feel part of something successful, and their work is publicly acknowledged and appreciated. Their work provides enjoyment, satisfaction, challenges, the chance to learn from and teach others, and the opportunity to make mistakes safely. They visit one another's classrooms to observe good practice, talk together and celebrate successes. They are keen to improve their own practice through professional development opportunities, and they are committed to doing the best that they can. They have become a group of highly competent, professional individuals who work well as a team.

Dispersal of leadership

From the outset, leadership was shared. Teachers became responsible and accountable for the program identified as their individual 'passion'. As the school grew, skills and talents of incoming staff were identified (usually by themselves), and they assumed responsibility for the implementation of that program. The principal took the view that whatever area of expertise was required, there was more than likely to be a person on staff who possessed that expertise. Though the principal usually had the final say (in the spirit of 'the buck stops here'), staff and students were, and still are, always involved in any decision.

Social relations within the school

The principal led the school with the fundamental belief that no one is better or worse than anyone else. This applied equally to children and adults and allowed her to honestly value others and their contribution. She endeavoured to be open and approachable and to never be too busy for anyone, particularly a child. The size of the school was important, because it meant not only that the principal knew everyone but that everyone knew everyone else, thus allowing a sense of what the children call 'family' to develop. At the same time, her leadership style was described in Lingard et al. (2001) as being a 'warm demandingness'. The energy put into student well-being has already been described, but the same energy was also expended on ensuring staff well-being. Adults and children relate to one another comfortably and respectfully.

A bias for reflective action

Reflection is fundamental. Dewey offered the insight that it is not what we learn by doing but what we learn by *thinking* about what we are doing (cited in Fullan 2006). The children reflect frequently and regularly – in philosophy sessions and at other times. So do the teachers and the principal. The changes at Buranda came about because of a continual process of teachers doing, reflecting, inquiring, and seeking and responding to evidence. They reflect on their own practice, the practice of others and the operation of the school as a whole. Reflection is a powerful practice.

Persistence and flexibility in staying the course

There was never any doubt about what all those associated with Buranda were trying to achieve. Teachers new to the school would be told they would be expected to teach philosophy and environmental education in mixed-age classes. That was not negotiable. However, they were also assured that any support needed would be forthcoming, and it was. The principal kept the focus on what was to be achieved and how, and deflected distractions. This allowed the teachers to be single-minded in their endeavours, in the knowledge that the core business was being attended to.

Conclusion

As has been described, the community that is Buranda State School today is very different from previously. The students are achieving excellent academic and social outcomes, the teachers are satisfied and productive in their work, and the parents are happy and supportive. What has been achieved is now being recognized and acknowledged by educators in Australia and overseas.

Sizer suggests a school 'must be a safe, inviting and joyful place for students and for adults' (1992: 143), and that 'the school's central focus must be on the intellect, on helping each young student learn to use his or her mind resourcefully and well' (1992: 142). It would appear that the focus on well-being and intellectual engagement is indeed contributing to the achievement of improved learning outcomes. Students are happy, motivated and achieving academic results that reflect their personal best in most instances. They have a good sense of themselves and are comfortable with their own abilities. They like coming to school. These students are also good at listening to and considering the points of view of others. They ask wonderful questions and will spend hours discussing alternative possibilities with their peers. They are comfortable with changing their mind and can engage in and accept respectful disagreement.

Schools exist to help all children become as good as they can be in everything they do. By experiencing effective pedagogy and learning philosophy, students at Buranda State School are well on the way.

References

Buranda State School Annual Report (2008) Available online at http://burandass. eq.edu.au/wcmss/images/stories/2008%20sar%20final.doc (Accessed 11 March 2010).

Department of Education, Science and Training (2003) *Australia's Teachers: Australia's Future: Advancing Innovation, Science, Technology and Mathematics, main report,* Committee for the Review of Teaching and Teacher Education. Available online at http://www.dest.gov.au/NR/rdonlyres/14C1A4EA-F405-4443-B6BB-395B5ACED1EA/1662/Main_Report.pdf (Accessed 11 March 2010).

Dewey, J. (1966) *Democracy and Education.* New York: Free Press.

Dewey, J. (1997) *How We Think.* Minolta: Dover Publications.

Fullan, M. (2006) *Change Theory: A Force for School Improvement.* Centre for Strategic Education Seminar Series Paper no. 157, November 2006. Available online at http://www.michaelfullan.ca/ (Accessed 11 March 2010).

Hinton, L. (2003) 'Reinventing a school.' *Critical and Creative Thinking: The Australasian Journal of Philosophy in Schools, 11*(2), 47–60.

Lingard, B., Hayes, D., Mills, M. and Christie, P. (2003) *Leading Learning: Making Hope Practical in Schools.* Maidenhead: Open University Press.

Lingard, B., Ladwig, J., Mills, M., Bahr, M., Chant, D., Warry, M., Ailwood, J., Capeness, R., Christie, P., Gore, J., Hayes, D. and Luke, A. (2001) *The Queensland School Reform Longitudinal Study,* vols. 1 and 2. Brisbane: Education Queensland.

Lipman, M. (2003) *Thinking in Education,* 2nd ed. New York: Cambridge University Press.

Lipman, M., Sharpe, A. and Oscanyan, F. (1980) *Philosophy in the Classroom.* Philadelphia: Temple University Press.

MCEETYA (2008) *Melbourne Declaration on Educational Goals for Young Australians.* Available online at http://www.mceetya.edu.au/verve/_resources/

National_Declaration_on_the_Educational_Goals_for_Young_Australians.pdf (Accessed 11 March 2010).

Peirce, C. S. (1955) *The Philosophical Writings of Peirce*. New York: Dover Publications.

Queensland Parliament (2006) Record of Proceedings First Session of the 53rd Parliament, Tuesday 9 February. Available online at http://www.parliament.qld.gov.au/hansard (Accessed 11 March 2010).

Sizer, T. R. (1992) *Horace's School. Redesigning the American High School*. New York: Houghton Mifflin.

Sizer, T. R. (1996) *Horace's Hope: What Works for the American High School*. New York: Houghton Mifflin.

Warner, D. (2006) *Schooling for the Knowledge Era*. Camberwell: ACER Press.

Suggested further readings

Cam, P. (1995) *Thinking Together: Philosophical Inquiry for the Classroom*. Sydney: Hale and Iremonger/PETA.

Cam, P., Fynes-Clinton, L., Harrison, K., Hinton, L., Scholl, R. and Vaseo, S. (2007) *Philosophy with Young Children – A Classroom Handbook*. Deakin West: Australian Curriculum Studies Association.

Institute for the Advancement of Philosophy for Children (2010) New Jersey: Montclair University. Available online at http://cehs.montclair.edu/academic/iapc/ (Accessed 14 October 2010).

Lipman, M. (1988) *Philosophy Goes to School*. Philadelphia: Temple University Press.

Splitter, L. and Sharp, A. (1995) *Teaching for Better Thinking: The Classroom Community of Inquiry*. Melbourne: The Australian Council for Educational Research.

Chapter 3

Development processes in a laboratory school
Germany

Susanne Thurn

School profile

The Laboratory School at the University of Bielefeld was founded by Professor Hartmut von Hentig and opened in 1974 after quite a long planning process. It is an officially designed 'experimental school' of the state of NorthRhine–Westfalia and simultaneously an academic branch of the University's faculty of education. It has the ongoing task of developing, trying out and evaluating new ways of teaching, learning and living in schools and of finding ways to disseminate these developments to other schools and academically. School development, self-evaluation, external evaluation and continually justifying to society have been parts of its core mission from the beginning – long before these practices were expected of other German schools. To live up to these expectations, the Laboratory School was freed of many official requirements and provided with some additional staffing.

At the Laboratory School, a carefully conceived 11-year educational process begins with the reception year (the year before compulsory school attendance) and continues to around age 16 (the end of compulsory attendance): years 0 to 10. It includes the primary phase and secondary Stage 1. There are around 600 pupils in the school altogether, 60 to 65 pupils in each year selected to ensure that the school population matches that of the entire city in terms of social class and ethnicity. Around 10 per cent have special educational needs; they learn in mainstream classes, not 'integration classes'. Few – but essential – principles and convictions underpin the life of the school:

1 The diversity of children and young people is welcomed and seen as an asset and a challenge.
2 All learn together without structural differentiation according to achievement: their learning is necessarily individualized.
3 The school is a *polis*, a society in embryo, a community in which everybody who belongs to it has a share in formulating its laws – everyday democracy shaped and experienced.

4 As learning and personal development are highly subjective processes, as much as possible is learned through experience and as little as possible through being told; learning is felt on the senses, often takes the form of projects and activities, and has visible results through learners' presentations of their findings and achievements.

5 To bring this about, subjects are joined together into areas of experience, sites for living and experience are developed in and near the school, and the school day has a rhythm, with time to develop and the leisure to learn.

6 Individual learning is not tested normatively and reported back comparatively. The Laboratory School entirely avoids giving marks or grades until the end of year 9 but reports on pupils' learning in terms of their own progress. We place a high expectation on ourselves as educators that we will challenge and help our pupils reach their highest possible achievements.

Each child's pathway through the school involves four stages that have their own characteristics: each new stage has something fundamentally new about it. Classes in the first two stages (years 0 to 2 and 3 to 5) are organized vertically; the core curriculum in the upper stages is organized in same-age classes but with mixed-age electives and 'achievement classes'. From the holistic learning of the early years, curriculum areas such as natural science or social studies emerge, connecting several traditional subjects. Pupils receive their first grades at the end of year 9 – needed for them to find a place in other schools after they leave or to begin training for a career.

The school's pedagogy is strongly experiential. As von Hentig always argues in his books and reports (or speeches), 'As far as possible, we should replace instruction with experience'. However, we should not forget the other half of his dialectic, 'The teacher's role is to bring experience into consciousness'. The curriculum is based strongly on learning experiences: for example, von Hentig proposed that children in the early years should

- pursue an interest together, show each other, talk about it;
- step back from the group – be alone;
- literally explore the elements: make a fire, dam water, dig a hole;
- build a hut, plant a garden, look after an animal;
- cook together and eat it – wash up afterwards;
- read quietly;
- observe something, observe others, follow your curiosity;
- celebrate special occasions, perform something, sing, give one another presents that you've made yourself;
- and all of that along with the normal school activities – writing, reading, calculating, drawing, cleaning up.

(cited in Thurn 2010)

Even when learning becomes more cognitive, the links with experience and the emotions are sustained – Pestalozzi's motto: 'head, heart and hands'. School spaces include the 'zoo' (pets can be cared for there and looked after at home during the holidays), a disco, media room, kitchen, allotments and a place for building huts. The staff include a master craftsman and a youth worker. Much of the learning is through practical projects such as a circus, film making, eco-gardening. Travel is also important, culminating in three-week international exchanges.

Children and young people are expected – and are given the time – to develop opinions on a daily basis, to reflect, extend or change them, to defend them courageously, or be influenced by others. We are a school that wants to be a *polis* in which politics in miniature and democracy in embryo can be learned and lived and responsibility accepted as part of our participation in one another. There are many opportunities to discuss and to learn responsibility:

- for everyday life (from second breakfast together to cooking for one another on residentials)
- from the agreed rules of working together in school to defending the rights of asylum seekers in the wider society
- for the local and global environment, whether this means ecology or the welfare of Turkish families after the earthquake
- for their own history – past, present and future – setting up a memorial at Bielefeld Station to the Jewish citizens who were deported in 1942, because without knowledge of history we are condemned to repeat it, but also exploring our desires and hopes for the future
- for the things that are important to us – culture, religion, aesthetics, responsibility for a good life.

This is a school where young people are accepted as they are, where they can always find a grownup to trust and who has time for them when they need it – but who doesn't interfere uninvited in their life. Young people need adults who take seriously what they think, feel, write, say, ask and mean – who can help, advise, encourage, correct, challenge and console. They should find adults who can perceive what makes them individual, interesting and lovable, not just what is disturbing and disruptive. This can happen only if the adults in the school also feel comfortable being there and respected in their individuality.

Within a fundamentally mixed-ability and inclusive environment, pupils are given many opportunities to excel in areas of interest. This can involve researching information and then presenting it through a publication or exhibition. Pupils in Stage 3 can begin Latin or French as their second elective, as an alternative to practical options such as climbing, cookery or carpentry. Each year of Stage 4, pupils embark on an individual research project or creative project, supervised by a teacher of their choice from anywhere in the school: from Jung's theory of dreams or Che Guevara to an exhibition of costume designs.

Evaluations have confirmed the benefit of the school's policy to delay giving numerical marks or grades until these are finally required for transition at age 16 to the next stage of education or training. Such competitive marks are regarded as humiliating and demotivating for many. They are part of a divisive system that, in Germany, involves socially linked selection after the fourth year of schooling – children having to stay behind and repeat years, being moved to a lower grade of secondary school. This led to the national shock of Germany's very weak Programme for International Student Assessment (PISA) results, showing not only a high proportion of poor results but also a strong pattern of social reproduction. After much debate, the Laboratory School finally agreed to its pupils sitting PISA tests, despite its very different curriculum; pupils were carefully matched for background, and the school was publicly recognized as highly successful.

School development as a responsibility of experimental schools

Learning Through Action, the title of a book by Hartmut von Hentig (1982), describes both our pedagogical theory for working with children and a development task for the schools he founded at the University of Bielefeld (the Laboratory School and the College (Oberstufenkolleg) for over-16s and mature students) learning to develop a better pedagogy should itself come first of all from practice. Pedagogical development for practice should occur through practical activity, close observation, collective reflection and careful evaluation of change. Critique must have consequences: the gulf between theory and practice, between research and teaching, must be closed. The development of these schools was seen as an experimental field for school development overall.

When von Hentig retired in 1987, this conception came under political threat. The 'teacher-researcher model' whereby all teachers had some hours free for researching their development work with little control or interference, was particularly disputed. After a tough fight and with crucial support from the University, a new model was established that guaranteed the future of its research and development work (Terhart and Tillmann 2007).

Now the school received a supplementary budget (equal to five full-time teacher salaries) to fund the part-time release of staff for agreed development projects and the accompanying research and publications. The University contributes three posts to accompanying this work. Elected representatives of school, university and regional government form a Common Leadership to agree on projects.

Research and development arise from and during practice. Teachers write proposals, sometimes with the University academics attached to the school or with external advisers. (However, it is important to understand that we regard ourselves as academics, too.) The plans and results are evaluated using three criteria. They must

- improve the practice of the school
- impact upon its overall development
- extend educational theory.

However, the school's development processes don't depend exclusively on such research projects. The school adopts a single key problem or task each year, running through all four stages and systematically worked on in all meetings and units. Other development processes are more specific but often have a reciprocal impact, enriching and supporting one another; for example, research projects can arise out of the annual theme, or research findings can give rise to a theme.

Development through annual themes

Annual themes might arise because the entire staff wishes to extend its knowledge and practice in a particular area. The staff hear experts from within the school, invite visiting experts, discuss and adapt texts, work on their own application plans, and begin with practical trials. A major past example has been inclusion – making education more inclusive and providing additional support, dialogic learning, pedagogical diagnosis, cooperative work, gender-specific teaching and problems relating to migration.

Another kind of annual theme arose from the desire to establish greater unity between the four stages, so that teachers understood one another's work better and were better able to support the progress of pupils throughout the school. Twice in the last 15 years, the staff have agreed to observe their colleagues in other stages, to give feedback on these observations as critical friends and to work together on new developments in the stages.

Annual themes can also arise from the need to ensure that the many local initiatives being tried out in the school are actually implemented and incorporated within the whole curriculum.

Development within curriculum areas

These developments help fulfil the school's commitment to develop and evaluate new ways of teaching and learning for sharing with other schools. One extended activity concerned developing curriculum units for integrated science teaching, trialling these at the Laboratory School and designing professional development for staff who had specialized in only a single science.

These curriculum units, along with professional development activities, were then published for use in other schools.

In various development projects, resources were developed, methods piloted, pedagogical justifications written, and experiences and theories shared through national events and finally disseminated through extensive curriculum guidelines and staff development. Primary English teaching has been continuing since the 1970s, well before there was political support for it. The development of physical education in Germany in the last 30 years has been shaped to a considerable extent by research and development at the Laboratory School and is clearly visible in the state's curriculum guidance. Other examples include music, textile design, drama, maths, literacy in Stage 1, story writing in Stage 2, 'literacy and achievement' projects with older pupils, project and workshop-based teaching in the primary stage, insights into the region's economic structure and world of work through a comprehensive programme of placements, and finally processes of 'life-planning'.

Broader developments

Another influential development involves gender. Some female teachers began to work on this 'against the tide', looking towards gender-specific needs rather than a simple homogenisation across the gender divide.

We first developed and tried out our own curriculum units, initially within the school and then in a national collaboration sponsored by the Equality Ministry. Male colleagues researched gender-specific perceptions of the school's own sports curriculum – certain that both boys and girls appreciated the school's co-educational teaching. The negative responses surprised the research team and led to a far-reaching revision of the sports curriculum and to further research. We gradually developed a spiral curriculum of gender-conscious life planning covering the entire school, implemented after further development and research. It has been adopted, at least partially, by many German schools. It contains, among other features:

- regular boys' and girls' conferences (every stage)
- a 'housekeeper passport' (Stage 2)
- the project 'Love, Friendship, Sexuality' (start of Stage 3)
- interviewing male and female workers about the relationship between paid work, family work and communal work during the three work placements (Stage 4)
- the 'boy strengthening' and 'girl strengthening' electives
- evaluating methodologies thought to be 'more suitable for boys'.

(A comprehensive reading list about these various gender-related school development processes can be found in Thurn 2009.)

This process also provides an excellent example of pupil-driven development. When a girls-only elective was introduced involving dance, drama, self-defence and massage, and discussion about health, sex and relationships, the boys insisted on their own provision. This included the housekeeping certificate based on skills acquired during a residential, and a childcare placement in nursery schools and playgroups that enables boys to understand the satisfaction of looking after children. These anti-sexist pedagogies are designed to be empowering rather than promoting a sense of male guilt, though unjust or violent relationships are critically discussed with boys and girls.

Assessment and report writing provide a very clear example of the reciprocity of school development processes and research. After more than 25 years of experience, the staff wanted to systematically clarify our own practice through an intensive process of reflection and work in all subjects, stages and pedagogical conferences. Parent and pupil representatives took part, and their various perceptions and critical comments were taken up. Two 'workshop volumes' were produced as source books: first a collection of essays critiquing marks and promoting assessment and reporting that fostered good learning; then a collection of exemplars of our own anonymized reports on pupils. This resulted in a consensus paper, agreed by the staff at the end of the year, which continues to give direction to teachers, parents and pupils.

A research project by the Academic Unit that was vigorously debated by the staff focused on the communicative and subjective aspects of report writing to analyse them linguistically and evaluate them empirically to gain academic knowledge (Lübke 1996). The staff chose to re-emphasize the subjective quality and communicative strength of the reports in the consensus paper but, at the same time, responded to the critique that comments on behaviour and attitudes to work tended to overshadow comments on progress in subject learning; we agreed to place greater stress on academic progress in the upper years.

A new discussion began: how could achievement be made more visible? How could a new achievement culture grow in the school by presenting achievement, including through portfolios, learning diaries and agreements, mentoring, and evaluation of achievement? With this in mind, the Laboratory School and the Sixth-Form College organized a well-documented conference in 2000, which gave us new motivation for our work while opening it up to critical reflection (Becker et al. 2002). New forms of mentoring and documentation are still being developed and tested out in new research projects. Three teacher-researchers investigated the effectiveness of reports in their subjective and communicative impact, using a sample of one boy and one girl in each of the four stages, over a two-year period:

1 how the reports could be interpreted hermeneutically
2 what pedagogical message the teachers wanted to communicate

3 what their parents read in the reports

4 how the pupils responded and followed up through action – the most important issue.

The results of this 'reception study' (Döpp et al. 2002) were reported back to the staff and discussed with the parent and pupil councils. As a result, a new evaluation and counselling culture has developed, including the following changes:

- Mid-year reports from each specialist teacher have been replaced by a comprehensive report from the form tutor.
- This report particularly evaluates the academic and social behaviour of the pupil in the various curriculum areas, based on meetings of the various teachers.
- The pupil and parents have a half-hour meeting with the form tutor, with conclusions agreed, recorded and signed by them all as a commitment to future action.

The school's work on assessment and reporting has become even more crucial because of politicians' preferred view of achievement based on standardisation, quantitative measurement and resulting selection criteria. This view of achievement contradicts a pedagogical practice that seeks to help each young person towards his or her best achievement in his or her own time; these young people should not be selected on the basis of quantitative surveys but must be challenged and supported as individuals.

Development that changes structures

Stage 1 has always been vertically grouped, with five- to eight-year-olds in each class. Moreover, Stage 3 and Stage 4 electives were open to all pupils in the stage. It was only in Stage 2 that pupils learned entirely in single-age classes. A group of teachers in that stage wanted to extend vertical grouping from Stage 1 to Stage 2 and to carry out the necessary development work. They studied and discussed the available literature, visited other 'reform schools' that used vertical grouping for this age range, informed the staff about these experiences and insights, undertook a research project, worked out a comprehensive concept and finally put a proposal to the school leadership groups to carry out a pilot for a third of the pupils in Stage 2 for a six-year period.

Even an experimental school finds it difficult to undertake such a major restructuring: its practice is well grounded, proven and a source of security (Demmer-Diekmann 2005). Staff resistance particularly concerned English (i.e. as a foreign language) and maths: how on earth could such sequential subjects be taught in mixed-age groups? A carefully worked out compromise included an agreement to test the progress and attainment of the vertically grouped pupils in these subjects against that of the other classes. The test results spoke powerfully in favour of mixed-age classes (Thurn 2006). Finally, there was a substantial vote in favour of extending this to all Stage 2 classes, with the others abstaining rather than opposing, saying they would prefer the evaluation period to be extended. The next challenging step is to support and evaluate the engagement of staff who had previously not been involved in carrying through this comprehensive restructuring.

Positive and negative process factors: problems and tasks

This restructuring had a number of process factors that are of wider relevance:

- The entire staff was involved in the discussion and development from the start.
- The proposal was clearly presented in writing, followed by regular written and oral information.
- The teachers involved in the pilot opened up their own practice to colleagues' observation.
- Public presentations were delivered about the project's results.
- Those leading the pilot showed a patient readiness to answer new critical questions from sectional meetings, to alter or extend the concept in response, to adjust curriculum content and to engage in discussion at subject meetings.
- They dealt modestly with regard to their own successes: requests to visit, give conference presentations or publish, and especially the comparative tests.
- They showed tolerance in dealing with one-sided complaints from colleagues who were opposed, for example, that the new year 6 pupils didn't have the usual competences.

The parents had also to be convinced afresh that they hadn't made a mistake in trusting their children to this 'experiment'. It is very important that the project group were well informed and coherent in their arguments, always checked their ideas with one another, supported one another through disappointments and setbacks, but remained convinced and were confirmed in practice.

Finally, the project group succeeded in finding supportive partners in the school leadership who maintained an active interest in the project, shielding and protecting it when necessary. It is certainly of the highest importance to take seriously the concerns of those who oppose change. Teachers' self-image and professional identity are put at risk by major structural change after they have taught in a particular way and with a secure working rhythm and in separate working spaces. Parents have a built-in picture of teaching from their own school experience, even if they remember it unfavourably; they become worried at deviations from this when concerned about their children's future.

More negative circumstances occur in our experience when a school recognizes clearly enough the need to develop but can't understand how to work this enthusiastically into its life. For example, as a staff, we recognized that we hadn't developed a clear sense of how to deal with new media, that it played only a marginal role in our practice, and that a process of experiencing and reflecting was lacking. This was adopted by a massive vote as a key aim in the school's research and development plan, with strong support from the staff, the Common Leadership and the Academic Unit. The university dedicated one of its staff to this project; we followed all the rules of the art of organisational development; and the staff were willing participants. However, it lacked an enthusiastic project group who could drag the rest of us along with their persuasive power, present their intentions and counter possible objections through forceful arguments that were 'practically pedagogical'. A few teachers tried out this-and-that in their teaching, but nothing emerged that could be articulated theoretically. Specific actions were foregrounded over a coherent research focus.

A major new development now faces the school. The entry stage (Stage 1) has operated for a long time on a mornings-only basis, with optional and separate childcare and activities during the afternoon run by different staff. These two groups of staff liaised with one another but mainly worked separately. We are moving towards an integrated whole-day pattern, partly because the parents of our youngest children need and, indeed, want this. This presents a great opportunity to develop a new rhythm for the entire day in which we can alternate meaningfully and comfortably between exertion and leisure, work and play, movement and quiet. How can teams be built that will take up this new challenge with enthusiasm? How can people who have shaped their work over the years with growing professionalism now take on something fundamentally new that will mean more work and also insecurity? How can people connect up who have their own personal interests in mind and might not even want to change their working hours?

Too much is in play: their own understanding of the work; the need for security and the routines they have grown used to; the new effort that is anticipated; the worry that they won't be able to succeed. How can a balance be achieved between the different interests without too much anxiety, as one thing is absolutely clear: good school development can work only with the willing cooperation of those involved; it cannot be forced – even when people won't 'do the right thing' voluntarily.

Good progress is being made, so that, from the start of 2010-2011, all children will be at school three days a week until 15.30, and the childcare staff are each attached to a group. The day is divided into three sections: 8.30-10.30; 11.00-12.30; and 13.30-15.00 (with meals, rest and play between and at the end). One part is organized by the teacher, one by the nursery teacher and one by both. All are enthusiastic about this change, and we are curious to find out how it really works. We have a sense of 'take-off' within the staff that we never even dared to dream of...

Development perspectives

How Do New Things Happen in Schools? is the title of a book by Christine Biermann (2007). It is important to re-present the many positive developments and research findings at the Laboratory School to its own staff as a whole. This happens through the annual themes; through study days that involve staff representatives with others covering their classes; through seminars and discussions with outside experts; through presentations to a variety of meetings for part or the entire staff, and the parents' council and sometimes the pupils' council; through short articles and references to the literature, including our own publications, in the weekly bulletin; through systematic reviews of all the school's publications (nearly 70 a year) within the Common Leadership; and through the annual plan of the Academic Unit and its reports. Despite this, it has to be said that the school suffers from too many research and development findings that we can't properly make use of.

The challenge of how to make this useful for other schools is just as big, but vitally important. Around 2,000 visitors, increasingly international, come to see us in a year. The practice of the Laboratory School is shared through teacher education, by means of lectures and through placements. The staff of other schools ask our teachers whether they will work with them as critical friends. Universities, teaching colleges and staff development centres, induction seminars for new teachers, teacher unions, the education units of political parties, the media, and increasingly educational foundations and alliances pressing for educational change invite us to give presentations. This has become particularly acute after the shock of Germany's poor PISA results. However, beyond this, the Laboratory School has to continue to develop. Because of its favourable conditions, the school and the Academic Unit have to react more quickly and appropriately – one could say, seismographically – to social change and childhoods that have been changed and need to change. That is the only way we can continue to live up to Johannes Rau's words of praise, after ten years of working with us: 'a thorn in the flesh of school change'.

References

Becker, K., von der Groeben, A., Lenzen, K.-D. and Winter, F. (eds) (2002) *Leistung sehen, fördern, werten. Tagungsdokumentation*. Bad Heilbrunn: Klinkhardt.
Biermann, C. (2007) *Wie kommt Neues in die Schule? Individuelle und organisationale Bedingungen nachhaltiger Schulentwicklung am Beispiel Geschlecht*. Weinheim und München: Juventa.

Demmer-Diekmann, I. (2005) *Wie reformiert sich eine Reformschule? Eine Studie zur Schulentwicklung an der Laborschule Bielefeld*. Bad Heilbrunn: Klinkhardt.

Döpp, W., von der Groeben, A. and Thurn, S. (2002) *Lernberichte statt Zensuren: Erfahrungen von Schülern, Lehrern und Eltern*. Bad Heilbrunn: Klinkhardt.

Lübke, S.-I. (1996) *Schule ohne Noten: Lernberichte in der Praxis der Laborschule*. Opladen: Leske und Budrich.

Terhart, E. and Tillmann, K.-J. (eds) (2007) *Schulentwicklung und Lehrerforschung*. Bad Heilbrunn: Klinkhardt.

Thurn, S. (ed.) (2006) *Englisch jahrgangsübergreifend unterrichten: Evaluation eines Schulversuchs in den Jahrgängen 3/4/5 der Laborschule Bielefeld*. Bielefeld: Impuls, Schriftenreihe der Laborschule, Band 42.

Thurn, S. (2009) 'Macht und Geld regiert die Welt – und Männer sind anfällig dafür!' Sechzehnjährige Mädchen und Junge über Macht und Geschlecht. In M. Löw (ed.) *Geschlecht und Macht: Analysen zum Spannungsfeld von Arbeit, Bildung und Familie*. Wiesbaden: VS-Verlag.

Thurn, S. (2010) 'Hartmut von Hentig'. In K. Zierer and W-T. Saalfrank (eds) *Zeitgemäße Klassiker der Pädagogik: Leben – Werk – Wirken*. Paderborn: Ferdinand Schöningh.

von Hentig, H. (1982) *Erkennen durch Handeln: Versuche über das Verhältnis von Pädagogik und Erziehungswissenschaft*. Stuttgart: Klett-Cotta.

Suggested further readings

Goodman, P. (1971) *Compulsory Miseducation*. Harmondsworth: Penguin.

Hollenbach, N. and Tillmann, K. J. (eds) (2010) *Teacher Research and School Development: German Approaches and International Perspectives*. Opladen: Barbara Budrich.

Thurn, S. and Tillmann, K. J. (eds) (1997) *Unsere Schule ist ein Haus des Lernens* [Our school is a home for learning]. Hamburg: Rowohlt.

von Hentig, H. (2008) *Die Schule neu denken: eine Übung in pädagogischer Vernunft* [Rethinking schools: An exercise in pedagogical reason], 5th ed. Landsberg: Beltz.

Chapter 4

Curriculum development and thematic learning

Norway

Bjørn Bolstad

Introduction

It's Wednesday morning. The low autumn sun shines in through the large glass windows of Ringstabekk School onto pupils of class 10a who are sitting in groups around tables. Four pupils around each table discuss keenly how they should present their chosen form of energy to the other 70 pupils in the class. The three teachers speak with groups and give advice on how they might make the presentation exciting and understandable for the other pupils. In Group 8, Ingvild and Mads have had a good idea that they introduce to their colleagues in the group. During the last three days, these pupils have really become absorbed with wind power, and now Mads suggests that they should demonstrate to the rest of the class how a wind farm works. It takes an hour for them to get their entire group to really understand how the propellers drive a generator and how movement becomes energy. Soon they will learn from other groups about different energy sources and will be able to build this wider knowledge on their understanding of wind power.

The pupils' work on the theme energy has been *exemplary*, in the sense of focusing on key examples to generate wider knowledge, but also *interdisciplinary*. They have learned, for example, how to write scientific articles and how to contact specialists by telephone. They have learned to calculate some average values, how the economy is dependent upon cheap energy, and naturally much detailed knowledge about electricity, power and energy.

Ringstabekk pupils work in a cross-curricular manner using methods such as project work, storyline and enterprise, among others. This is balanced against time for discrete academic subjects and (in concentrated time spans) practical and creative subjects. The school is organized in 'large classes', each with 60 to 75 pupils and a dedicated team of four to five teachers; there are two 'large classes' for each year.[1] The teaching team plan the cross-curricular learning together, involving pupils through steering groups for each theme. The intention is that the teachers in each team have sufficient specialist knowledge to cover the school curriculum, that they share their understanding with one another, and that they should teach only this one large class. This isn't always possible, but it happens to a large extent, so that the teachers in a team are free to develop a timetable for their class for each 'period' (see next paragraph) without affecting others. This means not only that they can plan appropriate timings for each activity without being interrupted by a bell but that they can concentrate on particular subjects over a given period. In that sense, we don't have a school *timetable*, but we do take time planning seriously. This flexible use of time also provides a framework for pupils to plan their own use of time for learning. We are convinced that this will become increasingly important in their working lives. The school is more like a modern media company than a centrally managed factory. Pupils work in different kinds of groups during the year, they meet various challenges through different interdisciplinary methods, and they learn to adapt to change.

The school year at Ringstabekk is divided into six *periods*, each five to six weeks long. Studies during each period consist of an interdisciplinary *theme*, a practical or creative subject, and some discrete subjects (particularly those that are not prominent in the theme). In each period, pupils study just one of the three practical 'zones': art and crafts, music, food and health. For example, pupils have music twice a year for a concentrated period (approximately three hours a week for five or six weeks).

The practical or creative subject is also taken into account when the team plans the interdisciplinary theme. For example, the theme can end with a concert or an exhibition. The pupils in 10a remember very well how they had an exhibition for parents one morning when pupils presented installations they had arranged about World War II. The parents experienced, among others, video installations about the growth of Nazism and posters of the resistance movement. They also remember a 'blues-show' where the pupils performed lyrics and songs they had composed themselves.

When the team of teachers plan for the year, they make sure that different subjects play a central role in the interdisciplinary themes of the year. For one period, natural science can play a major part, and then maybe the next themes are centred around history or language. The teachers don't try to squeeze every subject into every theme but teach the remaining subjects separately or during the next period.

Project method is the school's central approach to cross-curricular learning. Pupils are systematically trained in this method and develop the capacity to formulate research questions, to find information from different kinds of sources, and to present what they have discovered. These are competences that they will surely need later in life, both in future studies and in their working lives. When Ringstabekk teachers speak of project work, they don't just mean any old kind of work where pupils aren't just listening to the teacher or studying from the textbook. The staff have a clear conception of what can be called *project method* and what should be classified as another form of thematic approach. Planning a project begins with the team of teachers interpreting the National Curriculum.[2] Project work at Ringstabekk must start off from some kind of problem, for example, an issue that needs clarification and evaluation. The teachers have to sign off the pupils' research questions before they can pursue the research stage, and pupils obtain training to distinguish between specific research questions that are used for collecting information, and broader problems that can be solved only through analysis and reflection.

Further, a project must lead toward some kind of product. This is often linked to the practical subject (zone) being studied at the time. Projects have to be interdisciplinary, which also means that they must have a clear disciplinary content. To participate fully, pupils must have an involvement in leading the project. This is often achieved by including some pupils in the steering group along with the teaching team. These steering groups plan projects both before the work begins and within the project. Projects in the school are *exemplary*.[3] Instead of learning a little about everything, which pupils often forget later, pupils work in a concentrated way within a carefully bounded thematic field.

The Danish pedagogue Hans Jørgen Kristensen (1997) argues that project method is based on five key principles:

1 It is *problem*-orientated.
2 It is *product*-orientated.
3 *Participatory* or collective leadership.
4 *Interdisciplinarity* along with a high quality of *subject* teaching.
5 *Exemplary* content.

The teachers have, in recent years, worked to modernize and develop project method. Among other examples, by sharing experiences across the whole school staff, they have formulated a repertoire of methods to use for processing information, presenting the products of learning, and summing up and pulling together knowledge. Mads remembers clearly how they had a round table conference about diverse world conflicts and how to avoid such conflicts. The 'big class' was divided into two, so that 37 pupils sat in a circle. Two of each group presented briefly their conflict, and afterwards they discussed the possible solutions and how violence could be avoided. Teachers evaluated the pupils' achievements and gave everyone an individual evaluation based on agreed criteria. Mads can still remember a lot about this conference nearly a year later.

Ingvild especially liked making short films to illustrate different ideologies. Some groups made symbolic films, and others were more concrete. She remembers very clearly how they had a visit from a professional scriptwriter and then wrote their own scripts. She had never before so clearly experienced writing scripts in Norwegian lessons to incorporate ideas from religion or social studies, but this time she was fully engaged and recalls it well. The parents came to the film evening – they called it the Oscars – and each group had to say something about the film they were presenting. She remembers how much she enjoyed seeing everybody's films.

Ringstabekk pupils also encounter a range of other methods, for example, storyline, problem-based learning (PBL), pedagogical games, simulations and enterprise. The school has used *storyline* for more than ten years. This doesn't just provide a vehicle for exciting subject learning but engages learners in a catalytic way for learning at a very personal level. One example is a storyline in which pupils adopt different ethnic identities; they learn to see their own assumptions and prejudices and use their imagination to 'walk in somebody else's shoes'.

Many of the interdisciplinary forms are types of *simulation*, defined as situations where the pupils act as if they were somewhere other than school. Examples are political debates in which pupils represent different political parties or a conference about climate change in which pupils play experts in different fields.

PBL can be seen both as an introduction or training for a more extended project method or as a method in its own right. Texts such as newspaper articles or scientific articles can serve as case studies in PBL. Each group of pupils is handed a case study and proceeds through seven steps to work out what is problematic, to decide what information is needed to understand it, and finally to evaluate what they have learned.

The biggest enterprise event, which is also a simulation of reality, involves pupils setting up a company – usually in year 9. Under the general theme of *Work*, the class establishes a business. This takes about a week to develop. All the pupils apply for the positions they would like. The management group is established, after interviews, by the head teacher or representatives of local businesses. When this management group is confirmed, they interview the other pupils. Part of the preparation is to develop good ideas about products and designs. One of the most popular in the locality was the restaurant a class established. Ingvild remembers how she was appointed chef. She learned that she had to work long days to fulfil this responsibility but also how satisfying it was. However, she remembers with pride that the restaurant got good reviews, that she received good comments from her fellow workers and – not least – that they made a nice surplus income. Other examples include setting up a riding course for children, a computing course for older people, offering gardening help, and organising cultural events in a hospital. Many traditional school subjects can be connected to enterprise, including maths, writing a formal letter to apply for a job, and studying the history of the labour movement.

Aesthetic activities are also very prominent in the school. Every year the entire school arranges an activity week in which all pupils organise an exhibition or produce a musical. Twice a year all the pupils dance in the school yard. In addition, every class arranges concerts and displays for the rest of the school and the local community.

The school also promotes systematic teaching in various learning skills and reading strategies. Pupils shouldn't just be presented with subject content during their years at school but must also develop strong methodological competences – learning to learn. In recent years, many pupils work on learning strategies during the primary school years, but they are often not ready to use them integrated into subjects. It is useful, therefore, for pupils to have training in using Venn diagrams, columns and KWL (what we know, what we want to know, what we learned) to prepare, organize and evaluate their own learning. In year 10, pupils must choose for themselves which strategies they need. Ingvild often uses mindmaps, whereas Mads, who is a very systematic person, prefers columns.

Ringstabekk School has been working for a long time with cross-curricular themes to promote more holistic learning experiences. The school doesn't wish to divide up learning into separate subjects and thus create a fragmented version of reality but wants its pupils to experience the connectedness of real-world phenomena. The pupils do spend part of their time working within discrete subjects but, even then, teachers try to show the connections, for example by synchronising subject content.

The pupils' motivation to learn is substantially enhanced. Ringstabekk pupils tell how they are motivated by working on important themes in a cross-curricular manner, and that they like the challenge. Former pupils often come back to tell how they learned how to think at the school and how this prepared them for university studies.

A prime aim of education in Norway is to give pupils a desire and enthusiasm for learning and education (cf. Education Law 1–1 i.) If the purpose of schooling is personal development and the acquisition of a learning culture, pupils need to do more than just accumulate separate subject concepts and methods. They have to learn how to write and how cells function in their bodies, but school must also develop their methodological and social competences and help them grow as human beings. They and their teachers need time for this. Pupils need to talk together and write about the learning process and which strategies they use. They need to reflect on how they collaborate and live within a community. Each pupil has regular conversations with his or her contact teacher (tutor) in which they discuss both the formal learning and how they develop methodologies and the ability to work together.[4] The pupils also have to see good examples and role models, so it is very important that the staff also work together actively.

School development

Ringstabekk School's history is the story of nearly 40 years' school development. Since its opening in 1972, the staff have been very conscious that a school needs to develop to stay alive.

There have been some big leaps forward in the school's history. One example of 'double loop learning' was because teachers understood that they had to organize in teams and that every teacher could teach only within a team. This teamwork became an important condition for the pedagogical development within the school. Within the team, teachers are mutually dependent through their interdisciplinary work. No teachers can cast themselves adrift into individualistic practice. Team meetings are an important forum for pedagogical discussion and reflection, and the team gives teachers many possibilities to try out pedagogies in practice.

Another essential factor in development has been a strong focus on pedagogy and pedagogical theory. When teachers have tried out new methods, they ground them pedagogically and develop theory. The school is living and developing within a clear pedagogical tradition built on Dewey's activity learning supported by a constructivist understanding based on Piaget and into a socio-cultural sense of learning starting from Vygotsky.

In addition to team meetings, major vehicles for pedagogical development have been the Pedagogical Committee and the Common Arenas. The entire staff meet for two hours on one afternoon a week for the Common Arena. At these meetings, methods and theories are discussed. In the Pedagogical Committee, which also meets once a week, each team leader meets with the head and deputies, a total of nine people, and here, too, pedagogical discussion is central. These meetings are not merely to exchange practical information. In addition to the weekly meetings, a staff seminar takes place once a year, as do annual planning seminars for each year group. The staff seminars are important forums to introduce new methods and new pedagogical perspectives, but they have provided a context where praxis can be consolidated and theorized, leading towards the 'pedagogical platform'.

The Pedagogical Platform is an important instrument for securing the school's character. All teachers who work at the school have to sign up to it and work in conformity with it. The platform is revised or changes every three years, and all teachers are involved in the process. Thus, the teachers experience an active engagement with the school's pedagogical development and a close and lively communication between leaders and participants. For many years, 'inspectors'[5] were elected from among the staff, and even though this practice has ceased, there is still a close relationship between teachers and school 'leadership'.

Even Ringstabekk School has felt the pressure from the winds that have been blowing across the Western world. These winds have demanded a focus on 'basic skills', established test systems, and focused more on short-term results than long-term development. This has, for example, led to a condensation of time for thematic work and for a closer monitoring of subject knowledge within projects or storyline. However, the school's staff, and certainly its leadership, are determined to balance the demand for recordable outcomes with long-term development. They place great emphasis on sharing information and dialogue with parents. The parents in the school's immediate neighbourhood, Baerum, a relatively affluent Oslo dormitory suburb, see little sense in a 'tacking'[6] mentality in which pupils have to cram toward fortnightly tests. Parents, too, want school to be long-sighted and to help its pupils to develop good methods and strategies for learning.

Ringstabekk School is looking to the future with both strengths and challenges. An obvious strength is that the school is extremely flexible and easily copes with change. One reason for this is that the teachers have a sense of the school as an organisation and not just as individual praxis. They understand that they can't always do what they wish because there are other demands to satisfy, and they also understand how important it is for all the teachers in the school to be good teachers. It wouldn't do the school much good if some teachers were fantastically clever while others were mediocre or bad. A school is an organisation, and all teachers have to work collectively to be good teachers.

Another strength of the school is the extreme engagement of the teachers. Working as a team strengthens this commitment. All the teachers relate very well to their pupils, and they are all determined on pupils making as much progress as possible. The pupils, too, are engaged and ambitious, and so the pupils' and teachers' engagement is mutually reinforcing.

The inner sense of what a school can be is really different here than in many other schools. The teachers have a broad and holistic sense of what young people should learn, which is really important given a constantly changing future.

Every school needs to be clear about its weaknesses. People outside Ringstabekk have constantly been questioning its methods, and this has made the staff reflect on this and has made them conscious of possible weaknesses, such as the needs of pupils who need more structure and boundaries in their learning, including pupils with special needs. By working together in the team, teachers have a strong awareness both of who these pupils are and what kind of help they need, so they can meet this challenge well and give these pupils good support. In recent years, the parents of pupils with additional needs have made their satisfaction very clear with how the school relates to these pupils.

Another challenge for the school is to balance a focus on training in key skills and basic knowledge, on the one hand, with the need to develop reflection and deeper understanding on the other. The pupils come to school as children of 12 to 13 years and leave it as thinking young people of 15 or 16. During these years at 'youth school', pupils are expected to grow both cognitively and emotionally. In youth schools that just focus on training in basic skills or on drilling reproducible information, the young people grow up less than they ought. Conversely, if we just focused on reflectiveness and holistic thinking, many pupils would not develop the necessary strategies and skills. Meanwhile, schools should develop social citizens, so it is important that pupils experience connectedness so that they can participate well in a democratic society now and as they grow older.

The school's vision is: *We will face the future boldly and gladly.* We try to work each day toward this vision.

Notes

A comprehensive account of Ringstabekk School's curricular, pedagogical, and developmental practices and working theories has been published (Bolstad et al. 2001). Though unfortunately not available in English, it provides one of the most comprehensive and theorized accounts of a single school's development, reflecting the sustained interrelationship of theory and practice at the school.

1 As is normal in Norway, this 'youth school' lasts three years, from 13 to 16 years old. It is a fully comprehensive public school within the local authority. With around 400 pupils, Ringstabekk is quite large by Norwegian standards. It is not unusual in Norway, and with variants in other Nordic countries, for a team of teachers to have full responsibility for a year group of pupils, but Ringstabekk is a particularly strong example of how this structure can provide a framework for new ways of learning.
2 The Norwegian national curriculum or Laereplan is a relatively flexible and general document.
3 The term *exemplary* is used by a number of pedagogical theorists, for example, the German Klafki, to emphasise the importance of carefully selecting a specific example or set of content that will truly engage learners and to teach concepts or skills of wider application.
4 Every teacher in a class team is a personal tutor for around 15 pupils.
5 The term *inspector* in Norway is somewhat similar to a deputy head in English-speaking countries. In many schools, the inspector also leads a year team. They are not seen as remote figures or simple administrators.
6 *Tacking* is the yachting term for zigzagging forward for short distances in contrary directions. It is a revealing metaphor here, as it also signifies sailing against a wind.

References

Bolstad, B., Bonde, E., Haugerud, I. E., Jacobsen, I., Raaum, E. and Teigen, K. A. (2001) *Moderne pedagogikk – theori og praksis ved Ringstabekk skole* [Modern pedagogy – theory and practice at Ringstabekk School]. Oslo: Universitetsforlaget.

Kristensen, H. J. (1997) *En projektarbeidsbog* [A project workbook]. Undervisningsministeriet Copenhagen: Folkeskoleafdelingen.

Suggested further readings

Bell, S., Harkness, S. and White, G. (2007) *Storyline: Past, Present and Future.* Glasgow: University of Strathclyde.

Bolstad, B., Bonde, E., Haugerud, I. E., Jacobsen, I., Raaum, E. and Teigen, K. A. (2001) *Moderne pedagogikk – theori og praksis ved Ringstabekk skole* [Modern pedagogy – theory and practice at Ringstabekk School]. Oslo: Universitetsforlaget.

Lucas, B. and Claxton, G. (2010) *New Kinds of Smart: How the Science of Learnable Intelligence Is Changing Education.* Maidenhead: Open University Press.

Vygotsky, L. (1986) *Thought and Language.* Cambridge: MIT Press.

Chapter 5

Educating in the margins, lessons for the mainstream

Australia

Glenda McGregor, Martin Mills and Pat Thomson

Introduction

This chapter draws on research concerned with the educational opportunities taken up by young people who had been permanently excluded from or who had disengaged from mainstream schools in the United Kingdom and Australia (McGregor and Mills, forthcoming; Mills and McGregor 2010; Thomson and Russell 2007; see also Thomson and Russell, 2009; Russell and Thomson, 2011). The particular focus of the chapter concerns the insights that these alternative education settings provide for the mainstream sector in terms of addressing the needs of some of their most disadvantaged students.

The concept of alternative education is a slippery one. It can encompass behaviour management units (e.g. Pupil Referral Units); special schools, such as those catering to students with autism; fee-paying schools based on democratic philosophies (e.g. Summerhill); and non-fee-paying flexible learning centres that draw upon government and philanthropic funding sources (te Riele 2007). Some of these alternative education sites provide a range of insights into how mainstream schools might change their practices and structures to facilitate the re-engagement of those young people who appear to have given up on schooling. It is our view that the sites that can best inform change in mainstream schools are those that do not work with deficit models of young people. Such sites do not have as their intent a 'fixing up' or 'disciplining' of students to return them to the mainstream but rather work to construct supports, environments and learning activities that attract and retain disengaged students.

The chapter uses case studies from Australia but cross-references findings with similar research in the United Kingdom. We provide a brief outline of the Australian context: this includes a description of the case study sites and a review of some of the issues facing young people who attend these schools along with their reasons for re-engaging in the education process. It concludes with a discussion of some of the lessons for mainstream schooling indicated by the successes of these sites. However, while acknowledging the positive work undertaken within these sites, it also questions the social justice implications of proliferating such schools.

Contexts

In Australia, the landscape within which alternative educational sites operate is a busy one. The federal government, in conjunction with the states, has identified improving school retention as a national priority. The intention is to make the completion of secondary education nearly universal by dramatically improving the numbers of young people who stay and complete the full twelve years of formal education.[1] Not surprisingly, there is a strong relationship between attainment and levels of academic achievement (Taylor 2009; Teese and Polesel 2003). Data provided by the Organisation for Economic Co-operation and Development (OECD) indicate that the relationship between socio-economic status (SES) and educational outcomes is stronger in Australia than in many other comparable countries (OECD 2007). This confirms local research (Lamb et al. 2004; Ross and Gray 2005; Savelsberg and Martin-Giles 2008; Teese and Polesel 2003; White and Wyn 2008) that shows that, of those who have left school, there is an overwhelming representation of students from low SES and/or Indigenous backgrounds. The Prime Minister has acknowledged that currently only 59 per cent of students from low SES backgrounds in Australia finish year 12 (Gillard 2009). Indigenous students, who are overrepresented in low SES groups, are also faced with a range of challenges posed by geo-location, colonization, generational marginalisation, and cultural and language barriers: these affect their engagement with and retention in schools (see 'Closing the gap', Commonwealth of Australia 2009). International research (e.g. Alonso et al. 2009; Janosz et al. 2008; Milbourne 2002; Parsons 2009) suggests that it is generally the students who experience the most economic and social disadvantage who disengage from the mainstream schooling and whose future life opportunities are thus most negatively affected.

In Australia, various policies have been set in train to support the target levels of retention. Some of these have been based on incentives. However, the most evident measures are those that have come to be associated with the 'earning or learning' agenda where students are not legally allowed to leave school until they are 17 unless they have a job or a training institution to attend. There have also been measures[2] introduced into some low SES and Indigenous communities to withhold welfare payments from parents whose children are not in attendance at school. Ironically, in Queensland, the context for the cases in this chapter, at the same time as there is an attempt to retain students in the state schooling sector there has also been an increase in levels of power allocated to principals in terms of being able to suspend students who are not fitting in. When this is set alongside a system that is demonstrating a shift to high-stakes testing and the publication of school results on the internet (see

Lingard 2010), this is not a situation that bodes well for students already in the process of disengaging from schooling. The Queensland situation is parallelled in other locations; for example, English schools are simultaneously expected to be more inclusive and demonstrate no tolerance for 'poor' behaviour.

The Australian sites considered in this chapter are those that have provided young people who have been treated harshly by life, and then often had this treatment intensified in schools, with another opportunity to complete school.

The case study sites

The Australian cases considered here include a school that had its origins in a park and catered to homeless young people but, at the time of this research, had relocated to an old school building. This school, Victoria Meadows Flexi School, was supported by funds from a large metropolitan city council and a Catholic education provider. The student population consisted of about 90 young people aged from 15 to 21. The school was staffed by both teachers and youth workers and offered various combinations of vocational, academic and arts curricula. It also had a crèche for those young people (mostly young women) who were parents. Another school, Fernvale Education Centre, began in an old Queensland suburban house and had recently moved to a more traditional school setting in a nearby suburb. It was a girls' school with a very high Indigenous population. Fernvale had a strong focus on supporting young mothers and also provided a crèche. It had a student population of slightly more than 100, ranging in ages from 12 to 25. While offering a standard curriculum, including subjects necessary for university entry, it also provided the girls with an opportunity to undertake workplace certificates. The school was funded through support from a religious organisation. The third site, Woodlands Flexi School, was a flexible learning centre located in a regional area and, though located off campus in a community hall in the local town, was overseen by a local high school. Approximately 60 students ranging in ages from 14 to 18 attended this school. It offered a variety of workplace certificate courses and a standard curriculum and had a close relationship with a local university, thus providing a pathway for those students who wanted to do tertiary studies.

Who attends?

The young people who attended these sites came from a wide range of backgrounds but had in common a poor history of engagement with the mainstream sector. Many had left or been forced out of school after conflicts with teachers and administrators whereas others had gone because they felt schools had little to offer them or had particularly difficult personal circumstances that prevented them from meeting the attendance and/or assessment requirements of mainstream schools. This is not uncommon (Parsons 1999; Smyth and Hattam 2005), and evidence from our data clearly attests to this:

> Dena (Woodlands): When I was at [my last school] I couldn't make it to school on time sometimes because of family issues...

In Queensland, the 'earning or learning' (Education Queensland n.d.) rules mandate that young people younger than age 17 without a year 12 or equivalent qualification must be in school or training to qualify for a youth allowance. Thus, young people who leave school early often find themselves without financial support and ill-informed of places such as Victoria Meadows:

> Georgina: I was in a mainstream school ... from year 8 till year 10. I was having complications with bullying and stuff like that. I just couldn't deal with the way that they were teaching the kids. I wasn't getting enough attention so I stopped going to school. But 'cause like they have that thing, you know, you either got to go to school or you've got to work, I was looking for jobs or something alternative. I couldn't find anything and then my friends referred me to here.

In some cases, it was apparent that the young people attending the case study sites would have had difficulty in attending any school at their time of departure from the mainstream. For example, one student, in explaining some of the difficulties she had faced at her previous schools, stated:

> Alexis (Fernvale): I have a major depressive disorder and I went to a psych ward for a while and couldn't really deal with the mainstream schooling so searched around looking for a smaller school.

However, sometimes difficult, and often tragic, events in the young people's lives were not appropriately recognized within the mainstream school and often led to conflict with schooling authorities:

> Malcolm (Victoria Meadows Flexi School): I left school about three months before I finished year 12. I got expelled because I had a pretty big personal conflict with my old school principal at Bielby Creek. Pretty much he told me that I was useless... I was working and he was like, 'you're not attending school' and I was working my arse off. I didn't have no parents supporting me because my parents are deceased and he didn't want to believe that. I pretty much had to take in their death certificates to school to prove to him that they weren't alive ...

However, despite the difficult life circumstances of these young people, the vast majority of those interviewed were generous in their praise of their current schools and the opportunities that were presented to them. For instance, Susan from Woodlands, who had been suspended from her last school after swearing at a teacher and had come to Woodlands on the recommendation of a friend, told us about her current school:

> It's the best school ever because like [pause] 'cause it's like... I hate, like, teachers getting up you all the time – it's just really laidback and awesome.

This kind of praise was repeated regularly and often demonstrated on the part of the young people a commitment to furthering their education. The support that these students showed for their current schools was a consequence of the services and positive learning environments provided in addition to the education programs.

What these schools offered

Recognition of personal circumstance

There was recognition within these alternative schooling sites that various social and economic factors impacted upon young people's abilities to attend school. These factors included poverty, homelessness, parenting and other caring responsibilities. As a consequence, the various sites offered a variety of social and practical support in the form of youth advocacy, crèches, counsellors, breakfasts and lunches, transport vouchers, and assistance in finding furniture and accommodation. Having a supportive, caring environment for both mother and child proved vital to the lives of many of the young women:

> Marta (Victoria Meadows): I can bring my kids and they're really flexible about family circumstances. Because I've been on my own since I was 15 I've had to live by myself and had to move a lot so they've been really supportive trying to find somewhere to live.

Though the state department of education in which the Australian research was conducted has a policy requiring schools to support young mothers and pregnant schoolgirls (Education Queensland 2010), it became apparent that this support had rarely been provided by mainstream schools. For instance, Karen told us she had come to Fernvale because once she became pregnant, she was not allowed to continue past year 11:

> They wouldn't take my re-enrolment for the grade 12 because I was pregnant. So my counsellor at the time, or my youth worker – she sourced

a couple of places and came up with Fernvale as being the closest and easiest accessible for me.

The flexibility of the program at Fernvale also enabled her to continue with her education after taking time out to have her baby:

> I was here for five or six months but then stopped to have my daughter Kylie and I eventually came back at the end of last year

Schools such as Fernvale and Victoria Meadows also provided significant practical support once the girls enrolled. According to Brittany (Victoria Meadows):

> We can like come and make coffee and toast. It's so much easier so when I'm running late and I don't have time to feed my son then I can come here and have breakfast.

For Barbara at Fernvale Education, it was the social and emotional support that proved significant:

> Well they put a holiday program on for us and no other school does that and I find that really good because I'm a mother and I like to enjoy myself and have a bit of a break.

Recognition of the socio-economic circumstances of their students was clearly evident in the discussions around school assistance in respect to finances, transport, and housing and legal problems. According to Wayne (Victoria Meadows):

> They're happy to help but they do expect an effort to be put in. It's not just help for nothing – you've got to put something back you know – a couple of weeks back, I didn't have any money for transport and I didn't have any money for my medication and I said that and they actually gave us, me and Mary, 20 dollars so we've got transport and money for my medication.

And Chanel from Fernvale noted:

> Yeah there are youth workers that will help you with [welfare]. They've got Jean up there – she's the counsellor if, like, you have a problem with your parents or your partner or you need a home or something she'll help you do that. She just helped me leave a domestic violence relationship. She's got so many contacts for people who need counselling or legal aid or accommodation. They do awesome – a lot of things. They offer transport for people who can't get here.

Assistance with the many daily needs of these young people occurred within school cultures of non-judgmental trust and acceptance. The provision of such environments facilitated the re-engagement to learning.

Supportive environments

Noted at all of the alternative schools visited was the willingness of these young people to travel considerable distances to attend. Many now travelled for an hour or more, passing mainstream schools along the way. This effort may be attributed to their newfound sense of belonging to their chosen alternative school. Ashlee from Fernvale Education Centre put it this way:

> It's not just a school, it's like a second home. If you're wanting to get away from your family problems you just come to school, you know you can talk to one of the teachers or one of the youth workers and just nut it out.

The size of the schools was also seen as a positive factor by the students. For instance, as Mary from Victoria Meadows Flexi School stated:

> One of the biggest problems I had was getting attention... I think the teachers concentrate too much on the students who do really well and they kind of forget about the students who really need the help. I think that's why our mainstream schools need to learn [that] it's hard for a teacher to look after so many students.

Chanel from Fernvale agreed:

> Oh yeah here the classroom sizes are smaller whereas in normal schools they're like 30 and sometimes more people, and I was always falling behind...They just didn't have the time – there was no way to catch up. ... I wouldn't have bothered coming back if I didn't find this school. Like if my friend had never told me about it I would still probably be sitting at home.

Along with the small class sizes, the freedom to call teachers and workers by their first names contributed to a democratic, respectful environment:

> Georgina (Victoria Meadows): Well we're calling teachers by their first name because you have a connection with them. Like we get called by our first name and we call them by their first name so it's like equal ground and it makes it so much more easier to connect and be more friendly with them than calling them Mrs or Mr.

Other behavioural issues such as smoking and swearing were both approached from a perspective of negotiating with the young people. There was recognition of their life journeys, and students were given ways of dealing with these patterns of behaviour within the supportive environments of the schools. In respect to smoking, Georgina went on to say:

> I think with the smoking, you know, it's kind of telling us, 'you're growing up, you have the right to do this' ...

Wayne from Woodlands commented upon the issue of swearing:

> If you swear on accident, yeah. they'll just talk to you about it or something – like, at another the teacher went through my book and he said he couldn't find it [the work] but I actually did it and I was like, 'that's bullshit' and I got suspended for that.

The environments of these schools were shaped by the relationships of the people who went to them. According to Stacey of Victoria Meadows:

> I love it here. It's like, they're [teachers and workers] so much more respectful and they do really leave it up to you to act like an adult and be your own person which was how I was brought up.

As core components of schooling environments, the learning programs and pedagogical and assessment strategies at these sites were also crafted within the context of such relationships between the personnel and the students at each school.

Teaching and learning

At these sites, it was made clear to the young people that they had *chosen* to come there and, therefore, it was their responsibility to make it work. This was challenging but very much appreciated by the students, as noted by Ashlee from Fernvale:

> Like it allows us to be adults and make our own decisions. If we don't want to work then they'll say, 'OK well, at the end of the day it's your decision if you don't want to work, it's not going to be good for you but we're not going to force you'.

Additionally, the young people found that their commitment was rewarded by the personal attention and teaching that they had felt cheated of at their previous schools:

> Susan (Fernvale): They'll come [teachers/workers] and talk to you and check up on how you're doing. Like if you don't understand something they'll come and help you...

Understanding of the life challenges faced by these young people also influenced expectations around assessment:

> Skye (Victoria Meadows): It's flexible – you'll have assignments but ... like, people might have things going on at home and in a normal school they wouldn't take that into consideration, whereas here they'll take that into consideration, like personal things. There's, like, reasons you can't do your assignments. [Here] you don't have to come, you don't get detention or anything like that if you don't come.

The empathy that workers and teachers showed in their dealings with the students extended to respect for their differing opinions. Irene expresses a common view in the next exchange:

> Irene (Woodlands): Like they don't, they're still teachers but they talk to you more like, not teachering just like, more like a mate kind of ... As long as you're not going, 'oh that's stupid' and all that sort of stuff. Like as long as you're like, 'I disagree'...

When asked about her idea of 'good teaching', Georgina from Victoria Meadows gave this advice:

> The better personal connection you have with a student the more they're going to excel. So the more you help them personally not just in their work but them as a 'self' – like trying to make them a better person – will reflect in their work – that would be good advice.

Such insights sum up the sentiments of the research participants across the three Australian sites. Clearly 'what worked' was a combination of personally tailored learning programs, about which students had to take responsibility, taught within supportive schooling environments by dedicated and empathetic workers and teachers.

Lessons for mainstream schools

There is much that can be learned from the ways in which these alternative schools have worked to re-engage young people who have become disconnected from schooling. These lessons include the provision of services beyond classroom teaching; the need for flexible school rules; the development of curriculum and assessment practices that support the various demands that are often placed on young people operating from the margins of society; the need to create learning environments that support caring relationships between teachers/workers and young people; and, not least, the importance of utilising engaging pedagogical practices.

Early school leaving can be a consequence of personal circumstances, but research indicates that it is usually the product of a complex mix of factors (Mosen-Lowe et al. 2009; te Riele 2006; Savelsberg and Martin-Giles 2008; Smyth and Hattam 2005; Taylor 2009; White and Wyn 2008). School factors are often central in this mix. Research has, for example, demonstrated how the difficult circumstances of pregnant girls are often exacerbated by being stigmatized and encouraged to leave or change schools (Vincent and Thomson 2010). Various literatures also emphasize the lack of understanding within schools of the issues facing low SES students that directly contribute to youthful disengagement from education (see, for example, Alexander et al. 2008). Similarly, there is research evidence to suggest that the values that permeate all aspects of mainstream schooling alienate – and thus have worked to disengage – students from a variety of marginalized cultural backgrounds (see, for example, Gray and Beresford 2002). Disturbingly, some research has highlighted the ways in which many students who reject learning commonly select the metaphor of 'prison' to best describe their experiences at school (Teese and Polesel 2003). In short, many mainstream schools as they are currently constructed regularly fail to accommodate the needs of the most marginalized young people and, in the process, inculcate a sense of being oppressed by the very institutions that claim to be the means of furthering their life chances. This need not be so.

The lessons from the Australian alternative schools indicate that when schools are aware of the social and economic factors that prevent some young people from attending school and, for instance, provide support systems such as crèches, meal programs, counsellors and youth advocates, the young people will remain in or be attracted back to education. Within the research schools, rules were based on ensuring that the students had a safe and productive learning environment (no attention, for instance, was paid to uniforms), and the rules were flexible enough to cater to the varying personal circumstances of the students. Constructing an environment that accommodated their personal circumstances was critical for enabling these young people to remain in an educational institution. However, there were also significant educational reasons for them remaining.

These educational reasons included programs that were meaningful to the students and enabled them to pursue personally determined life goals and programs that opened up new and, for them, unthought-of possibilities. Such programs were founded upon pedagogical practices that engaged and challenged the students and provided them with opportunities for successes that had previously been out of reach. Central to the programs was an ethos of care that was made possible by the size of the schools and classes. Though the class size debate is a controversial one (see, for example, Blatchford 2003), many of the students at these schools spoke to us about how much easier it was for teachers to know and hence be able to support them within these smaller environments. There was also a commitment to giving students every opportunity to demonstrate their learning through flexible timelines and assessment regimes.

There are caveats to the positive picture we have painted of alternative provision. Case study research conducted on alternative provision in England by Thomson and Russell (2007) highlighted many of the same factors (see also Munn et al. 2000). Their research noted the importance for young people of feeling that they had some say in the kinds of programs that were on offer, a practice that the young people described as notably absent from the mainstream schools they had attended. However, Thomson and Russell observed that this agency was sometimes misdirected. They noted the tendency of some providers to offer recreational and leisure programs that were less able to be used for entry to ongoing further and higher education. They noted among providers a view that young people who were marginalized from school were good only for work with their hands, not their heads. Where providers did not have such a view, young people were able to continue with – and often make up ground – in educational programs that could lead to the kinds of futures they could increasingly imagine as possible. Russell and Thomson (2011) also noted the preponderance of boys in alternative provision and the ways in which this skewed the programs on offer. Many of the young women found themselves in highly stereotypical programs and thus prepared best for work in the hair and beauty industry and in children's services. Such restrictive offerings are, of course, not confined to alternative provision. However, what is on offer in alternative provision is not uniformly good, and we are not suggesting that this is the case.

A further caveat relates to the longer-term effects of a system that relies on alternative schools. We do suggest that they currently serve a very important purpose in (re)engaging young people in learning who otherwise would not be in education. However, we do not advocate the proliferation of such organisations in ways that would differentiate the education system with unjust consequences. Indeed, we are somewhat confronted by a Nancy Fraser (1997, 2009) style social justice dilemma in relation to these schools. A concern with social justice causes us to recognize that these schools provide a different and important service for those students schools do not serve well. Thus, we support the work that these schools do in terms of recognising the differences that matter for their students. However, by maintaining and expanding the existence of these 'different' schools, mainstream schools are let off the hook in terms of meeting the needs of their often most marginalized students. Potentially, alternative flexi-schools could be constructed as 'dumping grounds' for unwanted students. Thus, the creation of a fair and just system would seem to suggest that it is the business of state-provided education to put these 'alternative' schools 'out of business' by ensuring that all young people have free access to a high-quality education. This is a matter of distributive justice. However, this requires mainstream schools to change in ways that cater to those young people who are often operating on the margins of society. We would, therefore, suggest that the mainstream needs to look to the kinds of alternative schools we have foregrounded in this chapter to learn from them how best to ensure that government schooling is indeed for all. Until such time as this occurs, we tend to agree with Mary, a student from Victoria Meadows Flexi School:

> If they created more of these small schools – like say in just main suburban areas – then I reckon it would have a huge popular demand and kids would be saved from going down the wrong track.

Notes

1 The target is to reach 90 per cent year 12 attainment by 2015 (DEEWR, 2009) with the current overall year 12 attainment rate at 74 per cent (Australian Govt. Fact Sheet 2009).
2 The School Enrolment and Attendance Measure.

References

Alexander, K., Entwistle, D. and Kabbani, N. (2008) 'The dropout process in life course perspective: early risk factors at home and school.' *Teachers College Record*, *103*(5), 760–822.

Alonso, G., Anderson, N., Su, C. and Theoharis, J. (2009) *Students Talk Back to a Segregated Nation on the Failure of Urban Education Reform*. New York: New York University Press.

Australian Government Fact Sheet. (2009) Compact with Young Australians: Increasing Educational Attainment of Young People Aged 15–24. Online. Available at http://www.deewr.gov.au/Youth/YouthAttainmentandTransitions/Documents/CompactQAsWeb.pdf (Accessed 13 May 2010).

Blatchford, P. (2003) *The Class Size Debate: Is Small Better?* Maidenhead: Open University Press.

Commonwealth of Australia. (2009) *Closing the Gap on Indigenous Disadvantage: The Challenge for Australia.* Canberra: Commonwealth of Australia.

DEEWR (2009) 'Changes to Youth Allowance (Other).' [available online]

Education Queensland (n.d.) Senior Phase of Learning. Online. Available at http://education.qld.gov.au/etrf/senior.html (Accessed 23 October 2010).

Education Queensland. (2010) Pregnant and Parenting Students. Online. Available at http://education.qld.gov.au/studentservices/inclusive/gender/pregnant.html (Accessed 20 October 2010).

Fraser, N. (1997) *Justice Interruptus: Critical Reflections on the 'Postsocialist' Condition*. New York: Routledge.

Fraser, N. (2009) *Scales of Justice: Reimagining Political Space in a Globalizing World.* New York: Columbia University Press.

Gillard, J. (2009) Speech. Australian Financial Review – Higher Education Conference – 9 March.

Gray, J. and Beresford, Q. (2002) 'Aboriginal non-attendance at school: revisiting the debate.' *Australian Educational Researcher*, 29(1), 27–42.

Janosz, M., Archambault, I., Moprizot, J. and Pagani, L. (2008) 'School engagement: trajectories and their different predictive relations to drop-out.' *Social Issues*, 64(1), 21–40.

Lamb, S., Walstab, A., Teese, R., Vickers, M. and Rumberger, R. (2004) *Staying on at School: Improving Student Retention in Australia.* Melbourne: Centre for Postcompulsory Education and Lifelong Learning, The University of Melbourne.

Lingard, B. (2010) 'Policy borrowing, policy learning: testing times in Australian schooling.' *Critical Studies in Education*, 51(2), 129–147.

McGregor, G. and Mills, M. (forthcoming) 'Alternative education sites and marginalized young people: "I wish there were more schools like this one".' *International Journal of Inclusive Education.*

Milbourne, L. (2002) 'Unspoken exclusion: experiences of continued marginalisation form education among "hard to reach" groups of adults and children in the UK.' *British Journal of Sociology of Education*, 23(2), 287–305.

Mills, M. and McGregor, G. (2010) *Re-engaging Students in Education: Success Factors in Alternative Schools.* Brisbane: Youth Affairs Network Queensland.

Mosen-Lowe, L., Vidovich, L. and Chapman, A. (2009) 'Students "at-risk" policy: competing social and economic discourses.' *Journal of Education Policy*, 24(4), 461–476.

Munn, P., Lloyd, G. and Cullen, A. M. (2000) *Alternatives to Exclusion from School.* London: Sage.

OECD (2007) *Education at a Glance.* Paris: OECD.

Parsons, C. (1999) *Education, Exclusion and Citizenship.* London: Routledge.

Parsons, C. (2009) *Strategic Alternatives to Exclusion from School.* Stoke-on-Trent: Trentham Books.

Ross, S. and Gray, J. (2005) 'Transitions and re-engagement through second chance education.' *The Australian Educational Researcher*, 32(3), 103–140.

Russell, L. and Thomson, P. (2011) 'Girls in alternative education provision.' *Ethnography and Education*, 6(3).

Savelsberg, H. and Martin-Giles, B. (2008) 'Young people on the margins: Australian studies of social exclusion.' *Journal of Youth Studies*, 11(1), 17–31.

Smyth, J. and Hattam, R. (2005) '*Dropping out*', *Drifting off, Being Excluded: Becoming Somebody without School.* New York: Peter Lang.

Taylor, J. (2009) *Stories of Early School Leaving: Pointers for Policy and Practice.* Fitzroy: Brotherhood of St Laurence.

Teese, R. and Polesel, J. (2003) *Undemocratic Schooling: Equity and Quality in Mass Secondary Schooling in Australia.* Melbourne: Melbourne University Press.

te Riele, K. (2006) 'Youth "at risk": further marginalizing the marginalized?' *Journal of Education Policy*, 21(2), 129–145.

te Riele, K. (2007) 'Educational alternatives for marginalized youth.' *The Australian Educational Researcher*, 34(3), 53–68.

Thomson, P. and Russell, L. (2007) *Mapping the Alternatives to Permanent Exclusion.* York: Joseph Rowntree Foundation.

Thomson, P. and Russell, L. (2009) 'Data, data everywhere – but not all the numbers that count? Mapping alternative provisions for students excluded from school.' *International Journal of Inclusive Education, 13*(4), 423–438.

Vincent, K. and Thomson, P. (2010) '"Slappers like you don't belong in this school": The educational inclusion/exclusion of pregnant schoolgirls.' *International Journal of Inclusive Education, 14*(4), 371–385.

White, R. and Wyn, J. (2008) *Youth and Society: Exploring the Social Dynamics of Youth Experience,* 2nd ed. South Melbourne: Oxford University Press.

Suggested further readings

Meier, D. (2002) *The Power of Their Ideas. Lessons for America from a Small School in Harlem,* 2nd ed. Boston: Beacon Press.

Mosen-Lowe, L., Vidovich, L. and Chapman, A. (2009) 'Students "at-risk" policy: competing social and economic discourses.' *Journal of Education Policy, 24*(4), 461–476.

Munn, P., Lloyd, G. and Cullen, M. A. (2000) *Alternatives to Exclusion from School.* London: Routledge Falmer.

Smyth, J. and Hattam, R. (2005) *'Dropping out', Drifting off, Being Excluded: Becoming Somebody without School.* New York: Peter Lang.

te Riele, K. (ed.) (2009) *Making Schools Different: Alternative Approaches to Educating Young People.* London: Sage.

Chapter 6

Reflections of an Aboriginal school principal on leading change in an Aboriginal school

Australia

Chris Sarra

Introduction

From August 1998 until March 2005, I had the privilege of being principal of Cherbourg State School, an Aboriginal community school just three hours' drive northwest of Brisbane, Australia. At the time, it seemed a daunting task, as I had never been a school principal before but, as an Aboriginal academic getting frustrated by questions from undergraduates such as 'Are you a qualified lecturer?' I felt it was time to get on with the business of working with my own people and with my own ideas.

I went with a keen interest in Aboriginal identity as I was very much aware of how young Aboriginal students aspired downwards to confirm what they thought was their 'identity'; really all they were doing was conforming to mainstream Australia's negative stereotypes. I was determined to address this, remembering what it was like to be surrounded by stifled perceptions about who I was as an Aboriginal student and what I could achieve. If I was to lead a school with Aboriginal children, I was determined they would never be subjected to the stench of a school culture of low expectations.

Clearly the school faced many challenges, even talk about closing it down. It would have been easy to simply collude with a culture of low expectations. There was never a consequence for such collusion with low expectations of Aboriginal children; it was normal, a reality that was readily embraced and justified. After many lengthy discussions with children, parents, Elders and the Community Council, I challenged staff:

> What I believe, what the children, parents, Elders and the Council believe, is that our children can leave this school with academic outcomes comparable to any other school, and also leave here with a very strong and positive sense of what it means to be Aboriginal! If you don't believe that, then you should not be here!

Half of the teaching staff applied for a transfer within three weeks!

Positive change beyond such endemic collusion would certainly require something stronger: something smarter. It would take many years of hard work to create a new, stronger, smarter reality. With a new teaching team that worked exceptionally hard and in partnership with Aboriginal teacher aides and the community, we did create a new and more positive school culture that underpinned some profound change. Unexplained absenteeism was reduced by 94 per cent within 18 months; attendance rose from 63 per cent to 93 per cent. Year 2 literacy improved by 58 per cent within two years, and 81 per cent of students were within the state average band for literacy in 2004, compared to none in 1998.

Since leaving, I have been able to articulate what is now called this 'Stronger Smarter' philosophy – a strengths-based approach that signals a 'belief in the capacity' of indigenous children to perform as well as any other child regardless of the complexity of their social and cultural context. Also at its core is the belief that indigenous children are 'worthy of a quality education'.

The Stronger Smarter philosophy is as follows:

- acknowledging, embracing and developing a positive sense of Aboriginal identity in schools
- acknowledging and embracing Aboriginal leadership in schools and school communities
- 'high-expectations' leadership to ensure 'high-expectations' classrooms, with 'high-expectations' teacher/student relationships
- innovative and dynamic school modelling in complex social and cultural contexts
- innovative and dynamic school staffing models, especially for community schools.

I will elaborate on the first three points, to reflect on my role as school leader.

Acknowledging, embracing and developing a positive sense of Aboriginal identity in schools

Many head-teachers pride themselves in the rhetoric of 'All kids are the same in our school!' This rhetoric sounds so right, yet creates a binary that can undermine the well-being and esteem of those students who are obviously 'different'. The binary suggests that 'mainstream' or 'same' is good inside the school gate, and diversity should be ignored. It is like saying to children who are culturally different, 'Leave your cultural identity at the gate because it has no relevance here!' Instead, schools should be a place where identity is nurtured and embraced to give students self-esteem and enhance learning capacity. To avoid spurious argument about an 'overcrowded' curriculum, I am arguing that embracing and developing cultural identities are part of the process of delivering quality literacy and numeracy outcomes, *not instead* of it.

As educators, we either collude with negative stereotypes or we assert a belief in the capacity and worth of Aboriginal children. Aboriginal children also make a choice about where they stand in relation to this 'identity'. They can choose to collude with it by being lazy in class; by swearing at the teacher; and by saying 'You're picking on me because I'm black!' when the truth is they are simply being challenged about their behaviour and work ethic.

My clearest example was when a year 7 student ran out of my office shouting 'You're trying to run this place like a white school!' It was after I insisted the bells would ring twice: first at ten to nine, to signal time to stop playing and move to class, and the second to signal time to be in class and ready for work. Previously, teachers would look out of the staffroom window and ring the bell whenever they felt there were enough students around and they felt ready to get going.

The student somehow equated a school where bells rang on time with 'white', yet was strangely comfortable with the notion of an 'Aboriginal' school in which the bells rang whenever.

If I was to challenge children about their subscription to a negative stereotype, something had to replace it. Put simply, if the negative stereotype was not 'being Aboriginal', what was? Remembering what it was like to be an Aboriginal student located within stifled perceptions and recalling decades of reports on Aboriginal education, two essentials emerged:

- academic outcomes comparable to any other child in any other school
- a strong and positive cultural identity.

As principal, I took every opportunity – in assemblies, the playground, or classrooms – to talk about being Aboriginal as a tremendously positive thing that gave us all strength. We had a new school song in which we explicitly celebrated being Aboriginal:

Jingle Bells Jingle Bells,
Cherbourg School is here.
We're young and black and deadly,
So come and hear us cheer.
Bring on every challenge,
And put us to the test.
We're from Cherbourg State School,
And you know we're the best!

On school assembly, I would say to the entire school things such as 'Hands up if you're Aboriginal! Keep your hand up if you love being Aboriginal! When we leave this school what are we going to be?' The entire school would roar back to me from the pit of their gut, '*Strong and Smart!*'

I would then say to children, 'What does that mean?' They would reply enthusiastically, 'Work hard', 'be nice to the teachers', 'keep our school clean and tidy', *'don't let anyone put us down'*.

This was a powerful time. I explained to the children that our school would be a place where you could get power, that historically our people had been denied power, but we were never going to miss out. It really was an extraordinary time for all of us – staff, students and parents – to bask in the magic of taking control, by rejecting absolutely the negative stereotype held out for us, and embracing a new and positive sense of identity on our terms.

At some point, it was just words, but it clearly signalled to everyone that we would no longer collude with low expectations. Challenging students to see that they could be smarter was not the difficult part; getting the teachers to believe it was the toughest part.

We developed an Aboriginal studies program focusing on ancient, traditional and contemporary aspects of Aboriginal cultures and society. I further insisted the program should stare in the face some of the unpalatable challenges confronting Aboriginal communities, including assimilation policies of the past that had such a devastating effect on communities such as Cherbourg. I wanted our students to examine how this connected to contemporary dysfunctions and realize that things such as domestic violence, alcoholism and abuse were the legacy of such historical policies, *not* the consequence of being Aboriginal.

Some educators were critical of such explicit approaches to highlight and celebrate the differences about being Aboriginal. Perhaps this was borne more out of fear and anxiety about young Aboriginal people suddenly not fitting into the 'box' of a negative stereotype anymore. We had become so accustomed to seeing Aboriginal students as downtrodden. For me, it was a change that was long overdue and much appreciated by Aboriginal parents. I should add that there was never any attempt to put 'being white' down.

If we do nothing to enable Aboriginal children to feel positive about their identity, the wider society will subtly and not so subtly bombard them with messages that being Aboriginal means being inferior. These messages can sometimes be so prolific that it is difficult for a young mind to have the skill to reject them.

As a society, then, we are much poorer for failing to enable the capacity of Aboriginal students.

Acknowledging and embracing Aboriginal leadership in schools and communities

Acknowledging and embracing Aboriginal leadership was crucial: examples include special Elders' parades to showcase student work, a dedicated Elders' and parents' room, and employing more local Aboriginal people in the school.

On my arrival at the school, there was an older lady everyone referred to as 'Mum Rae' – an incredibly powerful and proud black woman with a detailed insight into just about every family. She was highly regarded by most people of Cherbourg. Yet, inside the school gate, any power she had seemed to be rendered useless. She had worked as a teacher aide for more than 15 years and was reduced to performing basic tasks such as photocopying, crowd controlling, colouring in posters and running messages on behalf of teachers.

It made no sense that one so powerful in the community should be neglected, and it must have been incredibly insulting. I said to Mum Rae, 'As long as I am here, you will never photocopy another piece of paper for anyone!' She had much more to offer. She became my 'right hand man' on school and community matters. She let me know who was who in the community; whom to visit when a child misbehaved; when to go easy on a child because things were not so good at home; when to push harder because they were trying to pull the wool over my eyes. It became an excellent partnership that saw me aligned with real authority in the community. It made life as the principal so much easier, especially when I had to push harder with particular issues.

There were many other examples of Aboriginal leadership in Cherbourg. Martina and Sophie had worked together in the school kindergarten for 20 years, watching young teachers come and go and basically ignoring them. Mrs Langton ('Nana Beryl') was in her fifties; she started out as a teacher aide and then, after much frustration, decided she should complete her own studies to become a teacher herself so that she could truly control what happened in class. Her highly functional classroom was an oasis among a sea of chaos and anarchy. I thought to myself, 'If it can happen in this classroom, it can happen in every classroom'.

Then, of course, there were the Aboriginal men of Cherbourg whom I recruited to the school; they really stood up for their community's children. Aboriginal men are often criticized for not getting involved in the business of schools, but I found them very keen to be involved once they were offered work in the school and convinced they had vital skills and presence.

Embracing Aboriginal leadership creates a series of exceptional school dynamics that can deliver exceptional returns, including classroom relationships. I made it clear to new teachers that they would be working with an Aboriginal teacher aide from the community who had an extensive knowledge of where students were coming from. I said quite firmly:

> You must reflect on how to maximize the knowledge they have of students. You might have the flash degree, but never treat them as inferior in the classroom. You must work with them as co-educators. I do not want to see them used as baby sitters, crowd controllers, or shields from grumpy parents. They have excellent knowledge and skills and you need to work

with them in a way that lets you better understand the children and how to get the best out of them!

When a teacher embraces the Aboriginal teacher aide in a positive and respectful way, Aboriginal students begin to see the teacher differently. Getting them to work becomes much easier, the teacher starts seeing Aboriginal students more positively, and so on. Because they were actually being asked what they thought about classroom planning and teaching and learning strategies, the aides and teachers started working late together, and the problem of teacher aides' going missing on Thursday and Friday was no longer an issue. They would turn up to work regularly, performing solidly, which in turn got students thinking, 'Maybe this strong and smart thing is real because I am seeing it in front of me every day in my classroom'.

High-expectations leadership to ensure high-expectations classrooms with high-expectations teacher–student relationships

To me as principal, it was clear that though I might drive a high-expectations agenda, the results would be delivered in the classroom, the place where teachers stare children in the face. The classroom is undoubtedly the most sacred place. The best I could do was exercise my authority to dramatically enhance what was occurring at that vital nexus: supporting and developing them, monitoring their performance and that of students, challenging them, and intervening if necessary (Sarra 2004).

Supporting teachers includes recognizing that it is hard work for teachers at the 'front line', and I had to be there for them.

In an effort to prevent new teachers being overwhelmed by a sense of 'culture shock', we developed an 'A–Z of Teaching at Cherbourg' handbook that listed a range of important and even trivial things worth noting.

At times, I felt like a coach trying to ensure quality performance by

- keeping the morale up,
- creating opportunities for teachers and aides to feel valued and learn from each other,
- enabling a collegial environment in which it was okay to admit you were struggling or hurting,
- ensuring generous resource support to enhance classroom activity, and
- encouraging them to be bold and try new approaches to learning.

More explicitly, this occurred in a range of ways, including fishbowl activities where teachers would share a challenge with colleagues, one-to-one meetings with myself or other senior colleagues, or visits to other schools to connect with other teachers. These were simple yet effective strategies that were well received by teaching colleagues.

Other ways of supporting teachers were not so simple. I recall once sitting with a teacher while an angry parent pointed her finger, saying, 'If my child comes home tomorrow and he is crying, I will come to this school and bash you!' Naturally, this was a confronting and volatile moment for all involved but, at that moment, the teacher had to know that I was there to support her:

> Let's just hang on for a minute. This young lady works extremely hard here at the school and works hard to get the best for your son. We can never work positively together and achieve something good for him with you making threats towards us. If we are going to get your boy stronger and smarter then we have to work together. This is not the way to do it and I won't let my hardworking colleagues be confronted by these kinds of threats.

After more discussion, the mother recognized that the teacher did work extremely hard and was pushing her son because she had very high expectations about his behaviour and learning potential.

Though supporting my teaching colleague was crucial here, the need for *developing* her understanding was equally vital. Given the nature of the conversation that had unfolded and in subsequent discussion, we established and understood that though the parent's threats were never tolerable or acceptable, they occurred because, underneath all her bravado, she was motivated by love for her child. The teacher understood this very well, which enabled her to move on easily. As colleagues, we understood the very 'deep' and important nature of the work we were doing within a community with a complex history and the very complex legacies, such as aggression and frustration with institutions such as school, resulting from that same history.

This meant instilling a sense of 'higher purpose' about our work and its impact not only on students within our classrooms but on the community – indeed, its influence on how schooling was done for Aboriginal children throughout Australia. At the time, this might have seemed ambitious thinking but, as time unfolded, our 'Strong and Smart' approach to indigenous schooling certainly did have a wider impact.

Developing teacher understanding was as important as developing teacher skill. In practical terms, I attended to this need by

- ensuring access to professional development,
- connecting teachers to colleagues of the same year to ensure professional dialogue,
- mentoring between experienced and new teachers,
- brokering relationships between Aboriginal aides and teachers,

- identifying and sharing teacher expertise, and
- creating and maintaining a school culture in which teachers were encouraged to 'take risks' to transform practice.

In many ways, this was pretty straightforward. In some schools, lack of teacher skill can be presented as a complexity that somehow justifies poor school performance. I was determined to have a 'no-excuses' environment; if teachers signalled they could not deliver improved student results because of 'language issues', for instance, or wanted to build their repertoire of behaviour management skills, I was responsible for attending to this need.

Similarly, I was responsible for *monitoring* teacher, student and school performance as part of my relationship with the people around me. As in any school this meant

- reading student profiles,
- scrutinizing teacher planning to ensure it responded to what school and student data is signalling,
- having regular meetings with teachers and teacher aides to discuss student data,
- checking on individual staff morale and well-being, and
- highlighting areas of concern in school or student data and trends.

Monitoring student data and overall school and teacher performance should lead to the need to *challenge* within a professional school leader/ teacher relationship.

It is important to acknowledge and celebrate any sense of progress, though apparently small. However, I felt strongly about the need to avoid overindulging 'soft' or 'fluffy' outcomes. I recall a teacher telling me to 'back off' when I challenged her about a particular student's performance. She explained that progress was good because he now had 25 'sight words' compared to just 12 six months prior. Though I acknowledged a sense of progress, I felt it was necessary to challenge the rate of progress and the adequacy of the 'measuring instrument'. Sight words is usually a performance measure for preschool and year 1 students; this student was year 7.

The dynamic of 'challenging' in a professional relationship creates tensions and is one I think school leaders find easier to stay away from. It is worth noting exchanges between myself as school leader and the teachers' union. The teachers I inherited on my arrival were all strong union members. Of course, my challenges resulted in some robust dialogue – and with the regional union representative. There were occasions when I had to concede but never on the pursuit of improved student outcomes. I am also a teachers' union member but believe I should protect and defend the integrity of the teaching profession, not shelter laziness and incompetence.

Though it may have been hard work and even gruelling, setting up a team environment in which all staff were prepared to be challenged and to challenge others made life immeasurably more satisfying for us all. New teachers knew there would be hard questions such as the following:

- What are you doing that is contributing to underachievement?
- What are you doing that is contributing to absenteeism?
- Would you accept these outcomes for your own children?

Against this background, the question changed from 'What do we do with these children?' to 'What would I want done if this was my child?' This is how serious we had to be about our roles at the school. The level of commitment also brought the need for *intervening* where teacher performance was below a level we would tolerate for our own children.

For example, I spent a long time supporting one teacher but ultimately decided she was not suited to the school. She told me, 'I am doing my best!' but I had to reply, 'If this is your best, then the children and parents of this school deserve better than what your best is!'

Such conversations were never easy but were essential to ensure an environment that had integrity. We were encouraging the children to be 'strong and smart', so we had to demonstrate and live the same.

Regrettably, I confess I was not always as strong as I should have been. Specifically I recall times when I should have intervened to remove an Aboriginal teacher aide and an Aboriginal teacher but failed to do so. Both were local community people, and I was concerned that such moves would create a tension and be counterproductive. Looking back, I am still not sure whether this is true, but ultimately I have to admit it was tolerating poor performance.

Conclusion

As noted earlier, having the courage to exercise the hard processes is draining and easy to avoid. Historically, very few educators have been demoted or sacked for their role in perpetuating the delivery of chronic and endemic educational failure to indigenous children. Indeed, many get promoted out after delivering failure that would not be tolerated in a mainstream school.

This has been a blemish on our profession. Though there has been no tangible consequence for educators, there continues to be a dramatic consequence for indigenous Australians and communities. This is rightfully changing as a result of demands for greater transparency and accountability.

Alongside the framework and the story, there is no escaping the need for hard work from individuals. At times, some of us might find it easier to blame 'the system' for indigenous children's failing. 'The system' is a nebulous term that holds no individual accountable for the change required. We forget sometimes that we as individuals are responsible for changing 'the system' and can be content only with high expectations of Indigenous – and indeed all – children.

Clearly, enormous challenges confront us and, at times, this might seem daunting. I hope the Cherbourg story and the Stronger Smarter framework can offer some insight into a way forward amid such challenges. It certainly was a tough journey but, as a team, we managed to make positive change by embracing a positive sense of Aboriginal identity, embracing Aboriginal leadership in school processes, and having an unrelenting high-expectations agenda with high-expectations teacher-student relationships.

References

Sarra, C. (2004) *Report on Indigenous Education: Recommendations to the Minister for Education and the Arts.* Brisbane: MACER for DETYA, Queensland Government.

Suggested further readings

Bishop, R. and Berryman, M. (2006) *Culture Speaks: Cultural Relationships and Classroom Learning.* Auckland: Huia Publishers.

Bourke, C., Rigby, K. and Burden, J. (2000) *Better Practice in School Attendance: Improving the School Attendance of Indigenous Students.* Canberra: Department of Education, Employment, Training and Youth Affairs.

Harrison, N. (2008) *Teaching and Learning in Indigenous Education.* Melbourne: Oxford University Press.

Littky, D. and Grabelle, S. (2004) *The Big Picture: Education Is Everyone's Business.* Crozet, VA: Association for Supervision and Curriculum Development.

Sarra, C. (2011) *Strong and Smart – Towards a Pedagogy for Emancipation: Education for First Peoples.* London: Routledge.

Pedagogy of the landless

Brazil

Roseli Salete Caldart and the Movement of Landless Workers

Introduction

We are living in an age when humanity is in danger and when capitalism, now hegemonic across the world, is showing itself ever more dehumanizing and cruel in its logic. As teachers, we need to look to the horizon and to open ourselves up as educators to the experiences of constructing alternatives for humanity. You cannot truly teach without this broader vision.

This chapter is about educating children, but not in the abstract. It deals with education as human development in relation to the dynamics of a contemporary social struggle: agrarian reform in Brazil. It focuses on the Landless, their social movement and their pedagogy, their experience of education and school. However, it also has wider significance.

Large areas of Brazil, as elsewhere in Latin America, belong to an elite group of private landowners, including the old slave-owning dynasties. The best land is used for export crops rather than to satisfy local needs, and much land is not used productively. From the 1950s onwards, forced off the land by the modernisation of agriculture, millions of families migrated to create *favelas* (shanty towns) in the cities. The alternative was to occupy and squat on the land, and out of this emerged the Landless Workers' Movement (Movimento dos Trabalhadores Rurais Sem Terra, MST). As this action involved entire families, the needs of children were critical from the start. The camps and settlements were full of children, and children needed caring for and educating.

It is common to speak of education in terms of the formation (*formação*) of children into humane and responsible adults, but this is not a process that takes place in the abstract. The chapter begins, therefore, by locating the formation or education of children and young people within the wider process of human development in struggle, which is itself an educative process. The context, therefore, is the formation of a new social subject that calls itself *Sem Terra* (people without land), and the task is to identify a pedagogy, a way of producing human beings who collectively take control of their own destiny. This is a pedagogy where the movement itself is the principal educator, educating the landless by rooting them in a strong collectivity and by putting them in motion in the struggle for their own humanity. In this dialectic between roots, movement and project, it is possible to read some important pedagogical lessons that help us think about the great pedagogical questions of our time.

The condition of being the Landless, of being a fieldworker who doesn't own the land of his work, is as old as private appropriation of this natural good. It is a collective identity. Children are always a part of this: thrown off the land with their parents, involved in the struggle to occupy, and a part of life on the land they have settled.

Education through struggle

What is educative about the Movement of Workers without Land, these lost beings astray from the earth, marginalized from everything and with life drifting away from between the toes of their bare feet, these miserable beings, seeming barely human, who suddenly (or not so suddenly) resolve, in thousands, to raise themselves up from the ground and struggle for the earth they have been torn from? In this moment, they are struggling for the return of their human condition itself, realising that they have rights and can say *no* to a project of nation and society that wants to deny them the possibility of existence and yet can't stop giving them a name, the 'excluded'. Now you know! It is for their future and for their children.

The MST has become a reference point among the social movements of Brazil and beyond, a model for those in struggle and, for the elites, a 'plague' that needs exterminating. And others are confused by them – such radical actions, but at the same time they appear so peaceful when they march singing their hymns through the cities. People ask where they get their energy and discipline from – to organize and occupy, to walk so many miles, to struggle ceaselessly. And even singing, holding flags, having festivals, raising their children, giving heart and grace to the cities through which they pass.

Although the law in Brazil recognizes the right to occupy unproductive land, it is widely recognized that 'if the landless don't occupy, the government will do nothing.' The MST is becoming a symbol of social contestation with enormous cultural and symbolic power because the history of Brazil has been marked by the big farms (*latifundia*) that historically were associated with slavery. There is a consensus that this is a just struggle because there is no moral argument against the idea that the earth, natural and charged with an almost magic symbolism, should be in the hands of those who want to work it and make it productive. This is necessary to satisfy the hunger of millions of people, another evil that is incompatible with the so-called 'modern' or 'post-modern' world that the Brazilian elites are desperate to join at any cost.

Struggles for land assume across history a prominent cultural position, with symbolic dimensions that have something to do with the mystic force of the relationship of people to the earth. 'The earth is more than earth' (or 'The land is more than land') in the expression of bishop Dom Pedro Casaldaliga. Struggles for land, connecting across time and space, also connect with a religious dimension. However, there are also contemporary resonances, linked to libertarian utopias that appeared dead.

The educational significance of the MST can be understood as part of its sociocultural significance. By this, I mean the significance of the MST in a wider political arena beyond the countryside. It is often understood in terms of a challenge to capitalism, because the nature and form of its struggle and the values it incorporates express something, socialize, contradict capitalism.

The formation of the landless children is a part of a bigger formation. We can see the MST as a space of formation, in the sense of 'making yourself' as in E.P. Thompson's *The Making of the English Working Class* (1963). As in nineteenth-century England, uprooted workers in modern Brazil are transformed into a collective in struggle. This auto-production of an identity is political but also cultural as it puts down roots, recreates relationships and traditions, cultivates values, invents and reworks symbols that demonstrate the new social connections, and thus makes history. The landless are making themselves a new social *subject* but also a sociocultural subject, a collective whose daily actions, connected to a concrete social struggle, are producing elements of a type of culture quite different from the hegemonic social and cultural patterns in present-day capitalist society. An example of this is the decision, taken at local levels in each settlement and often after much debate, to opt for collective rather than individual farming. This gives rise to the question whether children are to be brought up for self-interest or for solidarity. Culture is being formed through material and moral choices. As Thompson said, 'Every class struggle is also a struggle about values'. The MST has always been culturally rich, with many well-recognized symbols, and has a major symbolic impact across the wider society.

The occupation of schools

Education is a central aspect of the MST, including schools for children and young people. Without it, the occupation of land would be meaningless and unsustainable. We demand that state governments must fund schools but that they should be run according to MST principles. In places, this is resisted by conservative politicians, and struggles arise. Across Brazil, the MST now runs 2,000 schools for grades 1 to 4 and 500 for grades 5 to 8. There are also 50 post-compulsory senior high schools, and degree courses run in cooperation with several universities. Of course, that is in addition to much informal and adult education.

The entire struggle of the movement is deeply pedagogical and includes many learning processes, but this chapter specifically concerns schools for young people. The need to provide schools came very early on in the movement. Indeed, it soon became clear that without schools, people would abandon the occupied land or be forced to send their children to relatives in the cities. Even today, in places, the local authority tries to insist on bussing children into town, and parents protest to prevent this. It has to be understood that the entire family has been involved in the struggle and has been changed by it. Also, traditionally, education has been part of a process whereby young people are separated from the land and end up in the cities.

At first, it was a matter of finding things for the children to do, including organizing opportunities for play. This was a spontaneous event, principally the initiative of some mothers maybe assisted by teachers or sometimes nuns. Some of these children were in a traumatic state after witnessing the violent repression by the authorities in the 1980s. Settlers also insisted on their children's right to attend school and that this should be publicly provided. However, it soon became clear that this wasn't sufficient.

Often there were some experienced teachers in a camp or settlement, generally women married to landless men, but problems often arose when the state sent in teachers who were at odds with the struggle:

> Some of the teachers who came from outside spoke to our children like this: 'See, if your father is in favour of occupying land, that's a crime; other people own that land because they've worked for it.' We couldn't have people stirring up trouble like this, telling the children that their parents were thieves!

People wanted a different kind of school but didn't quite know what. There were many discussions. Many parents felt they had learned little in school to help them know their rights, that they were taught only what the government decided, and they wanted their children to 'understand the world quicker than they had'. One principle that emerged was 'People who don't know our struggle aren't fit to teach our children.' An early decision was made to develop our own teacher training courses, in collaboration with universities and other academic institutes.

From these many local discussions, a national meeting was called in 1987, and there have been many since. These have debated and agreed on common principles, but the diversity of implementation is also important. It gives a richness to our practice; reality interacts with common principles and makes a new synthesis.

So the term *occupying schools* is a rich metaphor, involving a mass movement defining purposes and practices and with continuing mass involvement in running the schools. The education group, like other work groups in each settlement, includes members chosen by each section of the settlement.

Pedagogy

Pedagogy of the movement

The starting point for our pedagogical thinking is that the MST is our greatest educator. We learn most from the historic struggle we are engaged in, and this struggle and the identities it forms are also an educative process. The movement is a big school.

The education of landless people – those torn from the earth – begins by forming roots in a collective that doesn't deny the past but projects a future that collectively they help to build. This is how fear is overcome.

The struggle educates, with all its contradictions, frustrations, conquests and defeats. It helps form attitudes to life: that for all the difficulties, nothing is impossible to change. Movement, not stagnation, is the normal condition of human life. Schools have to provide experiences that help form human beings who are sensitive, who refuse to accept injustice, who are creative when faced with difficult situations, who remain full of hope. Rather than being domesticated into tolerating the disorder created by exclusion as if this was order, it is possible to subvert disorder and reinvent order, starting from real and radically humanist values that regard life as a more important good than any property.

Other features of our practice are also rooted in pedagogical values and theories.

Pedagogy of collective organisation

We refer to learning through participation in the democracy of the community but also organising schools based on new forms of organisation. The school should function like a learning cooperative, a space of learning not only ways to cooperate but mainly a vision of the world or culture in which it is natural to think of the good of all and not just of yourself.

Pedagogy of the earth

Pedagogy of the earth flows from the way human beings are mixed with the earth: she is our mother, and if we are sons and daughters of the earth, we are earth, too. That is why we should learn the wisdom of working the earth, of taking care of life. The earth is where we live, work, produce, die and bury our dead. Working the earth teaches us that seeds and plants don't grow instantly, they need cultivating; the work of the labourer is valued. We also learn that the world is there to be made, that reality can be transformed. Our schools can also teach the history of how land has been cultivated, the careful farming of the earth to guarantee more life, environmental education, sowing and harvesting at the right time, responding with persistence to the damage done by storms and by those who regard themselves as lords of the earth. This involves learning from practice and not just theory.

Pedagogy of work and production

Pedagogy of work and production derives from the fundamental value of working to produce what is needed to guarantee the quality of social life. It identifies the landless with the working class. Human beings humanize or dehumanize themselves, educate or miseducate themselves, through work and the social relationships established in the process of production. New ways of working are developed in the camps and settlements. Learners develop knowledge, skills and consciousness through work. Work has educative potential in itself, and schools should make it more fully educative, linking it to other dimensions of human life, culture, values and politics.

Pedagogy of culture

Culture grows out of action and reflection on action. We need neither a blind activism nor learning without action. Pedagogy of culture has, as one of its key dimensions, learning associated with gestures and symbols. We learn by handling tools invented long ago, which are bearers of objectified memory: things speak and have a history. Material culture symbolizes life. We also learn through relationships, with dialogue that is more than an exchange of words. We learn by example, looking at how others do things. And pupils learn from the example of teachers and how they live their lives. The symbols, work equipment and the ceremonies of the MST are also important in our schools. School provides a space for reflection on the various dimensions of your life.

Pedagogy of choice

Human beings make choices every day, and being part of the Movement of Landless Workers is also an active choice. We speak of a pedagogy of choice because we recognize that people educate themselves and humanize themselves more when they exercise choice. They assume responsibility for their own decisions, learn to dominate impulses and influences, and see a coherence between the values they defend with words and the values that they live. School must involve many choices, big and small, so that young people learn to cultivate values and reflect on them.

Pedagogy of history

Pedagogy of history emerges from the cultivation of memory, from gaining a sense of history and perceiving ourselves a part of it. History is not just a repository for significant things but something to be cultivated and produced. Collective memory is fundamental for the construction of identity. To cultivate memory is more than coldly knowing one's own past; that is why there is often a close link between memory and ritual. Through rituals and ceremonies, the Movement celebrates its own memory. When a symbolic act is carried out in memory of a fallen comrade or an important occupation of land, you feel the past as your own and as a necessary reference point for the choices you have to make in life. Memory is collective; no one and nothing is remembered in itself, disconnected from social relationships. So, in school, history should not be just a discipline but an important dimension of the entire educative process.

Pedagogy of alternation

Pedagogy of alternation comes from the desire not to tear up roots with our family or community. We can think of schooling as composed of two parts. There is school time, where students have theoretical and practical classes, participate in numerous acts of learning, organize themselves to fulfil essential tasks, evaluate the process and participate in planning activities, live and deepen values. And there is community time, which is when students research their reality, record that experience and engage in the exchange of understanding. The wider community is important in assisting this second part of learning.

How school is organized

This chapter is not intended to record what happens in every school, nor is it limited to a single case study, but the following sections brings together what is typical of many schools.

Many of the organisational features of our schools reflect features of the wider democratic structures of the camps and settlements. They are based on principles such as democratic management, the self-organisation of students and the creation of pedagogical communities. Collective management is an important guarantee to avoid paternalism and presidentialism; the division of responsibilities helps to involve everybody while respecting their qualities and skills. In the camps and settlements, families are organized into basic groups where everyone meets periodically for discussion. Each basic group elects (with right of recall) a coordinator, and the coordinators form the camp coordination. At the same time, other individuals are chosen in each sector to form parts of settlement work-teams that are responsible for, for example, water or education.

Pupils in each class distribute themselves in activity groups, each with about five participants. Each group chooses a coordinator, a deputy and a secretary. The coordinators choose a class coordinator, a deputy and a secretary; this process is repeated at school level. However, decisions have to be ratified by a full class meeting. New coordinators are chosen about every two months. Teachers help groups reflect on their decisions. Typically, the activity groups can help one another by studying together, completing school tasks, reading and discussing together, decorating or cleaning the classroom, distributing lunch, preparing an event, or participating in a civic action. Sometimes all the groups do the same thing, sometimes different.

We call *educators* all who are directly involved in teaching and learning in schools. These are the teachers, whether from outside or inside; other school staff (secretaries, cooks) who educate by example and through their participation in management; volunteers; others engaged in a community activity that is integrated with school learning.

A large part of education is the development of an ethos (*mistica*) and values. Ethos is the soul of a people. The ethos of the MST involves a contagious passion, the ability to shake off the dust and find new ways of doing things and learning. School ethos should involve promoting a love of work and a sense of belonging. Ethos can be expressed through poetry, theatre, physical expression, words, music, song, symbols, tools for work and preserving the memory of great struggles across time and humanity. Passion irrigates reason, helping us to be more human, disposed to challenge our limitations. Our schools promote values that are different from the anti-human values of capitalist society, especially in its neoliberal version: individualism, consumerism, egoism. Our values include solidarity, doing things for others, the capacity to be angry at injustice and suffering, the satisfaction of being part of a working class, a confidence in the power to construct one's own destiny and overcome our inferiority complex, commitment to collective values and a belief in humanity. There are also major challenges, including overcoming macho and racist attitudes, respecting differences and helping those with special needs.

Time is organized according to the wishes of each school. It includes

a. class time – essential for formal study, including in circles or groups, but also outside (e.g. a walk for observation);
b. work time – engaging in productive activities arranged with the intention of learning (e.g. how production connects to markets, fruit growing, herbal remedies, caring for small animals, woodwork);
c. skills time – where individuals can choose to learn particular skills (ICT, dance, pottery, etc.);
d. leisure and sport time – a wide choice of activities including walks, picnics, toys;
e. study time – for quiet supervised study; and
f. time to care for the school, including cleaning and improving the public space.

In organising the curriculum, it is important not to see school as a centre for programmatic contents. Teachers are not there to cover lists of contents. At the centre should be the cycles of our students' human life and the community's values. Learning should be adjusted according to the cycles of nature, including the agricultural year and the location of the school. Inclusion is fundamental: ensuring that all pupils get to school, that special needs are provided for, that their schooling is socially satisfying and *a break with the logic of a poor school for poor people.*

Our schools draw upon the full range of academic disciplines of the common curriculum as required by each Brazilian state. Schools are advised that the human sciences, especially history, are very important, including philosophy from the earliest stage. We also study further disciplines, particularly agricultural science, rural management and health. Our curriculum also involves the interdisciplinary study of generative themes and projects to improve our reality.

Schools should also organize learning opportunities for the wider community, including seminars and lectures, educational visits such as to city schools and neighbourhoods, religious communities, sports activities and visits to other MST settlements.

Secondary schooling

Providing primary schooling (grades 1 to 4) was the starting point, but we also had to consider how best to provide the secondary stage (5 to 8). These can be integral with the primary stage and can also involve collaboration with neighbouring communities not part of the MST. One of the available models for us was other schools with an agricultural specialism.

Our aims included

a. developing skills for rural work, including an introduction to the techniques of agriculture, animal husbandry, and administration and accountancy;
b. assisting the implementation and sustainability of the agrarian reform through discussions and studying problems;
c. developing political understanding (a more coherent understanding of the MST, and responses to injustice across our greater country of Latin America);
d. strengthening collective organisation and cooperation;
e. developing a general education suitable for progression to the upper secondary stage; and
f. educating the various dimensions of personality and helping personal identity construction of young people.

Education for social transformation is central. We have an explicit historic commitment: we are part of the working class and aim for the radical transformation of society to restore human dignity to the majority of the population who are denied it. Our curriculum involves an entitlement to:

a. critical contents in various disciplines, assisting the ideological formation of young people;
b. teaching methods that encourage young people to express their ideas, ask questions, take a stance, and develop skills of expression, discussion and argument;
c. diverse politico-cultural activities in the community, to assist the formation of a collective cultural identity alongside other rural workers;
d. the systematic involvement of cadres from the MST and other social movements;
e. cultivating the art of self-expression in its many forms; and
f. sports as a form of leisure, of physical and motor development, of a spirit of initiative, discipline and healthy competition with priority to collective activities.

This stage of schooling is also essential for rural development. Through their struggles and experiences, the social movements and people's organizations are constructing an alternative project of rural development as an immediate task of social transformation. Schools cannot stay aloof from the struggle for land and for the agrarian reform, the challenges of new forms of organizing production and work in the settlements, alternative technologies and collective participation in decisions affecting community development. As students in grades 5 to 8 are already involved in the production processes of the settlements, it is possible and necessary to make a deeper link between school and the concrete problems of rural reality – through study and discussion of these problems and also through direct involvement of the school in solving some of them. If the settlement has a serious problem such as the low fertility of the soil, why cannot the school be involved in research and experimentation with alternative technologies? And why shouldn't production costs be looked at in maths classes?

The educative principle of collective work is one of the basic pillars of the MST's educational project, whether in courses of political formation or courses for technical qualifications, at school or university. Grades 5 to 8 should be a school of work. This implies that the curriculum includes technological disciplines and activities, a study of animal husbandry and how to provide for the needs of settlers in the region;

a. that the curriculum should also include experimentation with alternative technologies, both in school and in practical settings;
b. that pupils participate in planning for the administration of the school;
c. that, wherever possible, they are involved in organizing productive processes, which brings income to the school or the settlement;
d. that they reflect on work experiences; and
e. that the school year is responsive to the work patterns of the region.

We need to attend to certain key methodological principles. People learn only when they need to, so teachers should identify and prompt occasions for learning. The students' prior knowledge should be brought out, even to counter it. It is essential to start with familiar realities when constructing knowledge, but it's also essential not to get stuck there but to attain scientific knowledge that is based on relations between phenomena, facts and dimensions of reality. We need to provide our students with up-to-date knowledge, so we must take care with old textbooks that carry archaic knowledge or barely scientific attitudes. Research is a good instrument for producing knowledge. There should be opportunities to integrate disciplines, including through generative themes.

This stage of schooling should cover the accepted subjects (Portuguese, literature, maths, geography, history, sciences, arts, physical education, a foreign language, and health education and religion). In developing the optional supplementary part of the curriculum, we should consider philosophy, sociology, psychology, agriculture, rural administration, work organisation and environmental education.

Even standard school subjects need to be thought through in terms of local priorities. In arts, for example, which creative activities are of most interest to young people in the area (dance, sculpture, local crafts, etc.) and how students can set up theatre and music groups. There are many motivating issues upon which a chemistry curriculum can be built, such as water purity, soil analysis, erosion, fuels and the properties of metals. Geography provides the opportunity to study different ways in which societies appropriate nature, rural and urban uses of land, natural resources in Brazil, and patterns of poverty and migration.

The major problems and developmental issues of settlements provide an important basis for generative themes, which require the contribution of different disciplines. What follow are examples of popular issues and questions.

The MST and the struggle for agrarian reform

The history of struggle for land in Latin America; how the MST is organized in different parts of the country; what are the major challenges, forms of struggle, principles and norms; the symbols, songs and culture; who is for and against agrarian reform; the relationship between town and country.

Production in the settlements

Schools should focus on real local problems, alternative techniques and technologies, reducing production costs and generating income.

How work and life are organized

This provides an opportunity to compare life in MST settlements with other ways of organizing work and social living, including health, housing, family structures and power relationships, both nationally and internationally.

Conclusion

As readers will understand by now, the Movement is central to our pedagogical vision and practice, but also we must say that schools and pedagogical understanding are themselves in movement. They develop as part of a wider totality, within a perspective of human development (*formação*). It is important for teachers and their students to have a vision not just of the history of the MST but of human history. We have to evaluate the treasures we inherit from the past and have a presentiment of the future, the culture that produces us, which we reproduce and which we develop for posterity.

Our schools are located within the process of producing a new social subject, the Sem Terra (Landless People). However, we are not separate in this, for it is an identity constructed from the historical accumulation of many social struggles and an inheritance for those who will struggle in the future. Education at its best is about making the earth (land, soil) a place for human cultivation in a double sense: cultivation by human beings and the cultivation of humanity.

One of the principal lessons that can be learned from the MST is how pedagogy can be set in motion in a reality that mixes personal development, the production of social subjects, class struggle and a struggle for humanity. We should look for these dimensions in all educational practices to raise new questions and move pedagogy forward.

We need to pay special attention to childhood among the Landless and the pedagogical *care* that is devoted to children. It is significant that the children have adapted the name Sem Terra (Landless) to call themselves *Sem Terrinha* (little people without land). The suffix *–inha* in Portuguese is an expression of both affection and size. This expresses a feeling that 'we too want to be part of the Landless movement, but we don't want to stop being children. But we're not just children, we're Sem Terrinha! We are Sem Terrinha with love. That is how we want to be cared for by the Movement.' The demand for love and care is a universal right of children and young people in education.

It is fitting to situate the pedagogy of the Movement within the broad history of education and pedagogy. However, to do so, we need to turn the official history upside down. We need a 'pedagogical occupation' of the territory of educational history. Leonardo Boff (1999: 35), in his reflection on 'knowing how to care', tells us that attaching care to everything we plan and do is a singular characteristic of human beings. In this sense, we can reflect on how education also has the duty of constituting, in people and societies, what Boff calls the 'caring way of being'. And caring for things, he tells us, implies intimacy, sensing things from within, welcoming them, respecting them, giving them comfort and rest (Boff: 96). Caring is getting in tune with people, feeling the rhythm.

At this time in particular, we need to care a lot for the task of human development (formação). This is an essential part of the wider social project. We can rightly claim that school is one of the places where the landless learn to care about and for themselves and one another. However, this is possible only when schools can reach out from themselves and integrate with a broader network of educational experiences of the social movements. Certainly, we have to take account – when developing pedagogy in these difficult times – of the urgent need for our country to learn to take care of itself, of the people, of its historical project.

Thus, as earth is more than just earth, a school can become more than just a school. What answers can we give to the young people of our country and across the world who still trust in our care?

Acknowledgments

This chapter was edited from sections of the following works.

Caldart, R. S. (2004) *Pedagogia do Movimento Sem Terra* (pp. 17–31; 230–270; 410–419). São Paulo: Expressão Popular.
Cerioli, P. R. and Caldart, R. S. (1999) 'Como fazemos a escola de educação fundamental' [How to do school at the elementary stage]. In Dossiê MST Escola: documentos e estudos 1990–2001. *Caderno de Educação*, 13, edição especial [Collection of historic documents].
Equipe Setor de Educação MST. (1995) 'Ensino de 5a a 8a series em areas de assentamento: ensaiando uma proposta.' In Dossiê MST Escola: documentos e estudos 1990–2001. *Caderno de Educação*, 13, edição especial [Collection of historic documents].

However, all these texts derive from extensive and thoughtful discussions at gatherings of MST educators and from the initiatives taken and sustained in the many local settlements of this social movement.

References

Boff, L. (1999) *Saber cuidar: ética do humano – compaixão pela terra*. [Knowing how to care: human ethics – compassion for the earth]. Petrópolis: Vozes.
Thompson, E. P. (1963) *The Making of the English Working Class*. London: Gollancz.

Suggested further readings

Camini, I. (2009) *Escola itinerante: na fronteira de uma nova escola.* São Paulo: Expressão Popular.
Freire, P. (1972) *Pedagogy of the Oppressed.* Harmondsworth: Penguin.
Kane, L. (2001) *Popular Education and Social Change in Latin America.* London: Latin American Bureau.
Pistrak, M. M. (2009) *A escola comuna.* São Paulo: Expressão Popular.

The Landless Workers Movement (Movimento dos Trabalhadores Rurais Sem Terra) has an English-language website http://www.mstbrazil.org with many links to other sources. Their main website is www.mst.org.br.

Chapter 8

The promise of place- and community-based education

United States

Gregory Smith

Introduction

Place- and community-based education is an approach to teaching and learning that embodies a fundamental shift in perspective about the kinds of knowledge presented in schools, the roles of teachers and students, and the broader purposes of education itself. Its primary aims include helping children understand the characteristics of healthy social and natural environments and connecting them to their own communities and places in ways that inspire a desire to contribute to and sustain the well-being of these human and more-than-human systems. Place- and community-based education achieves these ends by grounding learning in the local, starting with the immediate and lived experiences of teachers and students and using these as the springboard to explore the national and global. Focusing on the application of skills and knowledge to local issues and problems, this approach provides the young with opportunities to do work that is meaningful and valued by people beyond the school. In doing so, it gives students a reason to learn and communities a reason to support public education.

Although not widespread, place- and community-based education is gaining a following of people drawn to its vision of diversity, responsibility, participation and sustainability. In schools where it has become a motivating vision for change, educators come to understand that beyond lectures, books, or worksheets, learning can be enhanced through more direct forms of involvement with people and phenomena outside the classroom. Making this shift is something that individual teachers can and do accomplish, but a change such as this can be much more meaningful and powerful when embraced by school teams or an entire faculty.

Two schools in Oregon, United States – one urban and one rural – and a suburban district provide examples of how educators are enacting this approach to educational reform. They exemplify very different contexts, starting points and trajectories. The Sunnyside Environmental School (SES) in Portland was created in 1995 as a 'special focus' middle school by a small group of educational innovators. The Al Kennedy High School in rural Cottage Grove began as a program for potential dropouts and has moved from being a last resort for struggling students to a well-thought-of and now desirable educational option. The West Linn/Wilsonville School District in two suburban communities south of Portland adopted sustainability as one of its priorities and has subsequently begun a program to develop cadres of educators at every school knowledgeable about sustainability and social justice issues and capable of using place- and community-based approaches to address them.

Sunnyside Environmental School

The SES is what is called a 'special focus' school. Founded in 1995, it has for nearly a decade been attracting students from throughout the city to educational experiences that regularly get them out of the classroom and into social service agencies, parks and wetlands of the Portland metropolitan area. The school's web page describes the unique characteristics of its program:

> The K–8 curriculum brings the beauty and magic of the natural world into the lives of children through an integrated, developmentally appropriate, art infused education. Creativity, love of learning, personal responsibility and family, are the cornerstones of an education that celebrates the many overlapping environments of Portland.

The city's wild and urban areas become sites for inquiry, exploration and understanding as children acquire personal and academic skills that lead to a satisfying life as thoughtful, active members of the larger community. In pursuit of this goal, students are involved in service learning efforts throughout their years at the school (www.sesptsa.com/about/about.php, retrieved July 2009).

The SES serves 560 students and has become one of the city's more desirable schools. It has sought from the beginning to serve a diverse range of students and has actively reached out to Portland's low-income neighborhoods.

The school is the brainchild of Portland Public Schools educator Sarah Taylor. During a course in the educational leadership program at Portland State University in the early 1990s, she was asked to imagine her ideal school. As mother and adoptive mother to numerous young people, she had become impressed by the mismatch between middle schools and many of her children's natures and needs. She took this opportunity to envision an education grounded in community and place that she believed would better recognize young adolescents' desire for meaningful social experiences and active and engaging learning opportunities. Her professor urged her to write up a proposal to the school district's superintendent and board of directors and, within a few months, she was assembling around her a group of advisors and fellow teachers to help her move from vision to implementation and looking for a site to house a middle school that would initially enroll 180 6th- through 8th-graders.

During spring and early summer, she and her advisory team (including myself) hired six teachers, two for each grade. Taylor and the teachers then shaped the broad outlines of a curriculum that has proven to be a lasting framework for the middle school students. They decided to create mixed-grade classrooms for the core subjects of language arts, social studies and science; math and Spanish would be taught separately on the basis of student level; art was integrated into other subjects; and physical education was taught to the entire core class. This arrangement means that students can remain with the same teacher for much of the day. Tuesdays or Thursdays can be devoted to daylong field study or service learning away from school. Students regularly engage in environmental monitoring in urban watersheds or travel to more distant sites such as Mt. St. Helens or the Oregon Coast on overnight trips. Scope and sequence challenges have been dealt with by establishing a common theme for each of the three years: forests, then rivers, and finally mountains. Science, social studies and language arts activities are linked to each of these broad topics.

The school incorporates the Scottish storyline approach to immerse students as players in more distant contexts. When, for example, students study the American Civil War, they become residents of either a northern city or southern town. They collectively create a mural representing their home community. When posters seeking the whereabouts of runaway slaves appear on the walls of buildings in the mural or battles are fought in their village streets, students must respond. This personalization of education characterizes learning experiences throughout the school.

Service learning is another critical component. Students regularly participate in litter cleanups, ivy pulls, planting of native species as part of the restoration of urban riparian zones, stocking shelves at the Oregon Food Bank, or helping out with all-school festivals. Eighth graders are expected to develop a service-learning project on their own that involves gaining the participation of others in a common activity, such as a canned food drive or creating a pocket park on otherwise unused neighborhood property. Service in its varied forms becomes one of the primary ways that the SES links its students to the broader community.

The school exemplifies a number of opportunities and challenges that face educators interested in incorporating place- and community-based approaches. Opportunities included the chance to build a school from the ground up, to develop a truly innovative educational program with like-minded colleagues, and to work with other teachers and families committed to a purposeful and meaningful vision of learning and community and environmental responsibility.

However, there were also serious challenges. Once agreement was given to create the school, it was ignored by the district office to the extent of having neither books nor desks. It shared a building with an elementary school when it first opened, and, in year 4, a new principal of the host school assumed responsibility. This created difficulties as the school was technically a special focus *program*, and Sarah Taylor did not possess the full authority of a school principal. Struggle continued for a few more years; she was accredited as principal, but the school remained formally a 'program' rather than a school.

However, during these years, it attracted more and more attention throughout the district, and its enrollment grew to 240 students. Under pressure to become even larger, Taylor and her teachers decided to become a Kindergarten to Grade 8 school in 2003 and moved to another building, the Sunnyside School, in a neighborhood where enrollments had been declining. Student enrollment doubled, and the special focus program finally became a special focus school, eligible for a higher level of financial support.

The move entailed negotiating relationships with a handful of teachers from the former school who needed to be integrated into the Sunnyside faculty and the development of a Kindergarten to Grade 5 curriculum. The gardens had to be reestablished. Student enrolment, previously determined by a district-wide lottery, changed; Sunnyside became first a neighborhood school, then a special focus school, with neighborhood students given priority in admissions decisions. At first, the number of neighborhood students available to fill classroom seats was low, meaning that Black, Latino and Native American students from other Portland neighborhoods could still easily gain access to its program. The school has subsequently attracted a growing number of young families to its catchment area, mostly White and middle income, reducing access to students from less-privileged neighborhoods. This has become an ongoing issue of concern to Taylor and her teachers.

Sunnyside has continued to struggle in a variety of ways in its relationship with the Portland Public Schools but has now become a well-recognized and highly thought of educational option. District-level conversations over the past three years have considered the possibility of creating an additional environmentally focused school in another neighborhood, one that was lower income. Taylor, assisted by the teachers and site council, has written a curriculum guideline to share with district officials and school board members to help others better understand the unique characteristics of its offerings.

Although always part of the Portland Public Schools, the SES bears some resemblance to charter schools created by educators and/or parents. Like a charter school, it was a new institution and did not have to deal with inherited practices or staff. Though at first it had to accommodate some transferred teachers with limited interest, central office administrators eventually realized the need for a more selective hiring process. Unlike a charter school, Sunnyside has had to work within a complex organizational network where jealousy about the school's flexible structures and public attention, or administrative determination to make it conform to conventional practice, has been the source of ongoing struggle. This has moderated to some extent as the school has proven its staying power, but the struggle has taken its toll on Sunnyside staff.

The nature of the program itself also places significant demands on everyone who works there. Educators value its vitality and the sense of purpose and community, but they must also defer to their colleagues and the school's own traditions when it comes to curricular decisions. Working in a school such as this also requires a high level of creativity and energy; it's not possible to go on autopilot and maintain the appearance of success. Despite the challenges, the school continues to thrive and implements remarkable and innovative events such as a two-day teach-in about the Iraq War in the spring of 2008 and a four-day teach-in about global warming and climate change during the spring of 2009. It demonstrates what can happen when a district allows principals and teachers to pursue their imaginations and sense of personal calling to create a school that addresses important social and environmental issues and aims to develop citizens who believe in their own capacity to make the world a better and more just place.

The Al Kennedy High School

Unlike Sunnyside, the Al Kennedy High School had already existed for a number of years when it embarked on a reform strategy. The school was a last resort for students who get lost in conventional classrooms and become seriously credit-deficient. Many are from families who struggle economically in a community that once depended on the lumber industry for jobs and income. In 2007, a new administrator, Tom Horn, was persuaded by the district's superintendent (in 2007, the U.S. superintendent of the year) to become its principal. Horn found a school in disarray. During the first month, he dealt with four drug overdoses. Three years later, there is little if any drug use at the school, and students are graduating and going on to post-secondary education. Much of this transformation can be ascribed to Horn's leadership coupled with his ability to persuade the school's staff – teachers, custodian and secretary – to create a supportive and educationally meaningful environment for its students.

A former special education teacher, Horn was well positioned to develop an approach to schooling that was both personalized and engaging. Before becoming a teacher, Horn had worked as a professional surfer and a yurt builder. As a student growing up on Maui who'd come to love the waves more than classrooms, he had personally understood what it means to inhabit the margins of a school. Early on during his tenure at Al Kennedy, he decided to focus on learning activities that would take students outside the classroom and gain them some positive visibility in the community. One of the first projects involved clearing invasive species along a section of the Coast Fork of the Willamette River that ran through town. Beneath the brambles, students uncovered the millrace of the flour mill that was the site around which the community of Cottage Grove originally formed. Local residents became excited, and news stories featured this discovery.

A committed environmentalist and social justice activist, Horn began exploring other possibilities and invited me to make a presentation about place- and community-based education to his fellow teachers. That talk and subsequent conversations have resulted in a burgeoning of ideas that Horn has been able to share with his teachers and members of the community. Drawing on John Cleveland's paper, 'The Rural Sustainable School' (2007), a curriculum has been shaped focusing on agriculture, architecture, energy, forestry and community. This has enabled the creation of multiple partnerships with local agencies and the pursuit of sizeable grants.

The school, for example, has entered into a long-term relationship with the city of Cottage Grove to complete wetlands mitigation projects required when already existing wetlands are zoned for industrial use. Students clear invasive species and plant native trees, and the school is paid as a result. Horn sees this as an 80-year project. This additional income is used to pay for field trips to locations such as Canyonlands in Utah, places to which many of the school's low-income students may have only dreamed of going. Students are also encouraged to identify landowners with property adjoining local streams and rivers. Small grants are available for people interested in removing Scotch broom and Himalayan blackberries. Students volunteer to write the grants and not infrequently are asked to form the crews who then do the grunt work – providing students with a source of income and the satisfaction of knowing that they're bettering the local environment.

In 2008, Horn decided to take the school's nursery and garden projects to another level. Students were already involved in maintaining a garden and distributed produce to the local food bank, one of many ways that the school enacts its vision of social justice. To develop this even further, the school now collaborates with Healing Harvest, a nonprofit organization that provides gardening experiences for individuals who face a variety of physical and mental challenges; together, students and Healing Harvest staff and participants design and build organic gardens at elementary schools throughout the South Lane School District. According to Horn:

> Using the model of the Kennedy Community Garden, Kennedy students are providing schools with a place to share, a place to grow healthy food, and a place to develop a lifelong dedication to the environment. Real learning is accomplished by doing and discovering... Through this process, Kennedy [School] has found that the achievement of organizing and planting a school garden far exceeds the value of the produce harvested.
>
> (Horn, 2009)

Visits to the trailer parks where a significant share of his students live led Horn to adopt another set of strategies aimed at addressing the poverty faced by many residents of this former lumber town. He saw trailers that were sinking into the ground. He wondered about alternatives and whether it would be possible to design and construct housing kits – such as the Katrina Cottages sold by Loews – that were affordable and environmentally friendly, kits that included solar panels, rainwater catchment systems and composting toilets. He found architects in nearby Eugene and the University of Oregon interested in the idea, then wrote and received a $67,000 grant to come up with a prototype design. With that design, Horn is meeting with Lane County officials to find ways to use U.S. Department of Housing and Urban Development stimulus dollars to start a business prefabricating the modular structures. He is also initiating a collaborative arrangement with the local community college to establish a program for construction technologies and 'green building' management at the Kennedy School.

Horn is committed to making sure that the work students encounter in school is both academic and physical. He wants his students to be thinkers and doers. To this end, he also seeks grants that engage students in scientific analysis. In December of 2008, he received news that he'd received a $30,000 grant from the Weyerhauser Foundation to investigate microbial organisms in local forest soils over a five-year period. Such experiences give students the opportunity to learn how to engage in on-the-ground scientific research that can potentially contribute to the development of more sustainable forestry practices. Doing so ensures that the school helps students address its central academic goals to

- evaluate, discuss, question, analyze and apply;
- understand that knowledge and intellect should accompany goodness and commitment to community; and
- develop the intellectual and physical capacity that ensures a love of learning.

(http://blogs.slane.k12.or.us/kennedy/about/)

A school that previously had received little positive recognition by the community and whose students had been cast into the role of losers has now become a model of progressive sustainability education for the district as a whole. How did this happen?

Central is Horn's ability both to dream of new possibilities and to invite his teachers, parents and community members into that dream in ways that encourage their participation and enthusiasm. In an effort to get a community garden started at one of the trailer parks, one Saturday Horn knocked on the doors of every trailer and invited people to a meeting that would begin in 20 minutes about starting a community garden. Met by burly men with well-tattooed arms behind one screen door after another, he was unsure who would show up, but more than 40 people came. Horn began by asking how many people liked vegetables. One man said he loved tomatoes and recalled eating sandwiches made of two slices of beefsteak tomato with cucumbers in the middle when he was a kid. This primed the conversation and, by the time the meeting ended, plans had been laid to dig and plant the garden.

Horn's approach with his teachers and the community has been similar. He brings in articles and books or speakers and encourages people at school to talk about what they've learned, what excites them, what possibilities they can imagine. He goes to Rotary and Kiwanis Club meetings and speaks with local business and agency people, finding out what kinds of projects are attractive to them. The next step is to bring his teachers and these community members together. To advance the vision that now propels the school, he then organizes symposia during which educators and agency staff can talk about sustainability issues and projects that would benefit from their collaboration. To date, he has attracted the participation of numerous organizations throughout the community and garnered more than $700,000 in grant support.

Much of this can be attributed to his energy and vision and basic human decency. Horn's enthusiasm and honesty inspire enthusiasm and trust; this coupled with his talent for creating networks of people who want to work with one another is leading to the formation of an educational and community development effort that is giving young people and a town that have been treated by either their former teachers or the broader economy as unimportant a sense of their own capacity to create a viable and purposeful future.

West Linn/Wilsonville school district

The West Linn/Wilsonville school district serves a very different clientele. Located on the southern boundary of the Portland metropolitan region's urban growth boundary, the community became a desirable location for the construction of upscale homes in the 1980s and 1990s. Students come from middle- to upper-income families and are predominantly White. Not unlike similar districts, its schools are known for their progressive instructional practices and its students for their academic achievement. In 2007, superintendent Roger Woehl announced his interest in supporting a district-wide initiative aimed at raising the profile of sustainability issues. A newcomer to the field, Woehl had become concerned about issues related to climate change and resource exhaustion and the impact these developments would have on his own grandchildren. He sent an e-mail to teachers throughout the district inviting them to participate in a sustainability task force. More than 90 people responded. The task force was formed, and a number of its members were sent to an international conference in Mexico a few weeks later to learn more about the issues.

At its meetings in the fall and winter, the task force decided to focus on the topic of sustainability at an annual daylong in-service event during which teachers present sessions about their own innovative practice to colleagues from other schools. I was asked to give a keynote speech about sustainability education. To keep the momentum alive, a core group of teachers who had been addressing environmental and social justice topics for a number of years met with me in the weeks after this in-service event to design a grant proposal aimed at creating a course that investigated these issues in more depth. Our intention was to develop four- to six-person teams in every school who were knowledgeable about sustainability and place- and community-based learning practices and able to begin integrating these into their work with students. We wrote a grant proposal to the Oregon Community Foundation and Gray Family Fund, received partial funding and initiated the first of two iterations of the course in January, 2009.

Thanks to the superintendent's support and the active involvement of well-respected educators throughout the district, the course attracted 26 participants from all but one of the district's schools. Meeting for three hours after school on Wednesdays from January to May, participants deepened their knowledge of the variety of factors that are now calling into question the sustainability of industrialized and industrializing countries from the United States and Europe to China and India. We then moved on to a consideration of innovations that are arising globally to address many of these problems, exploring the domains of business practices, water management, forestry, food production, rangeland, fisheries, transportation, urban design and education – not with the idea of turning participants into experts but of giving them a sense of possibility and hope. This segment of the course culminated with a daylong tour of various organizations in Portland that are creating business, governmental, agricultural and educational institutions that promise to be more just and sustainable. Lester Brown's *Plan B, 3.0* (2008) and David Suzuki and Holly Dressel's *Good News for a Change* (2003) supported this investigation.

The second half of the course moved on to a consideration of the contributions educators could make. In my own work, I have argued that place- and community-based education can play a central role in this process by drawing children into an experience of affiliation with the places and communities where they live and by presenting them with opportunities to gain the knowledge, skills and disposition to become active in efforts to maintain the health of surrounding social and natural environments. Without this willingness to care and become involved, information about the unsustainability of current human beliefs and practices and the need to do things differently will remain only that: information. It is critical to find ways to give young people a sense that, working with others, they can in small ways take actions that hold the promise of addressing some of the challenges that now face humanity and the planet.

The final assignment of the course involved creating a study unit that addressed one of the three legs of sustainability – equity, environment, or the economy – in ways that would allow students to become more knowledgeable about their own place and that would ideally also give them an opportunity to address these issues practically. Participants whose jobs did not involve classroom teaching (instructional coordinators, librarians or administrators) were asked to create half-day learning experiences situated within the district that could be presented to people who enrolled in a sustainability education institute to be held two weeks after the end of K–12 classes. Following are some of the topics of units of instruction developed by individuals or teams of teachers.

- Restoration of a dry creek bed on the campus of a district primary school
- Development of proposals to the superintendent and school board about ways to reduce the carbon and ecological footprints of one of the district's high schools
- Reforestation in Oregon and elsewhere
- Investigation of native plants as part of a biology unit and the creation of a native plant garden
- Storyline exploration of Wilsonville, Oregon and its history
- Using gardening to transform a school's curriculum
- Building compost makers appropriate for homes and apartments
- Maintaining and learning about an urban loop trail near the school
- Designing and leading a school-wide fund raiser and celebration, with the specific intent of involving low-income students.

Some of these units were implemented during the spring course, others during the next academic year. Teachers reported that the units elicited much student interest, often from young people whose previous participation had been less than exemplary.

When asked what they had learned about sustainability, teachers responded in the following ways:

The class shifted my perspective about what really should be taught in schools. I feel this kind of work is imperative to change structures/ practices that are in place that are destructive and unjust.

I have a much better sense of the wide variety of issues that are linked to sustainability and a much broader sense of what sustainability encompasses. I have also gotten a greater sense of the urgency in teaching all of our kids about sustainability.

I have learned that educating for sustainability is not just about creating more sustainable communities. It is about better, more effective education. It is about creating better people by any measure. It is about cultivating hope, happiness, strength and peace.

When teachers were asked about how they might approach their work differently as a result of this course, one observed that

While sustainability, particularly the environmental aspect, was always part of my teaching, I've never felt as empowered to make sustainability part of my day-to-day work. I am convinced that my biggest goal is to help my students be systems thinkers, caring citizens and inspired young people who can make a difference.

Another wrote:

The key question for me will be 'How do I, as a teacher, better allow kids to make and strengthen connections, to be observant, to think critically, to empathize, to find joy in the real?'

It is too soon to say what impact this course and the two-day summer institute that followed its conclusion will have on teaching and curricular practices throughout the district. The hope is that by creating teams of teachers knowledgeable about sustainability in each school, educators will encourage one another to experiment with lessons and instructional approaches in ways that will deepen students' connections to their place and provide them with opportunities to do work that both they and their communities will view as useful and worthwhile. Another group of 24 teachers enrolled in the second iteration of the course in the fall of 2009, potentially creating enough people to advance a sustainability agenda and keep it alive.

Acting now for the future

Introducing sustainability or place- and community-based education into schools during a period when policy makers and the public are primarily concerned about accountability and standardization is not easy. Doing so requires imagination and a degree of courage to move in directions that are not part of national or even international conversations about educational priorities. Fortunately, learning experiences grounded in local places that address issues significant to community health and well-being often are engaging for students and valued by adults. Although research so far does not show that such learning experiences can consistently be associated with higher test scores, findings do indicate that an education that attends to local social and environmental concerns does not diminish those scores. Furthermore, these experiences are tied to increases in students' commitment to citizen participation and environmental stewardship – two dispositions critical to the development of a more sustainable and just society (Duffin et al. 2004; Smith and Sobel 2010).

The change strategies described in the preceding pages demonstrate different ways that educators are confronting this challenge. What characterizes work in each of these settings is a combination of hopefulness, determination and sometimes stubbornness in the face of difficult odds. In each instance, however, teachers and administrators committed to sustainability and social justice benefit from the support of central office leaders and community members. Moving schools in this new direction does not seem like something individuals acting in isolation can accomplish on their own. Just as in healthy ecosystems, the maintenance of relationships is crucial. Finding ways to extend networks of interested and supportive people – both inside and outside school systems – may provide the most productive course of action for people in other communities interested in accomplishing what is described in this chapter. Even in the face of what can seem intractable odds, school leaders and teachers like those described here are implementing a vision of sustainability and social justice education that has genuine promise. This is not an agenda that can be enacted only in the future. It is being enacted right now.

References

Brown, L. (2008) *Plan B, 3.0: Mobilizing to Save Civilization*. New York: W.W. Norton.

Cleveland, J. (2007) 'The rural sustainable school'. http://www.nupolis.com/public/item/230818 (accessed July 2009).

Duffin, M., Powers, A., Tremblay, G. and PEER Associates. (2004) *An Evaluation of Project CO-SEED: Community-Based School Environmental Education, 2003–4 Interim Report*. Richmond, VT: PEER Associates.

Horn, T. (2009). Personal communication.

Smith, G. and Sobel, D. (2010) *Place-and Community-Based Education in Schools*. New York: Routledge.

Suzuki, D. and Dressel, H. (2003) *Good News for a Change: Hope for a Troubled Planet*. Vancouver, BC: Greystone Press.

Suggested further readings

Gruenewald, D. and Smith, G. (2008) *Place-Based Education in the Global Age: Local Diversity*. New York: Routledge.

Smith, G. and Sobel, D. (2010) 'Bring it on home.' *Educational Leadership*, 68(1), 39–43.

Smith, G. and Sobel, D. (2010) *Place- and Community-Based Education in Schools.* New York: Routledge.

Smith, G. and Williams, D. (1999) *Ecological Education in Action: On Weaving Education, Culture, and the Environment.* Albany: State University of New York Press.

Sobel, D. (2004) *Place-Based Education: Connecting Classrooms to Communities.* Great Barrington, MA: Orion Press.

Chapter 9

Approaching school change through 'learning lives'

Norway

Ola Erstad

Introduction

The challenges and opportunities facing schools in the 21st century are apparent. Several discourses point to the failures of traditional education in responding to future challenges. The dominant discourse focuses on the basic skills of core subjects in schools and curricula as we know them today, for example in policy debates in various countries following the different PISA studies, beginning in 2000. An alternative discourse presents a re-imagining of schooling (Egan 2008), or a critique of the way we organize education today (Claxton 2008). A third discourse represents a middle ground, redefining school in line with ongoing cultural and technological developments, for example, as seen in *the Assessment and Teaching of 21st Century Skills* initiative (www.atc21s.org) and the *New Millenium Learners* project by the OECD.

In this chapter, I propose to challenge traditional conceptions of schooling as the places and spaces of learning in what I describe as a *learning lives* approach. These include studies of the interrelationship between different contexts of learning, where school is one of several, and studies more related to the complexities of schools themselves, as mixtures of formal and informal ways of learning. In this chapter I focus on the latter. The concept of *learning lives* is meant as a way of moving beyond simplistic conceptions of formal or informal/non-formal ways of learning. As such, my focus is on the learner as the unit of analysis, and learning is understood as lifelong, life-wide and life-deep (Banks et al. 2007).

For more than ten years I have been leading large-scale programs and projects in Norway focusing on school development and the implementation and use of new information and communication technologies (ICT). Rather than reporting on these developments here, I prefer to orient myself towards the future, building on insights about school change gained from these large-scale intervention studies. In the first section of this chapter I present an outline for a learning lives approach related to school change. And in the subsequent section I present a couple of examples from Norwegian schools I have been working with, showing how some schools are starting to break contextual boundaries of learning activities and mixing socio-spatial practices of formal and informal ways of engaging students in learning pathways.

Socio-spatial conceptions of learning lives

In this section, I outline some key theoretical underpinnings from sociocultural perspectives on learning and some key aspects of a learning lives approach. In my orientation towards school change, I have written about how schools have very different 'capacities for change' (Erstad 2009); how some school cultures are more developmentally oriented than others, or more systematic in their developmental strategies, and how schools make different uses of new technologies in these change processes. More importantly I believe that we need to look at different levels of how schools work in order to fully understand such 'capacities for change' (Erstad 2010). Olson explains the issue as follows:

> The problem, I believe, is that the theories that gave us insight into children's understanding, motivation, learning and thinking have never come to terms with schooling as an institutional practice with its duties and responsibilities for basic skills, disciplinary knowledges, grades, standards and credentials... What is required, then, is an advance in our understanding of schools as bureaucratic institutions that corresponds to the advances in our understanding of the development of the mind.
>
> (Olson 2003: x–xi)

However, the argument in this chapter goes a step further. I believe we need to move beyond discussing change within the confines of school *per se*, to take a more in-depth look at the ways schools relate to other contexts of learning and how young people mix the formal and informal in different ways, including at school.

Sociocultural learning beyond the school

I highlight four points of importance, building on a sociocultural perspective on learning (Wertsch et al. 1995). The first point concerns the importance of studying the tools and resources used for human development in social practices. Development of material resources goes hand in hand with the development of ideas and intellectual knowledge. Certain tools have traditionally been adapted to school-based learning, such as the book, but digital resources open up new possibilities of where and how people learn.

The second point is that learning should be studied in terms of the interdependence between collective and individual processes in specific situations. Another implication is that knowledge is negotiated and not something that is simply available for the person out there in the world. Knowledge is a result of struggle and engagement and is deeply related to argumentation and mediated action in social context.

The third issue of relevance concerns the way we organize and understand the changes in learning over time in relation to broader cultural change (Schwartz et al. 2009). These changes could be both the result of developments in tool structures, and related to broader social and cultural developments, for example the changing roles of young people in society over time.

The fourth element is the concept of 'mediated action' elaborated on by James Wertsch (1998). One of his questions on mediated action is 'how the introduction of novel cultural tools transforms the action' (Wertsch 1998: 42). Transformations of mediated action can be seen in the introduction of the calculator and the computer, and the controversies these developments have raised among educationalists, also with consequences for the organization of learning activities in schools.

The above points indicate the importance of studying how new technologies represent new cultural tools that create new meaning structures. These tools create new possibilities for how people relate to one another, how knowledge is defined in negotiation between actors, and also how this changes our conception of learning environments in which actors negotiate meaning.

The gap between school as a learning environment and media use outside of schools is something that students are acutely aware of. The following quotations express some conceptions about the role of schooling among students:

> The things you learn in school are to do with education and getting jobs. You're not really using them in actual real life.
>
> (18-year-old; Bentley 1998)

> I guess I could call myself smart. I mean I can usually get good grades. Sometimes I worry though, that I'm not equipped to achieve what I want, that I'm just a tape recorder repeating back what I've heard. I worry that once I'm out of school and people don't keep handing me information with questions ... I'll be lost.
>
> (15-year-old; Bentley 1998)

There will always be a gap between these two settings. The issue is, though, that the experiences and the competencies that young people acquire outside of schools become increasingly important related to learning processes, and ways of understanding learning between different contexts of learning.

'Learning lives'

The term *learning lives* is meant to encompass the longer trajectories of learning that people are involved in, moving from one setting to another and different kinds of transitions and across the life cycle (Barton et al. 2007; Ecclestone et al. 2010).

In the research literature, there has been a growing interest in socio-spatial aspects of how learners learn. Some focus on how students are tangled up in the web of practices defining schooling (Nespor 1997); some are about informal learning and place (Banks et al. 2007; Bekerman et al. 2006); some focus on literacy practices in and out of school (Hull and Schultz 2002); some focus on spatial literacies (Comber and Nixon 2008); and some focus on new mobilities online and offline (Leander et al. 2010). In relation to these theoretical positions and empirical orientations, I highlight four issues that are central to contemporary debates concerning a learning lives approach.

Learning identity

The concept of identity has been contested in different ways (Moje and Luke 2009). Also, there has been an increasing interest in trying to link learning and identity formation as interrelated terms. The two terms are understood as the capacity to adapt to changing roles within different contexts, as 'figured worlds' (Holland et al. 1998). Wortham (2006) has made an important contribution in the way he describes how social identification and academic learning deeply depend on each other, by closely following the 'learning identity' among a few students during an academic year.

Toward contextualizing

The concept of 'context' is important because it informs us in an analytical sense of the way we interpret and understand the interrelationship between people and the circumstances they are involved in at different times and places. I relate to Cole's (1996) definition of context as 'that which weaves together':

> When context is thought of in this way, it cannot be reduced to that which surrounds. It is, rather, a qualitative relation between a minimum of two analytical entities (threads), which are two moments in a single process. The boundaries between 'task and its context' are not clear-cut and static but ambiguous and dynamic.
>
> (Cole 1996: 135)

Van Oers argues for using the concept of *contextualizing* rather than context:

Context, then, is the result of this process of identification of a situation as a particular activity-setting. Or to put it differently: the basic process here is the process of context making (which I will call contextualizing), which is an intellectual activity by itself, embedded in a current sociocultural activity.

(Van Oers 1998: 482)

The school then represents one of several ways of contextualizing.

Participating across time and space

In their research on interventions aimed at preventing social exclusion among adults in the United Kingdom, Anne Edwards and Lin Mackenzie argue for a 'detailed analysis of the formation, disruption, reformation and support of trajectories of participation in the opportunities for action provided' (Edwards and Mackenzie 2008: 165). We ought then to explore how participants are not merely situated in space and time but actively networking learning resources across space-time in the course of their activity (Leander et al. 2010: 8).

Creating connections

The concept of transfer is traditionally applied to a person, in a cognitive sense, carrying the product of learning from one task, problem, situation or institution to another (Beach 1999: 101). Such an interpretation of transfer has been criticized for not taking the contextual aspects into consideration, as transfer is not simply a matter of units being transported from one situation to another. Beach argues for leaving the transfer metaphor behind due to several limitations, and instead for establishing a metaphor that broadens our vision of generalisation across changing forms of social organisation based on a sociocultural view of 'generalisation as consequential transition' (1999: 111). This involves multiple interrelated processes rather than a single general procedure. The main point is to help students make connections between contents and contexts along different timescales (Lemke 2000).

Studies of learning lives in schools

This section draws on cases from different projects I have been involved in during the last decade. Even though they were collected at different times, they are quite similar in trying to understand the use of digital media as part of pedagogical practices and school development initiatives. They have in common the fact that they raise issues about socio-spatial aspects of learning and the learning lives of students across different contexts. That was not the main research orientation of these projects but rather an outcome that I have built on in my more recent research interests. The data were collected by interviews and video observations at each school.

Case 1: Reaching out of the classroom

At one lower secondary or 'youth school' just outside Oslo, a couple of teachers initiated the 'Antarctica project'. The overall focus of the project was 'to make a dream come true'. It all started in October 1999 when the explorers Liv Arnesen (Norwegian) and Ann Bancroft (American) presented their ideas for an education program connected to their Antarctica 2000–2001 expedition. This was presented as a global activity in which schools in different countries could participate. A special database was developed whereby anyone could follow the expedition. In addition, the school had a special arrangement with one of the explorers, Liv Arnesen, involving direct interaction before, during and after the expedition. This was to get both factual and research-based information, and information of a more personal nature about the experiences of the two women in Antarctica.

The principal said about using new technologies in the school:

> It relates to being able to use many senses, and to doing things and seeing that it works. To learn about another country by reading about it in a book, compared to getting it presented through the internet. Images and sound and experiences, you might say, and communication with students in other countries directly through e-mail and chatting and all that which now is possible.

The first step in the project was for the students to write a short essay about their 'secret' dream. They discussed these dreams among themselves and to what extent it was possible to make them come true. As part of this, they went on to exchange dreams with students in other countries. Some teachers had gone on the internet and found some schools in the United States, Poland, Finland and Palestine. One teacher explained the impact of this: 'The students got input on how to understand youth culture, to understand life conditions, that they are different'.

As a result of this activity, the students saw that young people have different dreams in different countries. Though some of the students in Norway dreamed about becoming better at snowboarding, a Palestinian girl dreamed about a stable and secure school.

The next step was that a couple of teachers started an activity of following the two women crossing the Antarctic. A group of eight students joined in for this specific activity. The aim was to create a web page that would contain different kinds of reports and information gathered by the students about the expedition and Antarctica.

One collaborator was a major Norwegian newspaper that had a special agreement with the expedition organizers to get up-to-date information. The newspaper also put up a link to the students´ web page on its web pages. In addition to that, the students have used the internet to get access to more general information about Antarctica, and they have downloaded some video-presentation programs and also digital programs to edit the interviews with the explorers and put it as a link to their web page.

The importance of critically evaluating sources was something the students themselves became aware of when journalists from the local newspaper interviewed them about the project. The students became conscious that they had to know the theme they were working on well when being interviewed, and they saw how the journalists used the information from these interviews and how they changed it. In this way, the students got a meta-cognitive perspective on the meaning of their own project. The same can be said about the consequence of publishing their own knowledge on the internet so that everybody, potentially, could see what they had written. It became very important for the students that the quality of the text was good enough.

The students gained different kinds of knowledge in this project. In terms of factual knowledge, several of the students stated that they had learned a lot about Antarctica. The method by which they had approached the information was also pertinent; they had been very active in finding relevant information and evaluating what to use. All the students had learned a lot about using computers for different purposes. In one conversation the students reflected on their own learning:

> Girl: I think it is very exciting to hear how they [the explorers] can get data, and also about the technical part, how we can get information from them, where they are.
> Boy 1: You learn that, because on the internet a lot is in English, and then you have to translate it into Norwegian.
> Boy 2: Yes and then, where we get information about how far they have walked. It is formulated in miles, and then we have to calculate from [English] miles to [Norwegian] miles.
> Boy 1: We are also going to make a press release that we are going to give to ...

In this conversation, the students mentioned several outcomes that illustrate an integrated view of knowledge acquisition. They got to practise English and to use mathematics and natural science in a realistic, real-world way. And as the principal mentioned: 'In the Antarctica project the students have to work with problem formulations about health, nutrition, pollution/ozone, whaling and weather/meteorology'.

In addition they got a different feeling for the processes of writing and expressing themselves by putting different kinds of information on the internet, by writing press releases, and so forth.

For the students, the project created some new perspectives on school as a knowledge institution. Commenting on the use of technology in such a project, some students mentioned that:

Boy: It becomes more fun to be at school. When you split it up a bit more. Instead of having six hours in one stretch, then it becomes easier to get through the day.

Girl: For some it might be a big shock when they get into the work market, because you do not sit and make mathematical assignments as such. When we work on projects you get a better grasp on what is happening in real companies and such.

Boy: We should get more experience on how it is in real working life.

Commenting on the Antarctica project, the teacher mentioned another meta-cognitive outcome: 'I think they have seen a bit more of reality. I think they have seen that if you are going to accomplish something you have to fight for it'.

This is not something the students just learn through the use of new technology. They have projects at the school where they use art, music and other resources. However, in relation to this project, the technology has given some opportunities and arenas for negotiation that creates exciting consequences for the students' learning, and conceives learning at schools as different kinds of learning trajectories or pathways.

Case 2: Building bridges to the community

This upper secondary school is situated in a small rural community in the west of Norway. It is the only upper secondary school in the municipality, so they have students from islands and other rural areas quite far from the school. The school building has a traditional structure, with one classroom for each class. There are 240 students at the school, divided between three year groups (16 to 19 years old). The vision for teaching and learning at the school is 'collaborative learning'. How students learn from one another, build understanding, and become active responsible students, are important aspects of their pedagogical vision.

An important aspect of the municipality's strategic plan is to see education from primary school to college as a whole, with the local industry as an integrated part. Maritime industry is very important for the community. During recent years, this industry has had challenges in getting competent workers because young people are moving out. So the local maritime industry and the school have a joint interest in creating better prospects and conditions for young people and in getting them interested in pursuing a career within this industry. Their ambition is to create more flexible learning environments through the use of new digital media and ways of engaging students in learning trajectories in and out of school and online/offline.

The curriculum unit presented here was based on storyline methods, but leading into real-life problem-solving. Storyline, through its use of narratives, enables knowledge to be obtained in a meaningful and realistic context. The teacher constructed an outline narrative about local businesses facing fictitious problems and seeking help from a consultancy firm (i.e. the class). The students had to define the problem and identify resources in the community in order to solve it. Groups of 3–4 students each chose to identify with a particular role, for example a job seeker; a customer in a bank, insurance company or tax office; or people needing help from the local council. They explored their role and made presentations to the class about what they discovered.

One of the groups developed a story about a financially troubled family with a handicapped child. The father had to look for a better-paid job, and needed to enquire about the benefits they were entitled to from health and social services. The students said they learned a lot because they played realistic roles.

The second part of the unit involved students actually serving as consultants for local businesses or for the municipality itself. Each group of students became a 'consultancy firm' and was asked for advice on a genuine problem. An electrical engineering firm consulted one group over whether to lease or buy cars. Local government officers asked another group to consider whether a new power plant should be built. The students were asked to look closely at social and environmental consequences as well as economic. Each group wrote a report for the company, as well as giving a presentation at school. The students found this real-life activity 'serious', 'exciting' and 'challenging'.

In both parts, the students were introduced to relevant theory before moving on to more practical activities. The subjects addressed were primarily economics and Norwegian, also drawing on ICT, but other subjects such as English, mathematics and science were included when relevant.

The aims of this unit were outlined in the following curriculum proposal written by the teacher:

The company

The students will develop an understanding of both possibilities and demands in relation to establishing a company and running a business. They will acquire an understanding of handling actual priorities to be made and conflicts of interests within a company. In addition to this, the students should develop an understanding of the company's role in managing resources related to economics, ecology and technology. The students will learn how to use ICT to solve problems if such equipment is available.

Society

The students will develop an understanding of society's limited resources and that priorities made will have consequences for both humans and environment at present and in the future.

The students were given a group evaluation of their written report and their oral presentation. They also received an individual evaluation of their achievement, the quality of the Powerpoint Presentation, how they presented it and the content of their report. The principal stressed the importance of changing the assessment strategy:

> It is no use doing project-based learning or collaborative work and then have an individual five-hour written exam. I think that it is very important to have a relation between the pedagogical method used and the assessment strategy.

The teachers were organized in teams, with one team for each grade. The team discussed teaching methods, projects and other questions related to the teaching. The teachers and the principal all said they found such collaboration very important for finding a connection between the pedagogical and organizational development.

One teacher defined his role as a teacher to be to facilitate, organize, evaluate and give feedback. He stressed that 'if the students do not know what to do, it is important to give suggestions according to what it is possible for the student to achieve. You come up with different suggestions for the student to choose from.'

The students said the teacher helped them '*organize ourselves*'. If the students have problems with the company (e.g. if it does not respond to e-mail), the teacher contacts the company, though the students stress that they have the main responsibility to follow up on things, not the teacher. They mentioned being taken seriously and treated like adults by the local firms: 'They treat us as real consultants. And at the same time they know that we are just students. So it is done quite professionally.'

Speaking about the activities, one teacher stated: 'When they work outside school, they get the same business plan we have in the real world. What they learn is not just parts of a whole, but the true facts of the case'.

The students said, 'You are treated like an adult in a real job interview!... He went through everything, ordinary job contract as they do to regular employees. This was real!'

The students believe they become more realistic and independent in facing the challenges and problems in adult life: they learn how to take up a loan, they know how to handle bad financing, how to inquire about benefits they are entitled to according to the National Health Services, and the like. Both the teacher engaged in the project and other teachers report that students are more independent. As one of the social science teachers stated: 'They get more references to what happens in society. When they are writing essays they are more realistic and discuss rather than moralizing and describing.'

An important aspect of the activity is collaboration. As one of the teachers put it:

When the students leave the school as a learning arena, and meet the real working life, as they do in 'Storyline', it is important that they know how to collaborate, have self confidence and have learned some techniques for solving tasks.

All the students we talked to liked collaborative learning and thought they learned more than working individually:

> You have to collaborate when you are in working life. You have to collaborate with your colleagues. With collaboration I really think you learn that other people can contribute where you do not have so much competence, and then you can contribute in another area.

All the teachers involved in the storyline referred to positive student outcomes, for example claiming that the students have much better computer skills and their critical ability towards the findings is getting better: 'The students who have used internet for a while have seen that they have to evaluate their findings and what they can use' (ICT coordinator).

The students seem to enjoy school, which is supported by a survey done by the municipality among all students. It seems as if their motivation for the activity is that they do not have to listen to a teacher for hours on end and that they work on something meaningful:

> Girl 1: It is so much more fun when we can work independently, and you have to! We do not have to sit and listen to the teacher for two hours. Now we can use computers, internet and other learning resources we need and in this way we can acquire good knowledge in the way we find best.
> Girl 2: We can work at our own speed. In this way, you know what you are doing, you really understand it.
> Girl 1: We are learning through what we are doing. In a way you are living it out. You are doing things in the company and when you have a test at school, you know it. You have done it so many times in the company, you have seen it. Instead of reading and reading and forgetting what you read. That is the problem with just reading books, suddenly you are not concentrating and then, 'What did I read?'

Before they started the activity, the teacher said their students had more fragmented knowledge. Teachers, students and the principal also stress that the students have improved their ways of presenting knowledge. The students say they do not have any problems with giving presentations:

> I do not see that as a problem. We are so used to it. But when we did it the first time for the class, we were really nervous, we looked down and stuttered. Now we have done it so many times, so it is not a big deal.

The principal says he thinks the students learn a lot from presentations because they have to think through what they are going to present and how they are going to do it.

Opening the 'classroom-as-container'

The cases presented here show ways of opening up the learning activities at school – what some describe as 'classroom-as-container' (Leander et al. 2010). These are simple cases from ordinary public schools in different parts of Norway and in different levels of schooling. They have in common that they use new digital technologies as a way of breaking away from more traditional classroom activities, building on the students' competences from outside the school, and as a way of reaching beyond the boundaries of school, understood as a place where students are passive and reproduce knowledge. However, these are not presented as technology projects but rather as ways of conceiving other ways of 'doing school'. As such, they are future oriented as ways of thinking about learning activities happening between different contexts and locations.

Both cases show how real life is defined as part of the learning situation and becomes more relevant for the students. Tearing down the physical and mental barriers of the classroom brings the real world directly into the learning environment. At the same time, they reach out into the real world through the communication possibilities of new technology. An atmosphere of individual responsibility and communal sharing was created.

Learning lives as an approach toward schooling opens up the learning environment, both in the way experiences and knowledge gained outside the school are made relevant as part of learning activities in school and in the ways students move in and out of school, and online/offline as learning pathways. Their learning identities are made relevant in both an ontological and epistemological sense (Wortham 2006).

One might say that the use of ICT creates possibilities for more variation and differentiation. It makes it easier for teachers to let the students investigate different sources of information and use it for their own knowledge production. One of the main conclusions from these case studies is that it is not a simple technological application that is the most important to stimulate change but rather an integration of different resources and methods in the learning environment. In the examples presented, the use of technology is an integrated part of the pedagogical processes and works to support a student-centred vision of learning and teaching.

To conclude, one might interpret the consequences of such student-centred learning environments on three levels. First, there were consequences at a personal level. The students said that they had had positive experiences of working in open learning environments and working with the resources that the technology offered. These students changed their opinions about school and learning; how well the students handled such an independent student role varied. Second, when the students used different digital artifacts, they used their cultural competence in other areas much more than before in more traditional classroom settings. So, the students got a broader comprehension of knowledge and how it had meaning outside the school. Third, there was a change among both students and teachers in the way they conceived of school as an institution for learning, from the way it traditionally decontextualizes students as learners toward perceiving them as learners moving between different contexts of learning. It then becomes one of several places and spaces for learning, structured in certain ways and more or less self-initiated by the students themselves.

Towards new mobilities

The socio-spatial approach to learning presented in this chapter, described as learning lives, presumes a new way of perceiving school as a place and a space organizing certain ways of learning. I believe schools are important institutions in our societies, but it has to become more apparent how schools relate to the overall learning lives of students, with their learning identities and trajectories of participation across different contexts of learning. Also, we need a better understanding of how learners draw on different cultural resources and how contexts are structured and initiated in different ways by the institutions themselves, either as part of the curriculum or as self-initiated for no other apparent purpose than to have fun, as when playing computer games.

'New mobilities' is becoming the new slogan (Leander et al. 2010). More than changing physical boundaries, and conceptions of the school of the future (Walden 2009), change is created through supporting students in their learning lives. The support is in how students can use technologies in different ways, not as a tool within teacher-initiated knowledge reproduction but as a tool supporting mobilities and learning identities.

References

Banks, J. A., Au, K. H., Ball, A. F., Bell, P., Gordon, E. W., Gutierrez, K. D., Heath, S. B., Lee, C. D., Lee, Y., Mahiri, J., Nasir, N. S., Valdés, G. and Zhou, M. (2007) *Learning in and out of School in Diverse Environments: Lifelong, Life-wide, Life-deep.* Seattle: University of Washington, LIFE Center and the Center for Multicultural Education.

Barton, D., Ivanic, R., Appleby, Y., Hodge, R. and Tusting, K. (2007) *Literacy, Lives and Learning.* London: Routledge.

Beach, K. (1999) 'Consequential transitions: a sociocultural expedition beyond transfer in education.' *Review of Research in Education,* 24(1), 101–139.

Bekerman, Z., Burbules, N. C. and Silberman-Keller, D. (eds) (2006) *Learning in Places: The Informal Education Reader.* New York: Peter Lang.

Bentley, T. (1998) *Learning beyond the Classroom. Education for a Changing World*. London: Routledge.

Claxton, G. (2008) *What's the Point of School? Rediscovering the Heart of Education*. Oxford: OneWorld.

Cole, M. (1996) *Cultural Psychology: A Once and Future Discipline*. Cambridge, MA: The Belknap Press, Harvard University Press.

Comber, B. and Nixon, H. (2008) 'Spatial literacies, design texts, and emergent pedagogies in purposeful literacy curriculum.' *Pedagogies: An International Journal*, 3(4), 221–240.

Ecclestone, K., Biesta, G. and Hughes, M. (2010) *Transitions and Learning through the Lifecourse*. London: Routledge.

Edwards, A. and Mackenzie, L. (2008) 'Identity shifts in informal learning trajectories.' In B. van Oers, W. Wardekker, E. Elbers and R. van der Veer (eds) *The Transformation of Learning* (pp. 163–181). Cambridge: Cambridge University Press.

Egan, K. (2008) *The Future of Education: Reimagining Our Schools from the Ground up*. New Haven, CT: Yale University Press.

Erstad, O. (2009) '"Learning networks"—capacity building for school development and ICT.' In R. Krumsvik (ed.) *Learning in the Networked Society and the Digitized School*. New York: Nova Science Publishers.

Erstad, O. (2010) 'Addressing the complexity of impact—a multilevel approach towards ICT in education.' In F. Scheuermann and F. Pedro (eds) *Assessing the Effects of ICT in Education: Indicators, Criteria and Benchmarks for International Comparisons*. European Commision and OECD.

Holland, D., Lachicotte, W., Skinner, D. and Cain, C. (1998) *Identity and Agency in Cultural Worlds*. Cambridge, MA: Harvard University Press.

Hull, G. and Shultz, K. (eds) (2002) *School's out! Bridging Out-of-school Literacy with Classroom Practice*. New York: Teachers College Press.

Leander, K., Phillips, N. C. and Taylor, K. H. (2010) 'The changing social spaces of learning: mapping new mobilities.' *Review of Research in Education*, 34(1), 329–394.

Lemke, J. (2000) 'Across the scales of time: artifacts, activities and meanings in ecosocial systems.' *Mind, Culture and Activity*, 7(4), 273–290.

Moje, E. and Luke, A. (2009) 'Literacy and identity: examining the metaphors in history and contemporary research.' *Reading Research Quarterly*, 44(4), 415–437.

Nespor, J. (1997) *Tangled up in School: Politics, Space, Bodies, and Signs in the Educational Process*. Mahwah, NJ: Lawrence Erlbaum.

Olson, D. R. (2003) *Psychological Theory and Educational Reform: How School Remakes Mind and Society*. Cambridge: Cambridge University Press.

Schwartz, B., Dreyfus, T. and Hershkowitz, R. (ed.) (2009). *Transformation of Knowledge through Classroom Interaction*. London: Routledge.

van Oers, B. (1998) 'From context to contextualizing.' *Learning and Instruction*, 8(6), 473–488.

Walden, R. (ed.) (2009) *Schools for the Future: Design Proposals from Architectural Psychology*. Cambridge, MA: Hogrefe and Huber.

Wertsch, J. (1998) *Mind as Action*. Oxford: Oxford University Press.

Wertsch, J., del Rio, P. and Alvarez, A. (1995) *Sociocultural Studies of Mind*. Cambridge: Cambridge University Press.

Wortham, S. (2006) *Learning Identity: The Joint Emergence of Social Identification and Academic Learning.* Boston: Cambridge University Press.

Suggested further readings

Bentley, T. (1998) *Learning beyond the Classroom: Education for a Changing World.* London: Routledge.

Edwards, R., Biesta, G. and Thorpe, M. (eds) *Rethinking Contexts for Learning and Teaching: Communities, Activities and Networks.* London: Routledge.

Erstad, O., Gilje, O., Sefton-Green, J. and Vasbo, K. (2009) 'Exploring "learning lives": community, identity, literacy and meaning.' *Literacy, 43*(2), 100–106.

Hull, G. and Shultz, K. (eds) (2002) *School's out! Bridging Out-of-school Literacy with Classroom Practice.* New York: Teachers College Press.

Nespor, J. (1997) *Tangled up in School: Politics, Space, Bodies, and Signs in the Educational Process.* Mahwah, NJ: Lawrence Erlbaum.

Chapter 10

Storythread pedagogy for environmental education

Australia

Ron Tooth and Peter Renshaw

Introduction

It was early in 1978 and I (Ron Tooth) was in my eighth year of teaching. As I walked toward the edge of the gully near the school, I could hear children squealing and playing. I had already decided that this was not a safe place for them to be and fully intended to call everyone out from among the shrubs and the trees. As I came closer, I could see who was involved and I was surprised that most of the children were from my own year 3 class. My first inclination was to interrupt and ask them to climb out from under the fallen branches, makeshift cubbies and pieces of cardboard and cloth. Instead, I just stood there and watched, captivated by what was happening. I was transported back to my own childhood, remembering the sense of wonder and adventure of playing in the bush near my home. With difficulty I resisted my 'teacher urge' to take control. I was a privileged observer of a powerful and exciting learning episode in action.

In the period that followed the gully experience and before I arrived at Pullenvale Environmental Education Centre (PEEC) in 1982, it become normal for me to spend hours with my class each week in the local bushland. We worked like natural scientists *and* artists, collecting information and filling our journals with information, detailed sketches, observations, poetry and personal reflections about what was happening around us each day. Sometimes, I set half-days aside for our expeditions as we climbed local hills and scrambled through creek gullies. As the standard of student work improved, I began to use narratives to introduce new concepts, knowledge and problems while I also focused students on the processes of direct scientific observation to heighten their understanding through personal encounters with their local landscape. I soon found that this mixing of story, drama and outdoor experiences in nature worked well as a way of developing deep knowledge and values. I remember thinking that if only I could continue to make these kinds of connections, something good would have to come from it.

The 'gully experience' was a professional turning point and represented a pivotal moment in the emergence of the storythread approach in 1982 at the PEEC. This Centre is set against a backdrop of forests, foothills and distant mountains on the western outskirts of Brisbane and exists today as a dynamic educational hub where students and teachers visit to participate in Storythread programs.

Storythreads are mediated 'environmental narratives' that allow students to engage emotionally and imaginatively with natural places. Environmental narratives, as they are embodied with storythread programs, are, quite simply, stories about people and landscapes and how each has shaped the other.

Decades later in 2007, I (Peter Renshaw) visited the PEEC to find out more about the storythread pedagogy that had been iteratively designed by Ron and his team and then implemented and refined through various research collaborations with teachers both from local schools in Brisbane and across the state of Queensland in other environmental education centres.[1] As a researcher, I brought an interest in collaborative learning inspired by a Vygotskian sociocultural theory (Vygotsky 1993), and as a citizen I brought a set of values and concerns for the environment. I discerned that various kinds of knowledge were integrated within each storythread unit: conceptual knowledge of the natural world and its interacting systems; process knowledge of how to investigate the natural world in disciplined and thoughtful ways; and knowledge of how to act strategically to protect and sustain the natural world. Storythread also engaged students imaginatively and creatively with natural places in ways that enabled them to see, hear and feel more deeply and attentively and to appreciate in an embodied manner why protecting and sustaining natural places was crucial for their future and that of humankind.

Storythread was powerful pedagogy: that was clear from my first visit to the PEEC. This insight was not merely an academic one for me. I participated in a workshop on storythread where I pretended to be a 4th-grader doing the storythread unit called *Bugs*. In doing *Bugs* I recalled, informed, designed, labelled, collected, categorized, imagined, argued and engaged in deep listening to the natural environment. With regard to the latter, I sat quietly in the bush during the workshop for about 30 minutes trying to see and hear nature in a different way. Afterward, I shared *my* novel insight that butterflies fly in complete silence (at least to the human ear) in contrast to noisy flies and other insects. I began to understand that paying attention to nature – listening and seeing deeply – was a powerful experience that was emotionally engaging and interesting. I pondered the evolutionary advantages of different types of wings and the physics of wing designs and the sensory systems associated with gliding and floating through the air (butterflies) versus motoring ahead with vibrating wings (flies). Clearly, young students experienced this as well in their own particular ways. Even in this pretend mode, as an adult I found the elements of storythread engaging intellectually and emotionally quite moving.

What I added to this collaboration with Ron and his team was a research focus on the mediating tools and social scaffolds that had been seamlessly incorporated into storythread over the years. Our ongoing collaboration has enabled us to analyse students' learning in relation to the variety of meditational means embedded in the storythread pedagogy. Briefly, the key insight for us is that there are distinct pathways to learning embedded in Storythread: some students are influenced powerfully by the characters and the narrative, others by the firsthand experience of the natural place, others by gaining interesting knowledge about nature, and others by their aesthetic sensibility to the beauty of the natural world. We explore and explicate this insight further next.

Storythread as environmental narrative

Storythread pedagogy builds on the environmental narrative genre. Environmental narratives are designed on the basis of deeply personal experiences of the world. The narrative genre affords particular insights into the complexity of life and relationships between humankind and the natural world (Slicer 2003). In Australia, environmental narrative appears in the oral traditions of Aboriginal people and the writings of environmental historians. Chatwin (1987) points to Aboriginal communities in central Australia who use their 'song lines' as flowing environmental narratives about the people and creatures that inhabit particular places. These narratives function as topographical maps that a singer can use to travel through a landscape as he or she locates particular physical and natural features of spiritual significance. Environmental historians such as Bolton (1981), Dovers (1994), Greider and Garkovich (1994) and Rolls (1993) reframe environmental history as a network of stories about wild and dramatic landscapes, the wilderness we have lost, entire species of animals and plants that have disappeared, and the exceptional individuals who have struggled to protect our environment for future generations. Traditionally, societies all over the world have used environmental narratives as 'objects' or 'tools' to deal with the complexity of life, to celebrate culture and land, and to apply knowledge and skills learned over generations.

Storythread pedagogy is a particular adaptation of the environmental narrative. It combines the story journey with deep attentive listening to take learners into a deepened awareness of themselves as they connect to and begin to understand the complexity, beauty and fragility that exist within any natural place. By engaging students and teachers directly with natural places in this way, they become more attentive to what is actually happening around them, and this can have profound implications for them as individuals and for how they learn. When students are inspired to look closely and attentively, they begin to see the world quite differently – with fresh eyes. Storythread pedagogy has, over the last 20 years, been profoundly shaped by this idea that listening and attending to nature and to place is central to achieving education for sustainability because it develops the kind of humility that is required for purposeful and meaningful education in the twenty-first century. This form of 'deep listening' (McNeill et al. 2004) and 'profound attentiveness' (Clark 2004) has been alluded to by many cultures over time.

All storythreads are built around six main elements, and when these are skilfully and consistently applied in both classroom and natural settings, they create a powerful context in which deep learning happens. These elements include: (1) the use of story and drama to create a sense in students of the significant others who have been there before them and with whom they can interact through imaginative and creative play; (2) the creation of 'personal knowledge' that develops as students experience a place firsthand and begin to construct new knowledge and theories for themselves based on what they have seen and experienced and what they hear from PEEC teachers and peers during the day; (3) the use of 'deep attentive listening' and close observation of small events in nature that are scaffolded by the teachers to create a sense of emotional, sensorial and ethical connection to place that opens students up to the complexity, beauty and diversity of the natural world; (4) the use of 'reflective responding' both in nature and then back in the classroom allows students to gain a much clearer understanding of their experiences in nature and the changes that are happening in their lives; (5) the development of an 'ethic of care' that often emerges, almost naturally, out of the attentiveness and reflection experience – all successful storythread journeys have this strong values dimension that runs from beginning to end, where the focus is on building respectful connections between self, others and place; and (6) finally there is the full mind–body sensory 'experience of place' with all its beauty and unpredictability as individuals are surprised by the unfolding complexity of nature as rain sweeps in, wind blows up and wildlife appear unexpectedly to catch the interest of a group or of a particular individual. Next, we exemplify storythread pedagogy by considering one program based on the beautiful bushland called Karawatha in the Australian city of Brisbane.

The Karawatha experience: an attentive and reflective journey into place

This example of Karawatha describes how a group of students and a committed teacher became part of a storythread journey that allowed them to step into the realm of a passionate environmental group, and particularly into the life of Bernice Volz,[2] who was one of the people who was instrumental in saving from development a string of endangered lagoons on the southern boundary of Brisbane. The lagoon system is now the centrepiece of the extensive Karawatha wetland conservation area that has been purchased by the Brisbane City Council and the state government as part of a land acquisition

Figure 10.1 Karawatha Lagoon

program. This remarkable woman is a self-taught ecologist with no secondary or university education. She is respected throughout local government and across a wide range of scientific circles for her local knowledge and ability to achieve change.

As part of the storythread experience, students and their teacher were invited to learn more about this woman, focusing in particular on her insights, values and actions, and why she so willingly committed herself to the long-term effort required to save Karawatha. Through a series of mediated environmental narrative experiences at school and then as part of a full-day expedition into Karawatha, students reflected further on her achievements, explored this wetland area for themselves and visited places that were important to her as they made their own personal connections to the place. Together they traversed Karawatha forest from one side to the other, imagining themselves walking in her shoes. Through this mediated

Figure 10.2 Ron with a group of students

experience, the students were drawn into this woman's life and into the story of Karawatha itself – its biodiversity, history and environmental significance. Students were invited by their classroom teacher to become environmental leaders in their school and to reflect on the life and actions of this woman as someone who had been an environmental leader throughout her life.

Throughout this extended environmental narrative experience, before, during and after the excursion to Karawatha, students were asked to record their journey in a visual diary and to reflect on the experience through an ongoing community of inquiry process. The community of inquiry circle (Cam 2006) became an important device that allowed students to think deeply about the experiences that they were having and how they might be relevant to them in their own lives. Students were asked to think about the total experience and whether it had changed them or their thinking in any way. The storythread experience culminated with the students working together with other classes in the school to coordinate an environmental week of activities and events where they created environmental art pieces to share with their school community that embodied their personal insights and reflections about Karawatha.

During the ten-week experience – but particularly on the day of the excursion to Karawatha Forest – the six storythread elements were very evident, beginning with stories and characters. These were deployed to create a sense of the presence of traditional Aboriginal owners across the centuries and the more recent passionate environmentalists, particularly Bernice and others who had been there before them making their own deep connections to this place. The students were scaffolded to create new knowledge of the natural systems as they saw, heard, felt and analysed what was happening around them and what was being shared with them. Included also were opportunities for 'deep attentive listening' both in Karawatha and in their school grounds and local environment where students refined their ability to observe and respond to the fine details of life that often remain hidden. Closely related to deep listening was the engagement of students in deep 'reflective responding' in Karawatha and elsewhere that allowed students to gain a much clearer understanding of the interconnected changes that were happening in their lives and in the natural world. Finally students could appreciate the centrality of an 'ethic of care' for the environment as they were enabled to see themselves, others and Karawatha as parts of a larger complex system.

The mentor teacher from the PEEC listens, responds and shapes the unfolding experience so that the elements of storythread are woven together to produce opportunities for full embodied learning. To achieve this, however, a storythread teacher needs to be skilled in using a wide range of quite specific 'micro-mediating tools' that can be applied at different times to shift student perception, spark the imagination and move individuals into alternative mind, body and sensory space where deep learning can happen. The students' experience of the natural environment is mediated by these quite specific sociocultural tools such as: (1) ocular devices including magnifiers, cameras and recorders that amplify perception; (2) imaginative visualizations and story moments that allow students to enter different times and spaces and experience events long past; (3) thought experiments such as reflecting on past events, present experiences and possible futures for the environment through deep reflection and communities of inquiry; (4) auditory snapshots such as the silent walk through the forest, deep attentive listening or adopting freeze postures suddenly to heighten awareness of this moment in a natural setting; and (5) tactile rituals conducted at the point of arrival into places of significance by placing hands on particular rocks or trees, applying clay to the face and skin, or sifting crystal rocks and soil from the bush path through the fingers – all work to heighten awareness, challenge perceptions and open the mind to the complexity of nature that is present all around them.

To summarize to this point, we have shown how storythread incorporates various mediational tools and social scaffolds to promote deep learning about nature and human connections to place. Next, we focus on evidence of changes in students following the Karawatha experience and other subsequent changes in how they began to view themselves, relate to family members at home and peers at school and how they now believe they should treat the living environment around them.

Evidence of change

The professional development of teachers involved in PEEC programs has been tracked over many years by the staff through examining and sharing professional journals, case writing about memorable insights and events and extended interviews (Ballantyne and Packer 2009; Tooth and Renshaw 2009; Tooth et al. 1988). During these interviews, teachers were asked about changes they had noticed in their students after the excursion to the PEEC. Incidents of compelling behavioural change both inside and outside the classroom were reported over the years by teachers, including an effort to increase respect for nature by fellow students and parents, a practical concern for litter reduction, a greater respect for small animals (such as lizards and ants) on school grounds, increased personal calmness and empathy for one another, and civic responsibility for looking after gardens and trees on the school site. Recently, we have collected evidence of change directly from students using a range of techniques such as KWH activities (What do we *k*now about this? What do we *w*ant to know? *H*ow can we find out?); inquiry circles focused on the experience at the PEEC; and small group interviews after the excursion. In examining the data, we were surprised by the depth and eloquence of some responses from students. For example, one student expressed herself as follows:

> Before I did this program I just saw myself as someone who is passionate about nature and, yeah, someone who cares about wildlife but after I'd done this program I see myself as a wildlife warrior and I feel more confident in myself and I've become more alert and observant with my surroundings and it has given me a new confidence to go out and see the environment, instead of – just sitting and think oh I like the environment, I like nature, but not actually doing anything about what's happening.
>
> (Interview with year 6 student)

In categorising students' responses to the inquiry circles and interviews, we searched the entire corpus for consistent foci and themes regarding the kinds of changes that had occurred. We abstracted three key foci: (1) changes in self; (2) changes in relationship to others and place; and (3) changes in learning at school. The changes to *self* were in terms of their personal qualities such as confidence and enthusiasm and an emerging new identity. The changes to their *relationship with others* were concerned especially with their sense of agency to influence others and do things to protect the environment and their realisation that even children have the power and responsibility to act for others and to protect the environment. *The changes with regard to school learning* were concerned primarily with more positive engagement and realising the relevance of school learning more. These changes were explicitly linked by some students to their realisation of the importance of direct experience of natural places for longer-lasting and deeper change to occur.

Changes to self

There were changes in how students viewed themselves at school and in the world generally. Sometimes, these were described in terms of change in relation to *personal qualities* or specific personal characteristics such as openness, confidence, alertness, attentiveness and passion. One boy could see that because of the entire Karawatha experience his openness to others had increased:

> I've noticed – I'm more open to new ideas from people because it used to be just like me, me, me but now I'm listening to others because what they say also matters and doing this program, yeah, has let me, like, open up my brain and allow other people's thoughts.
>
> (Interview with year 7 student)

Other students summarized their new sense of self as an identity shift – as in the eloquent initial quotation where the student says, '*after I'd done this program I see myself as a wildlife warrior*'. These self-identifying labels provide students with a strong well-formed schema for deciding how to act in spontaneous and proactive ways. For example, in the poetic comments following, a year 7 student imagines green leaves growing inside her – representing a new more passionate and exciting self.

> Well, this is a bit weird but I think that these, my inside of my body used to be dark and focused on one thing at a time. When I used to write, like, for English and stuff it would just be so boring and I wouldn't use the same sort of expression and passion that I do now because – but now inside where it used to be all dark and nothing special about it, it's sort of got these green leaves and it's just twirling around and I think that if people keep on doing this that's what will happen to them. And so I think that I've grown more exciting and passionate and not so dull and blank that I was before and so I think that this has improved

everything about me not just my nature smartness, so I think it's been really great.

(Interview with year 7 student)

Changes in relationship to others and place

A second category of changes we identified were in students' sense of agency to influence others and a concomitant heightened civic sense of responsibility to try to influence family members and other students and act for the good of future generations. This change is reflected in the following comment from a year 7 student:

Well, I think that even though we think of ourselves as a very small rock or pebble or whatever, we're actually quite big. We affect everything and even though we think of ourselves as very small the ripples will grow bigger after a while and then we can affect everyone and so the ripples will turn bad if we do something bad and then that will affect everyone so, see, even if it's just a little thing, even if we drop just a packet of chips on the ground that will, first it will just tell you that that is OK to do and then it will tell others that yes, OK, that's all right to do. Then if everyone starts doing it, then even if people don't think that it's OK people will do it anyway and so the ripple just grows bigger and bigger every time. But if we pick up that bit of rubbish then the ripples will grow in opposite and people will think OK, well that's OK for me to do that because it's good to pick up the litter and then it turns into other people picking up the litter and then it will become essential as the ripple grows bigger.

(Interview with year 7 student)

The ripple metaphor deployed by this student encapsulates the sense of connectedness that had been foregrounded throughout the storythread experience.

Changes regarding school and learning

The third category of changes involved specific aspects of the students' behaviour at school and their approach to learning. Participating in the PEEC excursion seemed to increase students' motivation and interest in school more generally besides providing an awareness that learning can occur in different ways and can be especially powerful when insights are established on firsthand experience. The following response from one student captures the notion that the PEEC program influenced his motivation at school.

Well before the program, yeah, I struggled to concentrate in class and just preferred to talk with friends in class, but now I've got a better understanding of my subjects now that I've learned to be attentive because I've found out that it's also very useful in class.

(Interview with year 7 student)

The importance of firsthand experience for deeper change to occur is captured in the delightful comment from one student who realizes that her family members are somewhat dismissive of her new concern for the environment. She suggests that they have to experience it for themselves (as she did) for real change to occur.

I have spoken to my mum and my sister and they think it's great and they think it's a good experience but they – they definitely are better than they were before I told them about it but I think they need to experience it for themselves, because they think, oh, that's great honey and then they just go along with their lives, they really need to do it for themselves.

(Interview with year 7 student)

The difference that the emotional engagement of firsthand experience can make to knowledge creation and learning was succinctly captured by one student in her distinction between 'feeling' and 'seeing' and her realization that this had moved her into a different kind of learning experience.

Before I saw the environment though visuals and now I see it through feelings. The trees were turning from green to yellow because the zone was changing and ….

(Interview with year 7 student)

This emotional connection to place influenced the way students saw Karawatha and how they applied what they had been researching at school. Concepts researched in the abstract at school about ecological zones, different types of trees and particular animals became vivid in Karawatha as they moved through the changing forest together. Abstract knowledge became embodied in a sensorial way that allowed students to create and remember detailed personal knowledge after the visit to Karawatha.

The moistness in like the ground was changing cause in Zone 1 the ground was drier and so it had um different trees and in Zone 2 the ground was a bit more moist so there was other different trees. The scribbly bark the um caterpillars, they um like the scribbly moths they plant their eggs in the tree and when they come out the the um scribbly caterpillar um eats it and when it gets bigger and it moves in like a squiggly line so when um the caterpillar gets bigger the um squiggles get bigger and um then it makes its cocoon and turns into a scribbly moth.

(Year 7 student in class community of inquiry reflection session)

As in the *Bugs* storythread, during the Karawatha experience students were introduced to scientific concepts and processes. In the preceding quotation, a student is coming to understand the relationship between ground moisture and tree adaptation and the life cycle of scribbly moths.

Conclusion

Just being in a natural place is not enough. The most successful storythread experiences depend on classroom teachers and PEEC teachers weaving together all the elements of storythread into a mediated learning experience. The experience of the natural places needs to be scaffolded so that students are able to see the world around them with fresh eyes and can develop the alternative knowledge, values and practices of sustainability that are the goal of all storythread journeys.

In reflecting on the data from the project, we are impressed by the transformational rather than simply incremental changes in students' thinking and their civic sense of responsibility. In student responses, we hear the authentic voice of children coming through into changed behaviour in very different ways. There appear to be 'multiple pathways' into learning and change from within a storythread experience that reflect and mirror the key elements of this pedagogy of place. These elements work independently and together as 'hooks' that capture the attention of students and engage different kinds of learners. It might be one pathway predominantly or a combination that leads to authentic engagement and deep learning in different students. Some are captivated by the sensuality and beauty of the place as it is experienced through deep attentive listening, others by the personal embodied knowledge and values that they create for themselves, and others by the imaginative power of the unfolding narrative in space and time.

In the responses of students, we have noted their awareness of the tension that exists between the abstraction and detachment typical of some classroom learning and the personal change and commitment to action that is associated with learning to care for the environment in a natural setting. We have also observed that when a storythread's multiple elements combine and unfold over extended periods of time as part of a single 'mediated experience', dramatic and transformational change can be achieved. It is the combination of its multiple elements, however, that we believe is the defining feature of a truly successful storythread experience and marks it out as a powerful expression of pedagogy and place that is able to deliver transformative learning.

It is the sensory reconnecting to place (Abram 1997) through narrative, where knowledge and values are 'embodied' experientially, that identifies storythread as a powerful expression of pedagogy and place and situates it as one of the new 'outdoor' body/mind doing and meaning-making pedagogies that engage students in learning beyond the classroom (Ballantyne and Packer 2008, 2009; Tooth and Renshaw, 2009; Tooth et al. 1988; Wattchow et al. 2008). This is why the generic elements of storythread can be so readily transferred to other contexts and places. They are reflections of a much broader and emerging vision of 'pedagogy and place' that focus on 'learning beyond the classroom'. Engaging students and teachers with this kind of pedagogy is what we urgently need to develop the knowledge, values and practices of environmental sustainability and to prepare them for living in our complex and changing world.

Final comment

PEEC is one of a network of 25 Outdoor and Environmental Education Centres (OEECs) distributed across Queensland. A study by Ballantyne and Packer (2009) demonstrated that the quality of teaching and learning in these centres is exceptional across key aspects of their performance. We would suggest that the OEECs benefited greatly from being on the margins for long periods of time. They were not directly subject to many policy changes and shifts that rolled through Queensland schools according to electoral cycles and the influence of different pressure groups. The blueprint for the OEECs was a single policy document written in 1989. This turned out to be a boon that allowed the highly committed teachers and principals in the OEEC network to experiment and iteratively design professional know-how through dialogue, commitment and sharing knowledge consistently over many years. The result is that there is now a network of Centres with strong but quite distinct experiential pedagogies running through all their programs. This coincidence of high quality and diversity of approach, we suggest, was made possible because the Centres were free to participate in long-term committed professional practice and research as design.

Notes

1 OEECPA (The Outdoor and Environmental Education Centre Principals' Alliance) is a network of principals from 25 Education Queensland State Government OEE Centres that work together to deliver 'learning beyond the classroom' experiences and programs for students, teachers and schools (http://education.qld.gov.au/schools/environment/outdoors/).

2 In the early 1990s, Bernice Volz was one of the founding members of the Concerned Residents Group, which later became the Karawatha Forest Protection Society Inc (www.karawatha.com).

References

Abram, D. (1997) *The Spell of the Sensuous: Perception and Language in a More-Than-Human World*. New York: Pantheon.

Ballantyne, R. and Packer, J. (2008) *Learning for Sustainability: The Role and Impact of Outdoor and Environmental Education Centres*. Online. Retrieved from http://tourism.uq.edu.au/learning-for-sustainability/docs/Learning-for-Sustainability-Final-Report-Jun08.pdf

Ballantyne, R. and Packer, J. (2009) 'Introducing a fifth pedagogy: experience-based strategies for facilitating learning in natural environments.' *Environmental Education Research*, 15(2), 243–262.

Bolton, G. (1981) *Spoils and Spoilers: Australians Make Their Environment 1788–1980*. Sydney: Allen and Unwin.

Cam, P. (2006) *20 Thinking Tools: Collaborative Inquiry for the Classroom*. Camberwell: ACER Press.

Chatwin, B. (1987) *The Songlines*. London: Jonathan Cape.

Clark, M. (2004, May 1) Falling in Love Again. *ABC Radio National Science Show*, interview by Alexandra de Blas.

Dovers, S. (1994) *Australian Environmental History*. Oxford: Oxford University Press.

Greider, T. and Garkovich, L. (1994) 'Landscapes: the social construction of nature and the environment.' *Rural Sociology*, 59, 1–24.

McNeill, M. P., Macklin, R., Wasunna, A. and Komesaroff, A. P. (2004) 'An expanding vista: bioethics from public health, indigenous and feminist perspectives.' Paper presented at the the 7th World Congress of Bioethics: Deep Listening – Bridging Divides in Local and Global Ethics, Sydney, Australia, November 9–12.

Rolls, E. (1993) *From Forest to Sea: Australia's Changing Environment*. Brisbane: University of Queensland Press.

Slicer, D. (2003) 'Environmental narrative.' *Ethics and the Environment*, 8(2), 1–7.

Tooth, R. and Renshaw, P. (2009) 'Reflections on pedagogy and place: a journey into learning for sustainability through environmental narrative and deep attentive reflection.' *Australian Journal of Environmental Education*, 25, 95–104.

Tooth, R., Wager, L. and Proellocks, T. (1988) 'Story, setting and drama – a new look at environmental education.' *Australian Journal of Environmental Education*, 4, 31–34.

Vygotsky, L. S. (1993) *The Collected Works of L. S. Vygotsky*, vols. 1 and 2. (Translated by Jane Knox and Carol Stevens.) New York: Plenum Press.

Wattchow, B., Burke, G. and Cutter-Mackenzie, A. (2008) 'Environment, place and social ecology in educational practice.' In P. Payne (ed.) *The Social Ecology of Movement, Environment and Community*. Frankston, Victoria: Monash University.

Suggested further readings

Abram, D. (1997) *The Spell of the Sensuous: Perception and Language in a More-Than-Human World*. New York: Pantheon.

Goulah, J. (2009) 'Tsunesaburo Makiguchi and Mikhail Bakhtin in dialogue: pedagogy for a spatial literacy of ecological selfhood.' *Asia Pacific Journal of Education, 29*(2), 265–279.

Louv, R. (2008) *Last Child in the Woods*. Chapel Hill, NC: Algonquin Books.

Payne, P. G. (2010) 'Remarkable-tracking, experiential education of the ecological imagination.' *Environmental Education Research, 16*(3), 295–310.

Thomashow, M. (1996) *Ecological Identity*. Cambridge, MA: MIT Press.

Chapter 11

Creative learning in an inner-city primary school

England

Pat Thomson and Lorna Rose

Introduction

Lillian de Lissa Nursery School is situated in the inner city in Birmingham. Its postal address in Edgbaston might suggest some association with the genteel game of cricket or with Millionaire's Row, a swathe of luxurious gated mansions that house some of the wealthiest families in the country. However, Lillian de Lissa is situated in one corner of the suburb, just off two major highways, and its families mostly live in rented flats. A handful of middle-class parents who are in the catchment area send their children to the school, but many of the families do have pressing economic needs and subsequent difficulties in managing everyday life. Approximately 90 per cent of children are of minority ethnic heritage, and nearly half of the 80 children in the nursery have English as an additional language; there are sometimes up to 20 different languages spoken across these children's homes. Some parents want to learn the English language, and this is provided through the Sure Start Children's Centre, together with support groups that help the parents to manage the range of new health, safety, financial and employment issues that they face. The school runs from 9.00 AM to 3.00 PM, when most children go home, but some stay on for school club until 5.30 PM.

The school's goal is to be fully inclusive and offer a rich range of opportunities to all children.

> At Lillian de Lissa Nursery School we encourage children to think independently, to become directly involved in their learning, have fun, communicate and develop trusting relationships with others. Children are given opportunities within a safe, secure and stimulating environment to explore, negotiate and take risks. They are encouraged to care, respect and be curious about the world around them. Creativity is at the heart of our school and is used every day to provide learning opportunities for all children, staff and families. This provides an exciting, purposeful and

challenging environment taking into consideration the rhythm, space and time needed for every type of learner.

(School Statement of Values)[1]

Staff are committed to providing an environment and support in which children can be curious, make significant discoveries and mistakes, and fully enjoy their time learning about the world whilst building positive relationships with other children and adults. The school is one of 57 national Schools of Creativity in recognition of its achievements in constructing and sustaining an environment in which curiosity, enquiry, investigation, experimentation and exploration are not only valued but are seen as the most appropriate way for young children to learn.

At the same time, the learnings mandated in the early years curriculum framework are being achieved to very high and still improving levels.

> The children have access to a well equipped art room; an artist is in residence for three days of the week; and a potter, a willow weaver, and engineers, musicians, storyteller and dancers are among the visiting practitioners with whom the children often develop close and rewarding ties. The environment is also suffused with creativity in the wider sense. At every turn, the staff are looking out for opportunities to open the children's minds, develop their interests and further their abilities to think and act in imaginative ways.
>
> (A celebration: creative childhoods, 2010, p. 2)[2]

The school draws a line from the thinking of Lillian de Lissa after whom it was named and from whose memorial fund it received an opening grant. Her emphasis on the importance of inside and outside play, storytelling and the use of multipurpose materials for exploration are key commitments in the school. Current school staff have also taken inspiration from the approaches used in Reggio Emilia[3] and in Danish preschools, but they have adapted their principles and ways of working to the specific location and population that they serve. They have also been enthusiastic about the creative learning approaches[4] that have been recently promoted in England.

The school staff are committed to

- reflective practice that leads to a deeper level of staff understanding about the learning of the children in the centre. This is manifest in the everyday practice of pedagogic documentation through which observations are made of the children's responses to each day's provocations, and these provide the basis for staff reflections and decisions about how to extend the learning. (We describe this in more detail in the next section.)
- the principle of '100 languages of children' – namely that children learn and express that learning in multiple ways, modes and genres[5].

- diversity and inclusion. Staff understand that using the children's ideas is strongly connected not only to promoting their well-being but also to the value of the rich mix of cultural resources from both immigrant and more established families that the children bring with them to school.
- extended projects – slow learning – through which children are able to explore and extend their understandings and tackle large projects normally assumed to be beyond the capabilities of young children.
- the notion that the environment is the third teacher (again drawn from Reggio Emilia), the first being the child and the second the practitioner. This approach to teaching puts the natural development of children and the relationships they have with their environment at the centre of its philosophy. The school offers its own small 'forest' nearby,[6] and the tiny school yard has been carefully organized so that it too offers small 'wild' and cultivated places for children to experience.
- ongoing adaptation. Because the needs of the children are different every year, the daily routine is tailored to suit the dynamics of the children in school at each particular moment.

The school also places high value on personal, social and emotional well-being, which is encouraged through the regular use of yoga, peer massage, cookery, therapeutic music, nurture groups and visits to local amenities such as galleries, parks and shops of interest.

Partnerships between teachers and creative practitioners

Creative practitioners are professionals who work in areas such as industrial design, horticulture and architecture as well as in the arts – storytellers, dancers, film-makers, visual and performing artists. They bring creative practices that complement the ways in which teaching staff work with children. The artists[7] that we work with are experienced in getting children to engage at a deep level by communicating in a different way to teachers. They have a finely tuned agenda which is supported by the techniques and provocations that they bring with them. The collaboration between artists and teachers requires joint planning and shared approaches to providing support for learning and observing children's developments. The emphasis that creative practitioners place on working with children's ideas, taking risks, exploring media is compatible with the school philosophy, but they bring additional skills and experiences to the task. Their work with the children also educates teachers and they thus play an important role in creating the most optimal conditions for engaging and re-engaging children.

(Rose and Carlin, 2011)

These principles and commitments infuse everyday activities. We now show how these appear as one day in the life of the school. In particular, we want to show how 'child-initiated education' works in one site.

How does Lillian de Lissa Nursery School enact 'being led by children'?

The conventional English way of planning educational experiences for children is to use the national curriculum framework and the guiding documents. On the basis of the kinds of things children are meant to achieve, activities are planned that will allow children to acquire the skills, behaviours and understandings that are expected. This kind of pre-planning usually anticipates not only the content and process of activities but also their sequencing and pacing. Of course, this kind of curriculum-driven pre-planning can be more or less flexible and more or less responsive to the particular children involved, depending on the beliefs and capacities of the particular staff and school.

The planning at Lillian de Lissa is of a different kind. It is 'led by children'. This doesn't mean that the national curriculum frameworks are abandoned or ignored. Rather, it means that the content, activities, and their sequencing and pacing are derived from close observation of and interaction with children, and the learnings from those activities are then plotted against the curriculum frameworks. The framework also serves as diagnostic, so that children who need particular kinds of support to learn particular things can be offered it, and so that teachers can check to see that a balance of activities are on offer over a period of time.

Perhaps the easiest way to understand how this works in practice is to look at a typical morning in the school.

The rhythm of activities

School starts officially at 9.00 AM, but teachers generally arrive from 7.00 AM onward. During the first part of the day, teachers talk to parents about any concerns they have and children often also present staff with something from home – a book, a toy, a story of something happening. Children are able to play all over the nursery at this time and, for some children who have been confined to a small flat since they left school the day before, the opportunity to be physically active is very important and enjoyable. During this time, teachers will adjust their thinking about the day's activities to cater for things that children have presented that morning. For example, if a child brings a book about dinosaurs to school, it will feature in the rest of the day's activities and, depending on the response from other children, may become incorporated into the activities on offer for the next day.

Figure 11.1 Playing in the nursery at the start of the day

At 9.30 AM, the children gather into their family group. Each family group consists of 13 children, and they each have a designated place in the school. This has shelves with books and objects, some seating, a clear 'mat' area next to a teacher's chair and a small whiteboard. Coat and bag hooks are nearby. On the whiteboard are photos of each of the activities that are on offer that day; each activity is organized onto a table or, in the case of the artist in residence, Lorna, in her room (the atelier). One of the children is appointed as daily helper; this is done in turns. Each child in the group chooses an activity for the day, and his or her name is written on the whiteboard by the helper. During this time, the teacher not only will explain the activities but also will talk about any particular books, toys, or stories that children have brought in that morning and how they are to be incorporated into the day. For example, children might be encouraged to read the book on dinosaurs with its owner (the expert), and there might be a story about dinosaurs to come later that day. Any particular events are also discussed so children know any variations to the usual routine. This might be music, drama, or forest school or new things in Lorna's room. After choosing an activity, children are offered a drink and a piece of fruit. All children are encouraged to take turns and to say please and thank you in words and signing (*Makaton*).

At around 10.00 AM children move into activities and the doors to the outside area are opened. While they are expected to commit to an activity, they are able to change during the hour of activity time. There is often a painting table on offer, but there is only room for four children at a time.

If more than four choose to do this, children are expected to do another activity until it is their turn to paint. Weather permitting, there is usually at least one outside activity on offer. A typical range of activities would include painting, making things in Lorna's room, use of outside equipment, manipulable building blocks, a writing/storying activity, a nature-based activity. Teachers distribute themselves around the activities and engage in meaningful conversations. Much verbal language and concept development occurs through these deliberative conversations. The painting table might discuss colour, for example, in relation to what the children have chosen to represent. The teacher will work to help the children understand how colours can be mixed as well as building vocabulary of different shades and hues. During activity time, teachers look for

1 'teachable moments', opportunities when children's immediate experiences can be connected with deeper learning, and
2 clues for things that lend themselves to further development. For example, if children talk a lot about the cars outside the school, then this could become an activity or series of activities based around cars that extends their knowledge.

Figure 11.2 Using the activities area

Teachers may also record what children are doing, using still or video photographs. These photographs are used to document key learning moments and stand as one avenue for profiling individual students' learning and providing feedback to parents. It is the totality of listening, watching and recording, known as 'pedagogic observation', that is the foundation of 'being led by children'.

At 11.00 AM, 'tidy up time', the bell rings and the children are all expected to pick up and organize resources they have been playing with in order to continue in the afternoon. At all times when the outside door is open, there are staff both inside and out. After the nursery is tidied, the children go to their home group space and sit on the floor in pairs. This is massage time. Soothing music is played through the school while teachers lead the children through a sequence of moves. Children are expected to ask permission to massage another child and to thank the child who has massaged them. Children are directed to listen to the music and to pay attention to the care with which they touch their massage partner. Halfway through the massage, they swap over so that each child has both massaged and been massaged.

After massage, more focused learning happens; sometimes a transition activity leads into this time. Something like standing up and forming a circle or sitting down and crossing legs segues into a more formal instruction period. Again, this is drawn from a lead from a child, although sometimes it will have a local or seasonal focus. For example, there might be an exercise in which children must remember and match pairs of Easter eggs. Again there is

Figure 11.3 Working in pairs during massage time

Figure 11.4 Outdoor play until it's time to eat

an emphasis not only on the substantive content but also the need for turn-taking and respect and encouragement for other children in the group. At around 11.45 AM, half of the children move to the lunchroom and the others go outside to play until it is their turn to eat.

Afternoons follow a similar pattern, with group time, activity time and then more formal group time before school ends for the day. The afternoons may well include activities derived from something that has happened during the morning. For example, a teacher might have the child with the book about dinosaurs lead a discussion of the group, followed by a set of stories about dinosaurs.

Informal discussions about what to do have taken place over lunch. If dinosaurs were popular, then one of the activities might be focused on dinosaurs and consist of an area with models and books that children can explore. This 'table' is prepared that night for the next day and a photo taken for the whiteboard choice activity.

After school, teachers prepare for the next day's activities. Every evening there is a short reflection meeting during which staff discuss things they have observed that lend themselves to further extension. For example, if children have been interested in models of dinosaurs, then this might be extended through looking at skeletons in a museum or visiting a Jurassic site. There is also discussion about any children who need particular support or who have made notable progress (behavioural or learning) during the day.

Student-led teaching is thus a combination of student choice and teacher-designed activities that are based on children's observed behaviours and conversations.

Teaching the Lillian de Lissa way

Working at Lillian de Lissa Nursery School and in this way requires a particular set of professional competencies. Some of the most important are listed here.

A pedagogic repertoire that is built around experience, conversation, coaching, judgement and observation

Teachers at Lillian de Lissa offer children choice but also scaffold their learning through

- talk (general verbal instruction, specific direction, questioning, introduction of new vocabulary, offering additional information), and
- action (modeling, 'doing with', showing where additional information can be found, moving the body for the child).

Teachers often combine more than one medium of communication, the most common of which are the written, verbal and visual. There is often a sequence of talk, experience, talk, write/record. This builds the basis on which children know; they've done it and they've used specific words and phrases to describe what happened. Teachers work both individually and with groups, also combining the two.

The capacity to successfully and seamlessly combine social and more discipline-based knowledge

Routines in the school depend on children operating cooperatively and as a group. This means teachers must pay attention to group processes at the same time as maintaining a rich dialogue with challenging intellectual content. While this intellectual content is relevant to what is happening that day and in the moment, it is also drawn from the teacher's understandings of where each child needs to go next. In this context, personalizing learning does not mean grouping the children by ability but working with and from deep understandings of each child's current learning profile combined with knowing how best to connect what is in the moment with the child's more general interests and existing knowledge. Group processes also allow children to extend one another's learning and to garner confidence and respect for the things that they know and can do.

Speaking and listening to children respectfully and seriously

It is not uncommon for adults to perform for young children. Indeed, at Lillian de Lissa this behaviour can be seen in some of the visiting instructors. However, Lillian de Lissa staff speak with children not as adults or as young people needing to be engaged or motivated but rather as sensible people with ideas, opinions and understandings that are to be taken seriously. Teachers also want to develop child–child communication. Children who want to talk only with adults are often gently moved so that they face everybody in their group, not just the teacher. Group times are the time when children learn how to talk authoritatively and/or persuasively and/or entertainingly to their peers. It is this respectful relational/interaction practice, a tangible expression of care, that seems to give Lillian de Lissa its particular ethos.

Attending to children with particular needs

All children have days when they are sad or cross and it is part of the school's job to deal with these. It is also the case that some children have more deep-seated problems that cause them to behave in ways that are disruptive to their own and others' learning. It is rare to hear staff at Lillian de Lissa raise their voices. The overall tone of voice that is used is at an ordinary pitch. This helps to maintain a feeling of calm and control. However, teachers at Lillian de Lissa know how to quietly remove a child from an activity and to do so without escalating the child's behaviour. Calming down and moving on often involves the gentle use of touch, moving the child away, moving him or her closer to a comforting adult, leading the child out of a room while holding him or her by the hand.

Continued development

The school operates in a challenging funding and political context. It has taken the view that while it must respond to new requirements and initiatives, it also must continue to build its own practice and knowledge base. This, however, is not a solitary pastime. Staff regularly work with neighbouring schools and with a range of national programmes; at the same time, Lillian de Lissa staff take every opportunity to learn from others.

A couple of years after the school took control of its own budget in 2004, it was decided to knock down the interior walls in order to create a more open environment through which children could move as they chose for much of the school day. Given that the school had just been judged outstanding by OfSTED, it would have been far safer to keep things as they were. But the risk paid off: the free-flow environment created by the new design has been vital to the children's ability to 'direct their own journeys' as they learn, and the school was again judged outstanding when it was inspected in 2009.

(A celebration. Creative childhoods (2010), Lillian de Lissa and Belgravia Childrens Centre, Edgbaston, UK, p. 16)

At the time of writing this chapter, the school was planning how it might work to produce and promote community cohesion, paying new and different attention to its families. It was also working on a plan to develop children's speaking and listening capabilities. Both of these priorities were to be effected through the use of storytelling and arts-based activities. There is no sign that the Lillian de Lissa learning journey is ended.

Notes

1 See http://www.ldelissa.bham.sch.uk/index.php?option=com_content&view=frontpage&Itemid=1
2 A celebration: creative childhoods, 2010, is available from the Lillian de Lissa and Belgravia Childrens Centre, Edgbaston, UK.
3 See for example Edwards et al. (1998); Hall et al. (2010); and Rinaldi (2005).
4 See www.creative-partnerships.com and also Thomson et al. (2009).
5 See the related work on multiple intelligences (Project Zero and Reggio Children, 2001).
6 See forest schools in Knight (2009).
7 See Reggio use of ateleristas (Gandini et al. 2005; Vecchi, 2010); Lorna Rose has this role at the Lillian de Lissa Nursery School.

References

Edwards, C., Gandini, L. and Forman, G. (eds) (1998) *The Hundred Languages of Children: The Reggio Emilia Approach. Advanced Reflections* (2nd ed.). Greenwich, CT: Ablex Publishing.

Gandini, L., Hill, L., Cadwell, L. and Schwall, C. (eds) (2005) *In the Spirit of the Studio: Learning from the Atelier of Reggio Emilia.* New York: Teachers College Press.

Hall, K., Horgan, M., Ridgway, A., Murphy, R.O., Cunneen, M. and Cunningham, D. (2010) *Loris Malaguzzi and the Reggio Emilia Experience.* London: Continuum.

Knight, S. (2009) *Forest Schools and Outdoor Learning in the Early Years.* London: Sage.

Project Zero and Reggio Children (2001) *Making Learning Visible: Children as Individual and Group Learners.* Reggio Emilia: Reggio Children.

Rinaldi, C. (2005) *In Dialogue with Reggio Emilia: Listening, Researching and Learning.* London: Routledge.

Rose, L. and Carlin, A. (2011) 'Ensuring equality with a focus on boys' learning.' In R. Elkington (ed.) *Turning Pupils onto Learning: Creative Classrooms in Action.* London: Routledge.

Thomson, P., Jones, K., and Hall, C. (2009) *Creative Whole School Change* (final report). London: Creativity, Culture and Education; Arts Council England. Also see www.artsandcreativityresearch.org.uk.

Vecchi, V. (2010) *Art and Creativity in Reggio Emilia*. New York: Routledge.

Suggested further readings

Dahlberg, G., Moss, P., and Pence, A. (2006) *Beyond Quality in Early Childhood Education and Care: Postmodern Perspectives*. London: Routledge Falmer.

Elkington, R. (ed.) (2011) *Turning Pupils onto Learning: Creative Classrooms in Action*. London: Routledge.

Gandini, L., Hill, L., Cadwell, L. and Schwall, C. (eds) (2005) *In the Spirit of the Studio: Learning from the Atelier of Reggio Emilia*. New York: Teachers College Press.

Knight, S. (2009) *Forest Schools and Outdoor Learning in the Early Years*. London: Sage.

Sefton Green, J., Jones, K., Thomson, P., and Bresler, L. (eds) (2011) *The Routledge International Handbook of Creative Learning*. London: Routledge.

Chapter 12

Talking honestly in a challenging primary school

England

Lori Beckett and Jill Wood

Introduction

This school had to change. A tough community primary school in a de-industrialized inner city in the north of England, it nestles beneath high-rise social-housing tower blocks and serves a very vulnerable local area noted for its high crime statistics and high alcohol and drug dependency and where a significant proportion of the population has never worked. Pupils came from a range of backgrounds – culturally, religiously and academically – with over 35 different languages spoken and seven faith groups represented. Needs were high and complex, relationships were tense and often confrontational, and aspirations were low. The entire neighbourhood was impoverished, marked by boarded-up buildings, litter, graffiti, abandoned cars and dumped old furniture. There was a resignation to the downward spiral. People had given up.

The school faced serious challenges. The 2003 Ofsted report, the government's measure of success, spoke favourably about what the school was trying to achieve, although an armed siege in one of the high-rise tower blocks helped convince inspectors of the difficulties. Then, the lack of a substantive school Head plunged the school into a reactive management regime, which contributed to a stressful and turbulent atmosphere. Lack of clarity of direction and a growing deficit budget meant that the school started to look and feel a little shabby, classrooms and corridors were cluttered and uninspiring, and many of the permanent staff were absent due to illness. The habit of pupils calling staff by their first name served to compound the lack of respect shown to all 'figures of authority'.

At the time of the school Head's appointment at Easter 2005, more serious challenges remained. The deficit budget was nearly £200K, pupil numbers had fallen dramatically, academic achievement was underwhelming, behaviour was a serious health and safety issue, and the school had the dubious position of sitting at the bottom of the local authority league table for primary schools – 243 out of 243. Staff morale was low, and there was an air of desperation. There was no substantive deputy Head and the governing body was out of touch with the real issues facing the school. Children were rude, behaviourally very challenging, and physically and verbally aggressive, and showed little interest in learning. The Index of Multiple Deprivation, another government measure, rated this electoral ward in the top 5 per cent of those most deprived in the country. Things could only get better!

Mapping the changes

The task of school reform looked daunting. The starting point was the very real health and safety issues followed by re-energising a committed teaching staff and subsequently raising expectations of the entire community. At first, the school embraced an intensified support plan that determined not only the focus but the pace of change. The school Head introduced a slogan of 'accountability, responsibility and rigour' to underpin the transformation. In a series of whole-school assemblies, the children set the rules for the school – only four – that started to give a sense of belonging. A new positive behaviour code was introduced, with rewards and clear sanctions for noncompliance. Children were given fixed term exclusions as a result of a zero tolerance policy on violence, racism, bullying, swearing and persistent disruption. The learning mentor delivered a two-hour, one-to-one learning session at the homes of excluded pupils so there was never a loss of focus on the purpose of coming to school. School uniforms were reintroduced to complement a sense of family bonds, and coffee sessions with parents allowed all the dissatisfaction that they had been harbouring to be aired and addressed. Within six months, pupils were addressing staff by their formal names to signify the relationship between teacher and learner.

We met 18 months into this new management regime to discuss a proposal for a school-university partnership called the Patterns of Learning project, specifically designed for a challenging school, with the main strategic intervention being teacher-led action inquiries developed in professional learning communities. This took direction from studies on the effects of poverty on education (see Connell 1993; Connell et al. 1991; Groundwater-Smith and Kemmis 2004) in concert with studies of critical school effectiveness and school improvement (Lupton 2004, 2005, 2006; Thrupp 1999, 2005), and school–university partnerships (see Beveridge et al. 2004; Cochran-Smith and Lytle 1999; Hayes et al. 2005; Lieberman and Miller 2001, 2008). Our project had utility in regards to school development, which dovetails with teacher learning and development, although the school Head insisted this be extended to include all staff: school executive, teachers, teaching assistants and nursery nurses. Coincidentally, we see this learning and development extending across the school–university partnership, because it is also about academics learning about working in challenging schools and local authority officials learning about contextualized school improvement and school quality.

Our respective biographies resonated, given that we are driven to working in challenging schools as teacher and academic partner, guided by a commitment to equity and social justice in and through schooling with the education system's support. We see the social justice challenge as one of 'complex hope' in terms of society's structural pressures and the possibilities of schools responding to those pressures (Thrupp and Tomlinson 2005) and agree there should be both teacher education for social justice and teaching for social justice (Cochran-Smith 2008). We have a mutual interest in socially just pedagogies (Lingard 2005) and we are both keen to change the experiences of schooling and education for pupils and parents living in poverty and to support staff building a better school for this community.

When we forged the terms of our work together, contained in a draft memorandum of understanding, the school had already 'turned a corner' insofar as the environment was ordered, welcoming and warm. The deficit budget had been addressed, staff were motivated, the governors had a better understanding of the complexities and challenges, parents were more trusting and there was a 'can do' ethos. Most important, the children's behaviour was conducive to learning, but there was a way to go.

With fewer than 30 per cent of the year 6 pupils reaching the expected level of attainment at the end of their primary schooling in both English and science and only 31 per cent achieving the required level in maths, the school was struggling to meet attainment targets. In the 2003 Ofsted inspection, attainment was a concern but was not as desperately low. From Easter 2005 to April 2007, everyone worked hard at raising standards in all core subjects. The introduction of a dedicated English as an additional language (EAL) staff member meant that for the first time newly arrived children were not just dropped into an alien classroom environment. They were assessed in a positive and empathetic way before being introduced to the entire class, with a supported programme to accelerate their learning in English. At the school level, the importance of the native tongue was retained; EAL children worked within small same-language groups so they could converse and share ideas. This certainly helped in securing their sense of self and reducing the number of behaviour incidents explained in terms of children's frustrations.

With the 2007 Ofsted inspection, results were improving and expectations from staff, children and parents were high. In 2008, the school was recognized as the twentieth most improved school in the country, the fourth most improved in Yorkshire, and the most improved in Leeds. It is important to note that although attainment was improving, it was actually the push to raise both social and academic learning outcomes for pupils that underpinned the successes. As a school, it was decided to take a pedagogical focus to ensure that the children were problem solvers, thinkers and collaborative workers and had the skills to find out for themselves what they needed to know. They were badged 'active learners' who contributed significantly to the 'can do' ethos, with results that reflected their willingness to learn and increasing taste of success.

Joint concerns

We share a twin concern with the emphasis on 'school effects' as it finds expression in the standards agenda and official school improvement plans. It is not enough to read local authority data such as the school's inclusion profile, the primary performance analyses, demographic charts, data and classifications, in an uncritical way, making simple correlations with pupil outcomes. Achieving results is not only a matter of predictions and targets, teaching practices and pupil performance are best steered by a managerial model: better management, better training and better monitoring (Lupton 2012). There needs to be a critical reading of school effects as regards identifying factors that contribute to pupil learning outcomes, so that we go past a crude identification of school practices in terms of contextual value-added measures and 'what works' (Angus 1993; Slee et al. 1998; Thrupp 1999).

A case in point is the use of Fischer Family Trust data, which takes national demographic data and school performance data to create sets of predictions and targets for English, maths and science for all children and young people in age-related year groups. Teachers use these data for every class and tabulate predictions and targets for all children, who are alert to expectations, with formative and summative assessment crucial to results. Though we see this as a tool to help raise achievement, used in the school to satisfy government dictates, we (along with a number of school staff) have reservations about the way statistical data intimates excuses for particular performances, and the way it deals with pupils' family and social backgrounds, cultural differences and British society in relation to learning outcomes. This is not to ignore the children's experiences of schooling and education.

From a management perspective, it is interesting to know how children from across the country compare but, actually, it is the success of your school's children that is more significant. The school uses the Fischer Family Trust data to support the drive for improvement, but this has not limited expectations. The children have shown a capability to learn as long as staff provide the right conditions to nurture their interest and energy and question what is taken for granted in everyday practices. Staff subscribe to the credo that success breeds success and, once the school accepted that, there were obvious improvements in children's academic learning, sports playing, singing and the like. There was an apparent yearning for repeated success, which grew and took on a momentum of its own. Children tried that bit harder, they started to attend the lunchtime and after-school homework clubs but, even more significantly, they became partners in their learning.

Another concern is that while the Fischer Family Trust acknowledges 'context' and pupil background factors in regard to achievement and performance, it buys into cultural deficit of the pupils because it recognizes difference in expectations but does not question the difference. As Angus (1993) pointed out, there is simply a mathematical connection between statistically equalized pupils and their performance but no sense of how the relationship works. This makes us think twice about family background, poverty, deprivation and local context – as Angus (1993) said, all typically regarded as 'noise', as 'outside' background factors that must be controlled for and then stripped away so that the researcher (read *teacher*) can concentrate on the important domain of school factors.

In this challenging primary school, the family's understanding of why children attended school was critical to the school's efforts. If staff are merely regarded as child minders or, worse, an institution to occupy children as part of the state's responsibility for parenting, then there is a need to examine the purpose of schooling. It is crucial to recognize that family background is not something that influences only input or that the teachers' task is to do the best they can with predictions and targets, implement best practices and improve teaching quality. It is not only a matter of high expectations, raising aspirations and regular testing because children are not just a statistic on a league table that measures only one aspect of development. Staff had to provide a progressive and productive curriculum that was not only accessible but also meaningful to the children and important to their parents and care givers. Staff also had to embrace a form of productive pedagogies (Hayes et al. 2005; Lingard 2005) because the purpose of schooling is not just to get children to age-related expectations but to equip them with knowledge and skills to make a significant contribution to their community and society as a whole. They need to be able to think, rationalize, prioritize, question and solve problems. The school aims to create a respect between culturally diverse populations of pupils and staff and empower families to respond positively to their responsibilities as parents or care givers and as global citizens.

This means connecting with the community and wider society and asking critical questions about the neighbourhood, pupil intake, pupils' family and social backgrounds and myriad other contextual considerations, not least what schoolteachers, pupils, and parents and care givers think is important. As Lupton (2012) noted, while the local context is objective and 'out there' and capable of strategic managerial responses, it is also evidently 'in' the school, shaping everyday interactions, expectations, activities and resource distributions. The school's location matters in multiple and fundamentally important ways.

This all speaks to the sociological emphasis in our Patterns of Learning project, because it draws attention to the school's location and the patterns of poverty and income inequalities that affect its work, as well as the patterns of student learning and school achievement, patterns of curriculum and pedagogies required for a richly rewarding learning experience, and patterns of staff learning with academics' and civil servants' learning. The measurement of poverty within the school's catchment area is tangible at 94.1 per cent on the Index of Multiple Deprivation. The school is at the heart of a disenfranchised, despondent and fragile community, and the school is potentially a catalyst for change.

This is where the utility of working with academic partners comes into play to tailor the school's improvement policy to its particular local community context. We approached the project mindful of Groundwater-Smith's (2002) caution to find the common ground between practitioner knowledge and academic knowledge in order to support the staff in theorizing their own work and developing localized responses to the challenges they confronted. This required sustained professional learning and development, initially a series of teacher-led seminars geared to identifying and naming concerns and developing our sociological perspectives on school achievement and capacity to engage professional reading and research.

As the sessions found support among the staff and the Patterns of Learning project took root, we took directions from the staff because our approach is very much open to their theoretical enterprise. From the outset, we all agreed staff would develop critical thinking about their work at the school using some suggested readings: Hayes et al. (2005), Lupton (2004), and Wrigley (2003). The task was to use these readings to build a shared understanding and theoretically informed vocabulary to critically interpret classroom work. To provide some guidance, we offered the following critical reading of Wrigley (2003), cognisant that he offered an alternative approach to school improvement. From Wrigley's work we created the following list of questions:

- Is there a sense of an alternative future for the children/student teachers at the school? What does this mean?
- In what ways can we go about the improvement of learning? How can we bring new life to learning?
- Can we list three ways we promote live engagement with the world? How do we combine head, heart and hand in the primary classroom and the initial teacher education classroom?
- Does Wrigley's concern about direct instruction speak to any of the concerns named last session? Does the school rely on transmission models?
- Do we embrace a constructivist theory of learning? What is the best way to describe this? When and why is this appropriate?

Honest talk

To argue the case for this sort of work with staff, we described our penchant for talking honestly about what needs to be done in this challenging primary school in these recessionary times. We took direction for honest talk from Lieberman and Miller (2008), who argue that professional learning communities as collegial cultures should be marked by bonds of trust to provide a forum for reflection and honest feedback, for challenge and disagreement, and for accepting responsibility without assigning blame. We have tried to move staff beyond consensus, so they resist the reassurances and quick fixes, to go deeper to uncover and analyse problems.

Foremost for staff was naming this particular challenging primary school as disadvantaged, which requires more open discussion and debate about poverty and the combination and concentration of social and economic disadvantage experienced in inner cities, and whether this automatically translates into educational disadvantage such as below-average performance and slow learning (Connell 1993). Staff reject any hint of impoverishment for children, alert to cultural deficit theories while keen to explore pupil characteristics and local area characteristics (Lupton 2004) in order to develop guides to practice in line with context-specific improvement approaches (see Thrupp 2005).

There were shifts in England toward a contextualized school improvement agenda. At the time of the Brown Labour government, which in May 2010 lost to the Cameron–Clegg Conservative–Liberal Democrat coalition government, the then Department for Children, Schools and Families (2009) published the *Analysis and Evidence Strategy 2009–10*. It documented research and analysis considered against each of the department's seven strategic objectives (DSOs): health and well-being, safeguarding, world-class standards, closing the gap in educational achievement for children from disadvantaged backgrounds, participation and achievement to 18 and beyond, keeping children and young people on the paths to success, and leading and managing the system. According to the then Secretary of State Ed Balls in the foreword, it was a response to *The Children's Plan* policy agenda, launched in 2007 and underpinned by the view that evidence and analysis is fundamental to tracking progress, to identify policies that are working and that could work better.

The fourth DSO – to close the gap in educational achievement for children from disadvantaged backgrounds – named the link between deprivation and achievement, especially between family income and achievement, and indicated the need to recognize this wider context for children's learning but also the importance of integrated service provision. It listed factors that promote attainment as socio-economic factors, parental involvement and teaching behaviours, and their interaction. At issue was school and preschool quality, with evidence pointing to the importance of early intervention and support and the development of aspirations as a mechanism for sustaining and improving attainment. Aspiration and its relationship with social mobility have been a theme for policy work and the then cross-government collaboration. The analytic priorities for this DSO included improving available information in regard to children and young people with special educational needs (SEN), improving SEN statementing and evaluating such departmental pilot studies as *The Extra Mile* project.

The *Analysis and Evidence Strategy 2009–10* was a most welcome initiative, though it speaks to Yates' (2004) concerns about hard-headed advocates of evidence-based quality research who take too little account of the *type of phenomenon* education research deals in, which is stark when it comes to the fourth DSO. The understanding of research linked to beliefs in evidence, tying equity to standards and underachievement, and listing teaching behaviours among contextual factors signals not only a lack of appreciation of the real world of challenging schools but a managerialist policy response. It goes some way towards engaging local community context but falls short of raising critical questions and maintained the then government's 'failing schools' agenda, which continues in the new coalition government. In this system, schools are subject to rigid inspections by often unannounced Ofsted inspectors and also so-called school improvement 'partners'. If judged to be not meeting standards, schools in challenging circumstances are subject to naming and shaming, more intense inspections and a host of recommended measures, including closure.

If a government, whatever its persuasion, is wedded to the idea of research as evidence, it must be open to reliable research undertaken in schools, including practitioner research done with academic partners. With research mentoring, staff can make their classrooms and school sites of inquiry, connecting their work to government policy agendas and critical readings of school effectiveness and school improvement. They produce many credible findings, with considered conclusions and recommendations for policy and practice, including contextualized school improvement plans.

For example, the school Head's action inquiry (Wood 2009) focused on white working-class underachievement and tied it closely to pupils' experiences of schooling. She concentrated on boys' attitudes to learning, self-belief and aspirations, noting one of them asked, 'What's the point of school?' Through school and classroom observations and semi-structured interviews with pupils, she found widespread disengagement from learning, certainly by the age of seven. In semi-structured interviews with parents and care givers, she found a total lack of aspiration for a positive future for these young boys, which lent itself to a self-fulfilling prophecy of nonachievement. The data were telling: 'He's alright, but let's face it, he's not the brightest button in the box, is he? I don't think there's 'owt he can do expect for gob off.' [there is nothing he can do except answer back]. 'Nobody does anything round here.' 'Nobody gets a job round here.'

In the data analysis, informed by reading 'The sociology of school effectiveness' (Angus 1993), Wood (2009) identified a lack of working-class role models; the poor concentration, attention and engagement of boys who meet such deprivation criteria as free school meals; feelings of hopelessness and lack of aspiration or positive image of the future and productive role in society; parents' lack of aspirations for their sons; and the lack of connectedness between schooling and home. While it might appear that local context and larger social and economic structures were being overlooked, she did not ignore poverty and social class and the way it is deeply ingrained in British society (Sveinsson 2009). By engaging action inquiry, the school Head investigated society's structural pressures in the local community and the school's capacity to respond. She looked past 'school effects' to 'poverty effects', recognized not just in the poor but in the way the school is organized (Connell 1993), and 'compositional effects' having to do with the local economy, histories of worklessness, and particular class structures and ethnicities, but alert to the significance of place because these things meant different things in this place (Lupton 2012).

The task was to take the conclusions about these boys' schooling experiences and these parents' and caregivers' lack of hope of improved outcomes, resignation to poverty, and overreliance on state support, and work them into building an alternative future for children. The school Head acknowledged this would begin to happen only when the school engaged parents and caregivers as partners in their children's learning and confronted the assumptions and constraints of deprivation. The contextualized response came in the form of differentiated school improvement: the school was in a situation in which only 13 per cent of parents made contact for consultation evenings but, with active encouragement, this rose to 98.4 per cent of parents genuinely wanting to be involved in their child's learning journey. In response to 33 per cent of boys indicating school was about 'doing boring stuff', the staff introduced an immersed curriculum, which is a creative, thematic and enquiry-based curriculum in which children are co-researchers who pose their own enquiry questions. A third contextualized response was the World of Work Wednesdays, an initiative through which a variety of local businesspeople come to school assemblies to talk about connecting school knowledge and skills to the world of work, and in which parents are encouraged into school or college training courses. The school Head's recommendations from this action inquiry were to continue building a practitioner research culture around curriculum and productive pedagogies and to continue raising critical questions about the school, its strategies and impact.

Conclusions

Reflecting on the school changes and what has taken shape through the work of our school–university partnership, we can see a more self-conscious sense of staff professionalism characterized by more progressive thinking about disadvantage and school change. In five years, the school has moved from being one with a falling roll to one with a waiting list. It must be said the task of developing locally owned improvement strategies is not without challenges and tensions, especially with the failing schools agenda operating in England. We argue that politicians and civil servants need to be more determined in regard to deprivation and underachievement and more actively engage the research evidence on context. We hope our work with staff in this challenging primary school can influence policy making and despite doubts about elected politicians, continue contributing evidence and analyses to the Department for Children, Schools and Families' *Analysis and Evidence Strategy 2009–10*, specifically DSO 4 to 'close the gap in educational achievement from disadvantaged backgrounds'. This requires a leap of faith because we fundamentally disagree with linking equity, standards and underachievement, but nonetheless we champion the idea of school practitioners doing action inquiries and demanding that current policy directions take into account existing conditions in challenging schools.

References

Angus, L. (1993) 'The sociology of school effectiveness.' *British Journal of Sociology of Education, 14*(3), 333–345.

Beveridge, S., Groundwater-Smith, S., Kemmis, S. and Wasson, D. (2004) 'Professional learning that makes a difference: successful strategies implemented by priority actions schools.' Paper presented at the Annual Conference of the Australian Association for Research in Education, Melbourne.

Cochran-Smith, M. (2008) 'Toward a theory of teacher education for social justice.' Paper prepared for the Annual Meeting of the American Educational Research Association, New York City, March.

Cochran-Smith, M. and Lytle, S. (1999) 'Relationships of knowledge and practice: teacher learning in communities.' *Review of Research in Education, 24*(1), 249–305.

Connell, R. W. (1993) *Schools and Social Justice.* Montreal: Our Schools/Our Selves Education Foundation.

Connell, R. W., White, V. and Johnston, K.M. (1991) *'Running Twice as Hard'. The Disadvantaged Schools Program in Australia.* Geelong: Deakin University Press.

Department for Children, Schools and Families (2009) *Analysis and Evidence Strategy 2009–10: Delivering Evidence Based Policy.* London: Author.

Groundwater-Smith, S. (2002) 'Evidence based practice in school education: some lessons for learning in museums.' Paper presented at *Why learning?* seminar, Australian Museum/University of Technology Sydney, 22 November. Available at http://australianmuseum.net.au/document/Evidence-Based-Practice-in-School-Education

Groundwater-Smith, S. and Kemmis, S. (2004) *Knowing Makes the Difference.* Sydney: New South Wales Department of Education and Training.

Hayes, D., Mills, M., Christie, P. and Lingard, B. (2005) *Teachers and Schooling: Making a Difference.* Sydney: Allen and Unwin.

Lieberman, A. and Miller, L. (2001) *Teachers Caught in the Action: Professional Development that Matters.* New York: Teachers College Press.

Lieberman, A. and Miller, L. (eds) (2008) *Teachers in Professional Communities: Improving Teaching and Learning.* New York: Teachers College, Columbia University.

Lingard, B. (2005) 'Socially just pedagogies in changing times.' *International Studies in Sociology of Education, 15*(2), 165–186.

Lupton, R. (2004) 'Understanding local contexts for schooling and their implications for school processes and quality.' British Educational Research Association newsletter *Research Intelligence, 89,* November.

Lupton, R. (2005) 'Social justice and school improvement: improving the quality of schooling in the poorest neighbourhoods.' *British Educational Research Journal, 31*(5), 589–604.

Lupton, R. (2006) 'Schools in disadvantaged areas: low attainment and a contextualized policy response.' In H. Lauder, P. Brown, J. Dillabough and A. H. Halsey (eds) *Education, Globalisation and Social Change.* Oxford: Oxford University Press.

Lupton, R. (2012) 'Local context, social relations and school organisation.' In C. Day (ed.) *Routledge International Handbook of School and Teacher Development.* London: Routledge.

Slee, R. and Weiner, G., with Tomlinson, S. (1998) *School Effectiveness for Whom? Challenges to the School Effectiveness and School Improvement Movements.* London: Falmer Press.

Sveinsson, K. P. (2009) *Who Cares about the White Working Class?* London: The Runnymede Trust.

Thrupp, M. (1999) *Schools Making a Difference: Let's Be Realistic.* Maidenhead: Open University Press.

Thrupp, M. (2005). *School Improvement: An Unofficial Approach.* London: Continuum.

Thrupp, M. and Tomlinson, S. (2005) 'Introduction: education policy, social justice and "complex hope".' *British Educational Research Journal, 31*(5), 549–556.

Wood, J. (2009) 'What's the point? A small scale study into factors affecting the underachievement of poor white boys in an inner city school.' Paper presented at Annual Conference of the British Educational Research Association, Manchester.

Wrigley, T. (2003) *Schools of Hope: A New Agenda for School Improvement.* Stoke-on-Trent: Trentham Books.

Yates, L. (2004) *What Does Good Educational Research Look Like?* Maidenhead: Open University Press.

Suggested further readings

Campbell, A. and Groundwater-Smith, S. (eds) (2010) *Connecting Inquiry and Professional Learning in Education: International Perspectives and Practical Solutions.* London: Routledge.

Connell, R. W. (2009) 'Good teachers on dangerous ground: towards a new view of teacher quality and professionalism.' *Critical Studies in Education, 50*(3), 213–229.

Lieberman, A. and Miller, L. (eds) (2008) *Teachers in Professional Communities Improving Teaching and Learning*. New York: Teachers College Press.

Thrupp, M. (2005) *School Improvement: An Unofficial Approach*. London: Continuum.

Wrigley, T. (2003) *Schools of Hope. A New Agenda for School Improvement*. Stoke-on-Trent: Trentham Books.

Chapter 13

Weaving the web of professional practice

Australia

Nicole Mockler and
Susan Groundwater-Smith

Introduction

In this chapter we outline the formation, processes and purposes of a dynamic hybrid network of schools working to create usable professional knowledge in a context of change. The Coalition of Knowledge-Building Schools, based in New South Wales, Australia, was formed in 2000 and over the past ten years has grown steadily and developed procedures for working collegially. Here, we trace the different phases of the Coalition's expansion and identify a number of turning points in the evolution of the network. We explore processes used for the invention and re-invention of professional knowledge within the community of practice, across varying social, geographic and educational contexts.

This chapter seeks to identify the conditions for building a joint enterprise through events and publications and highlights a range of strengths and challenges in creating this joint enterprise. As strengths, we examine issues of diversity and flexibility, academic support and goodwill. Among the challenges, we highlight matters associated with sustainability, capacity building and the need to remain 'critical'. We conclude not by offering a model but by suggesting a number of principles upon which successful hybrid networks can be established and maintained.

Network or web?

In his account of orb web construction, Zschokke (2009) outlines the moves that the spider makes in building its web. Briefly, the spider bridges an open space by attaching a dragline and traversing the gap; it then tightens the thread and uses it as a means to cross back to the other side. Slowly, but strategically, the spider establishes what is known as a 'proto-web', a star-shaped structure in which the threads come together in a hub enveloped within a frame, paying particular attention to balance. It then progresses to amplify the frame and to construct a 'sticky spiral' that will ultimately attract and capture its prey.

In seeking a metaphor for the establishment of the Coalition of Knowledge-Building Schools, the manufacture of a web most closely approximates the ways in which the community has been established – although clearly not with the purpose of preying upon its members! In our account of the history of the Coalition (developed below), it is clear that there were a number of steps analogous to the work of the spider. Initially, a modest bridge was built between a small number of participating schools. The Centre for Practitioner Research (CPR[1]) in the Faculty of Education and Social Work provided a hub and frame that would enable the web to be built and strengthened. The stickiness of the threads paralleled the agreed-on principles by which the Coalition would function.

The hub and frame: the Centre for Practitioner Research

The CPR was established in 1998, following the then Faculty of Education's successful hosting of the Inaugural International Practitioner Research Conference.[2] At that time, it was co-directed by Judyth Sachs and Susan Groundwater-Smith. It has always been unfunded and was seen as associated with the Division of Professional Learning's service to the community.

The two aims of the CPR were

- to validate and value the research-based knowledge created by practitioners in the field, and
- to develop cross-disciplinary networks to facilitate the production and circulation of new knowledge.

Its purposes were seen to be these:

- To foster, support and enhance practitioner research as a mode of inquiry to understand and improve practice in universities and schools locally, nationally and internationally.
- To contribute to the creation of situated knowledge regarding educational practices.
- To investigate and critique the outcomes of practitioner research.
- To encourage the development, validation and documentation of new methodologies in practitioner research.
- To act as a forum for the discussion of practitioner research via conferences and electronic and print media.
- To establish international affiliations with universities and schools similarly engaged.

The CPR's range of activities included conducting free-to-the-public 'twilight seminars', developing professional practice links with networked learning communities in the United Kingdom and mainland Europe and reaching out to other sites for learning beyond the classroom (such as the Australian Museum), and building and nurturing the Coalition of Knowledge-Building Schools. In any one year, these activities were seen to make a significant contribution to the education community. For example, twilight seminars would adopt a theme and pursue it with well-respected academics who were keen to make links between the academic and professional communities. One year the theme was focused upon the nature of identity formation, with bi-monthly meetings focusing upon

- professional identity in changing times;
- practitioner enquiry and professional identity formation;
- the public intellectual and social capital formation;
- the shift from pastoral to political identity;
- institutional identity and professional partnerships; and
- national identity formation in the context of polarised debates about the history curriculum.

Throughout the life of the CPR and, later, the Practitioner Research Special Interest Group (PRSIG), a wide variety of publications and conference presentations have been developed, often in association with school-based practitioners working in member schools of the Coalition or with such Friends of the Coalition as the Australian Museum. A number of these are inserted in the evolving history of the Coalition and its manifold activities outlined later in this chapter. Additionally, in partnership with MLC School, Burwood, Australia, the CPR published a resource (Groundwater-Smith and Mockler 2003b) designed to assist those engaged in practitioner research and drawing upon the wisdom and experience of members of the Coalition. *Learning to Listen: Listening to Learn* is in use by those supporting practitioner research in the United Kingdom, Netherlands, Austria, Singapore and the United States, as well as throughout Australia. Thus it may be seen that the CPR and PRSIG provided a robust frame and hub for the development of a web of interconnectivity between the members of the Coalition of Knowledge-Building Schools.

Developing the 'proto-web'

The initial dragline came as a result of the Innovative Links between Universities and Schools for Teacher Professional Development project, established as part of the Australian National Schools Network in the context of a school reform agenda in the early 1990s (Hartley and Whitehead 2006). Both Judyth Sachs and Susan Groundwater-Smith were able to establish sustained links with a range of schools with a commitment to ongoing teacher professional learning and to engage in what became known as facilitated practitioner inquiry whereby academic partners assisted in modest action research projects in schools (Groundwater-Smith 1998). The very beginning of the web was taking place.

The next important bridging line came through the Innovation and Best Practice Project, or IBPP (Cuttance et al. 2001). The IBPP, one of the largest educational research projects ever undertaken in Australia, was a large-scale research and development project that specifically focused on innovation in schools. Each of the 107 participating schools developed and implemented a significant innovation aimed at improving learning outcomes for students. Each school researched and provided a report on its innovation, with a specific focus on its success in improving student learning outcomes. Several of these were supported by academics from the CPR who sought to connect them to other schools with similar ambitions. At this point, the participation of Nicole Mockler, initially in the role of a practitioner researcher and later as a full-time academic, became critical as she served to further amplify the work of the partnership.

From these projects, a small number of schools were identified that clearly had an interest in engaging in systematic inquiry. Following some early meetings, these schools came together to form the nucleus of the Coalition. By 2002, seven schools (three independent and four government) had gathered together to more formally outline their shared purposes, which were

- to develop and enhance the notion of evidence-based practice;[3]
- to develop an interactive community of practice using appropriate technologies;
- to make a contribution to a broader professional knowledge base with respect to educational practice;
- to build research capability within their own and each other's schools by engaging both teachers and students in the research processes; and
- to share methodologies that are appropriate to practitioner inquiry as a means of transforming teacher professional learning.

(Groundwater-Smith and Mockler 2003b: 1).

By the time of this writing (2009), the Coalition had 13 members[4] – four independent girls schools (three metropolitan and one regional), two metropolitan comprehensive boys schools, one metropolitan comprehensive girls school, three coeducational high schools (one being regional), two metropolitan primary schools and one residential respite care school (accommodating young people from across the state of New South Wales). In addition, it is affiliated with what have been deemed 'Friends of the Coalition', namely the Australian Museum and Taronga Zoo Education Centre. It counts among these members some of the state's most privileged residents and those living in the most challenging of circumstances, all meeting in a climate of cooperation and goodwill. The Coalition's recently established website (www.ckbschools.org) includes further information about member schools, academic partners and 'Friends' of the Coalition.

Knowledge building within and beyond the coalition

By its very name, it is possible to detect the mission of the Coalition of Knowledge-Building Schools – that is, to create usable professional knowledge for employment within the participating schools and beyond into the wider educational community. In part this ambition was inspired by the David Hargreaves publication titled 'The knowledge creating school' (1999), in which he argued for schools to be sites for the generation of professional knowledge designed to enhance effective teaching and learning. Hargreaves (1999: 124) argued that such a school

- audits its professional working knowledge;
- manages the process of creating professional knowledge;
- validates the professional knowledge that is created; and
- disseminates the created professional knowledge.

Further, Hargreaves (1999: 126–127) outlines the conditions and factors that will favour knowledge creation in schools, *inter alia:* [5]

- A culture of and enthusiasm for continual improvement
- An awareness of the external environment
- A sensitivity to key stakeholders (including students)
- Coherent and flexible planning
- Flatter management structures
- Recognition of the expert knowledge held by teachers
- Knowledge creation as a whole school enterprise
- Regular opportunities for reflection, dialogue and enquiry
- A readiness to 'tinker', experiment and engage in partnerships and alliances
- A willingness to include diverse opinions
- An ethical culture embodying freedom and responsibility.

These factors and conditions can be seen as working principles for the Coalition members as they go about their business. In any one year, a number of the schools will be engaged in a diverse range of projects that they share with their colleagues through breakfast meetings once a term and through an annual one-day conference. This diversity is best illustrated by drawing upon an example of an email sent to members by the convenor following the most recent meeting.

First of all a 'big thank-you' to N. She has done a great job with the website and I know spent many, many hours on it...

We had a chance to hear about the Teachers' College and contribution that it made to planning in terms of both the actual and virtual museum. V. did a great job of reprising the report and you all have a copy to read at your leisure. L. indicated that at the end of the year the museum will be able to report on actions taken. She also foreshadowed that later in the year she would like to invite around 15 teachers to assist in working on the website, in particular a Teachers' Blog. At first she thought it might take a half a day; but the meeting indicated that release is for whole days and that the schools would be willing to work with the AM. A little later we also heard about the successful visit of G. Boys High School Pacific Island students, where the boys requested that the museum keep their cultural history safe!

A. Boys High School ... have worked with the museum on a number of exhibitions, Dinosaurs, Surviving Australia and Climate Change and a team comprising science, history, English and maths teachers worked to develop interdisciplinary units of inquiry using technologies, in particular Marvin, an animated program originally developed for indigenous students. Interestingly this application has also been used by S. H. in their Quality Teaching Indigenous Program (QTIP) project – it is another example of cross-over work that Coalition members have been so creative in implementing...

N. told us of the G.P. High School cluster's successful values project. Along with the High School, several primary schools, varying in size and location, have worked to engage in writing and publishing projects. I suggested that they take a look at the *Special Forever* environmental communication project managed by the Primary English Teachers Association (PETA) and the Murray-Darling Basin Commission – perhaps there would be the possibility of publishing beyond the cluster – it sounded very exciting and hopefully at our day conference we can look more closely at the products...

M. shared the G. Boys High School story in which boys have been active participants in developing the Positive Behaviours Intervention System (PBIS) for the school. The overall scaffold of all being safe, respectful learners (including teachers) was fleshed out by the boys and resulted in a matrix using students' own language. She showed us some great pictures from the launch where African and Lebanese drummers performed as well as rappers and a Pacific Island Haka. M. also outlined a peer reading program where year 10 students are trained by TAFE to act as tutors for years 7–9.

J. from St. M. College was able to report on the ongoing nature of their action research focus that is tied to the school's core values in relation to 'love of learning'. Currently there are eight projects underway, ranging from the effective use of laptops to J.'s own work on cultural diversity and inclusion. How, for example, does one teach about the Renaissance to Thai students with different cultural histories; and how does one learn from them? Currently she is interviewing Kenyan students and looks forward to reporting more of the progress at the next Coalition meeting...

We missed our primary school members and look forward to their contributions at our November day-long meeting where our focus will be on values education and where we are anticipating some contributions from students.

Turning points in creating the web

The strength of the web depends in part upon the moments when a new thread is cast and a turning point created. We would assert that a number of these can be identified. Early discussions and alliances, by happenstance, were conducted with a small number of independent girls' schools. Clearly, this could be seen as somewhat limiting. In seeking a broader representation of interests, several schools that had participated in past projects through the Australian National Schools Network and were known to the convener were approached.[6] In Australia's complex education environment where the funding of schools is highly contentious and there is a degree of ill will between the sectors, it was encouraging to find that such a diverse range of schools could see the benefit of working together. Other than the first meeting of each year that is held at the University of Sydney, the remaining meetings are conducted by host schools. Having representatives from privileged, generously funded schools spend time in schools of their colleagues, some of which were highly challenging physical environments, proved to be a new experience.

A second turning point occurred with the involvement of the Australian Museum and, subsequently, Taronga Zoo Education.[7] This engagement provided schools with opportunities to consider issues of education beyond the walls of the classroom and to more closely examine what it is to be a professional and engage in inquiry-based professional learning. Sachs (2007) observed that the Coalition provided teachers with rich professional learning opportunities that allowed them to focus on themselves as learners in the context of a learning community composed of colleagues similarly committed to taking a critical orientation to their practice. Working with the museum was particularly generative in the development of presentations and publications (Groundwater-Smith 2006a; Groundwater-Smith and Kelly 2003; Kelly and Groundwater-Smith 2009).

Indeed, it might be argued that the policy of making public the work of the Coalition has been a particularly distinctive feature, with presentations ranging from discussions of the employment of student voice in school-based research (Groundwater-Smith 2006b; Needham 2006; Needham and Groundwater-Smith 2003) to adopting mixed methods in research design (Groundwater-Smith et al. 2006). Publications have also focused upon documenting particular projects and initiatives within member schools (Elliott and Mockler 2008; Mockler 2001; Mockler and Groundwater-Smith 2010), on the broader professional learning implications of practitioner inquiry (Groundwater-Smith and Hunter 2000; Groundwater-Smith and Mockler 2002a, 2003a; Mockler 2005), on the ethical dimensions of quality in practitioner inquiry (Groundwater-Smith and Mockler 2006, 2007) and on the formation and development of the Coalition itself (Groundwater-Smith and Mockler 2002b, 2009).

So what kind of knowledge is being built here?

The strength of the web: challenges and tests

At this point in the evolution of the Coalition, it is possible to identify a range of strengths and challenges that impact upon the web: interestingly, but perhaps not surprisingly, the strengths and challenges of the Coalition can be conceived as 'flip sides' of each other, where each strength presents with a corresponding vulnerability or challenge, and for this reason we shall deal with the strengths and challenges together here.

The Coalition is an enormously diverse network, as noted earlier, where schools with radically different profiles and student populations come together, transcending some of the common barriers and obstacles to cooperation that can be observed within Australia and elsewhere. In addition, the contribution made by the Friends of the Coalition – both academic partners from a range of universities and the Australian Museum and Taronga Zoo Education – brings greater diversity to the web. While this diversity enables unusual conversations and collaborations to take place, it also demands of all participants an openness to one another's circumstances and life worlds and a willingness to 'inhabit each other's castles', to borrow Bridget Somekh's (1994) metaphor. This is particularly so when one considers the socio-economic diversity and its implications of this in terms of school resourcing and funding. The emphasis placed on the common aim of engaging deeply and critically with inquiry processes to the mutual benefit of students and teachers within schools assists Coalition members to transcend these barriers to a large degree, although this challenge is ever present.

Though the unfunded nature of the Coalition might be regarded by some as a challenge, in our view it is in fact a great strength. Within the audit culture that is currently so strong within Western societies, funding is often linked strongly to measures of compliance. As an unfunded web or network, the Coalition is accountable to no external body and, while members feel a strong sense of accountability to one another and their own school communities, this commitment comes with no external compliance agenda. As such, the Coalition operates based on goodwill. The willingness of members to contribute their time, share their ideas and experiences, and join together in collaborative projects with the intent of maintaining and focusing their capacity to critically inquire into practice, is a very evident strength.

The links between schools and universities fostered in the Coalition provide a foundation of academic support within which members operate. Schools can and do invite academic partners to support them from time to time in the gathering and analysis of evidence, and academic partners within the Coalition operate as resource people for members, supporting them in their professional learning and inquiry. This is not, however, a one-way street. Elsewhere (Groundwater-Smith and Mockler 2011), we have written of the potential of such endeavours to work as professional learning opportunities for all members, with university- and school-based colleagues operating within a reciprocal learning relationship.

The issue of sustainability is a critical and challenging one for the Coalition. Kemmis (2009: 35) has argued that practices will not be sustainable if they do not meet criteria necessary for their continuation in one or more of five dimensions:

- discursive sustainability (the comprehensibility of the practice);
- social and political sustainability (the inclusiveness of the practice in the interests of social harmony);
- material and environmental sustainability;
- economic sustainability; and
- personal sustainability (the practice does not drain the personal knowledge, capacities, resources and energy of its members).

We would argue that, indeed, the Coalition satisfies all five of these criteria in one way or another.

The Coalition has demonstrated a capacity to be self-sustaining for a decade now – an undeniable strength of the web – but we are also aware that sustainability cannot be taken for granted. Although in some member schools it is evident that a great deal of capacity building has taken place and that what Cochran-Smith and Lytle (2009) have termed 'inquiry as stance' has become embedded within the culture of the school, in most schools involvement in this work hinges upon the commitment of a small number of teachers. In the past, when key actors have departed from schools, a slow decline in involvement has occurred that has often seen schools slipping away. While in a number of cases this has given rise to involvement with new schools as those key actors have taken up roles in schools that they then brought into the Coalition, over the last few years we have worked to encourage schools to broaden their base of active participants.

The final challenge for the Coalition is that of becoming and remaining critical. Although sharing ideas and experiences is important, elsewhere we have written about the 'celebratory tendencies' inherent in some practitioner research contexts (Groundwater-Smith and Mockler 2005). For us, it is important that a willingness to celebrate the successes of practitioner inquiry is matched with a willingness to face some of the 'unwelcome truths' (Mockler and Groundwater-Smith 2009) that may come to light and to maintain a critical stance where development and learning is valued above celebration. The quality of relationships developed and sustained between schools over an extended period of time has helped to underwrite this criticality and, as a network, we are committed to remaining vigilant on this issue, asking the kinds of questions of one another that require honest and critical responses.

Lessons from the coalition: developing and sustaining communities of practice

As the Coalition of Knowledge-Building Schools approaches the end of its first decade, it is timely to reflect on the principles of operation that have enabled it to succeed and expand. In Groundwater-Smith and Mockler (2007), we developed a rationale for understanding 'quality' in practitioner inquiry through using the lens of ethics. We posed a series of ethical guidelines:

- That it should observe ethical protocols and processes
- That it should be transparent in its processes
- That it should be collaborative in its nature
- That it should be transformative in its intent and action
- That it should be able to justify itself to its community of practice.
                        (Groundwater-Smith and Mockler 2007: 205–06)

A strong concern for ethical processes and practices and a commitment to transformation is at the heart of the Coalition's work. As individuals and organisations, we share a common commitment to listening to and privileging the voices of students, to critically examining our own practice in order to develop it, and to creating pathways for equity and justice through education. These common commitments are what enable us to transcend our differences and the challenges we face as a community of practice, in the interests of knowledge creation both within and beyond the community itself.

We first wrote about the Coalition as an emerging community of practice many years ago now (Groundwater-Smith and Mockler 2002a), based on Wenger (1998: 73). Three key dimensions of practice provide the basis for the development of an authentic community of practice. They are (1) joint enterprise, (2) mutual engagement and (3) shared repertoire. We have quite deliberately worked to build and share each of these. Joint enterprise is developed through the collaborative work undertaken within schools and supported by academic partners and across schools with the Australian Museum and Taronga Zoo Education. Over time, we have built a negotiated understanding of purpose and process that is articulated in different ways in different contexts but is nevertheless common. Mutual engagement is built primarily through our once-a-term gatherings and annual conference, where we share our work broadly and open it up to one another's critique and questioning. Shared repertoire is partly about shared histories and discourses; this has built slowly over time as our experiences as a network have been shared and, just as importantly, documented.

Finally, membership of the Coalition is predicated not upon a mere interest in practitioner inquiry or knowledge creation but rather an *active and sustained commitment* to the work. As personnel and priorities change within schools, this commitment can either strengthen or weaken over time. One of the original three members of the Coalition left the network four years after its formation when the key staff member retired from the school. When a school's priorities shift such that this work becomes less important than other priorities, sometimes so does the commitment to the Coalition. Additionally, Coalition meetings are not a place where one can hide: members are accountable to one another, and part of that accountability is about being transparent about what is happening in schools and what is not. Members make a commitment to engage in inquiry and, while it is not uncommon for the intensity of this work to 'ebb and flow' throughout the course of the school year in any one school, membership requires a sustained and demonstrated commitment without which schools tend to self-select out of the network.

Conclusion

In her moving contribution to the tribute to the life and work of Orlando Fals Borda, the late Shirley Grundy argued for universities to reclaim their right to engage in partnerships with 'grass roots communities'. Grundy (2007: 81) concluded:

> In Australian Universities in the early 21st century the 'audit culture' is killing us softly and hastening the death of participation in social and intellectual life. Yet, as I suggest, participatory action research and the action of those of us who pursue it can help reform the audit culture and curb the current demise of higher education in Australia.

In some senses, the impact of cultures of audit and measurement have had just as deleterious an impact upon schools. Cultures of compliance demand that emphasis be placed on that which is easily measured, often to the detriment of that which is important. The Coalition of Knowledge-

Building Schools provides a small oasis in this desert, where schools and teachers who share a commitment to understanding and developing their practice and to the transformative capacities of schooling come together to share that which is, in our view, critically important but not so easily measured.

Notes

1 Renamed the Practitioner Research Special Interest Group (PRSIG) in 2006 in accordance with university policies regarding the naming and functioning of centres.
2 This conference built upon one held at the Institute of Education, Cambridge, UK, at which both Sachs and Groundwater-Smith presented keynote addresses.
3 This term is one that the Coalition has embraced in its broadest sense, seeking to problematize its current usage and redefine it to mean evidence that is gathered in a forensic rather than adversarial sense. For further discussion, see Groundwater-Smith and Mockler 2002b.
4 It also has an additional nominal member from remote New South Wales whose students take part in consultations with the Australian Museum.
5 In the interests of brevity, these have been paraphrased.
6 The Australian National Schools Network at this time was in abeyance, having had its funding reduced considerably owing to a change of federal government policy.
7 While we have made anonymous the schools and participating teachers, it is not possible to do the same for these two institutions, in that they are each 'one of a kind'.

References

Cochran-Smith, M. and Lytle, S. (2009) *Inquiry as Stance: Practitioner Research for the Next Generation.* New York: Teachers College Press.

Cuttance, P., Department of Education, Training and Youth Affairs, and The Innovation and Best Practice Consortium (2001) *School Innovation: Pathway to the Knowledge Society.* Canberra: Department of Education, Training and Youth Affairs.

Elliott, G. and Mockler, N. (2008) 'Practitioner inquiry for whole school change: possibilities and pitfalls.' Paper presented at the Annual Collaborative Action Research Network Conference, Liverpool, October.

Groundwater-Smith, S. (1998) 'Putting teacher professional judgement to work.' *Educational Action Research,* 6(1), 21–37.

Groundwater-Smith, S. (2006a) 'Millennials in museums: consulting Australian adolescents when designing for learning.' Invitational address presented to the Museum Directors' Forum, National Museum of History, Taipei, October.

Groundwater-Smith, S. (2006b) 'Professional knowledge formation in the Australian educational market place: changing the perspective.' *Scottish Educational Review,* 37(Special Edition), 124–131.

Groundwater-Smith, S. and Hunter, J. (2000) 'Whole school inquiry: evidence-based practice.' *Journal of In-Service Education, 26*(3), 583–600.

Groundwater-Smith, S. and Kelly, L. (2003) 'As we see it: improving learning at the museum.' Paper presented to the Annual Conference of the British Educational Research Association, Edinburgh, Scotland, September.

Groundwater-Smith, S. and Mockler, N. (2002a) 'Building knowledge, building professionalism.' Paper presented to the Annual Conference of the Australian Association for Research in Education, University of Queensland, Australia, December.

Groundwater-Smith, S. and Mockler, N. (2002b) 'The knowledge building school: from the outside in, from the inside out.' *Change, 5*(2), 15–24.

Groundwater-Smith, S. and Mockler, N. (2003a) 'Holding a mirror to professional learning.' Paper presented to the Annual Conference of the Australian Association for Research in Education and the New Zealand Association for Research in Education, Auckland, New Zealand, November/December.

Groundwater-Smith, S. and Mockler, N. (2003b) *Learning to Listen: Listening to Learn.* Sydney: University of Sydney Faculty of Education and Social Work/MLC School.

Groundwater-Smith, S. and Mockler, N. (2005) 'Practitioner research in education, beyond celebration.' Refereed paper presented to the Australian Association for Research in Education Focus Conference, Cairns, Australia, July.

Groundwater-Smith, S. and Mockler, N. (2006) 'Research that counts: practitioner research and the academy.' In J. Blackmore, J. Wright and V. Harwood (eds) *Counterpoints on the Quality and Impact of Educational Research. Review of Australian Research in Education,* (6), 105–118.

Groundwater-Smith, S. and Mockler, N. (2007) 'Ethics in practitioner research: an issue of quality.' *Research Papers in Education, 22*(2), 199–211.

Groundwater-Smith, S. and Mockler, N. (2009) *Teacher Professional Learning in an Age of Compliance: Mind the Gap.* Rotterdam: Springer.

Groundwater-Smith, S. and Mockler, N. (2011) 'Sustaining professional learning networks – the Australasian challenge.' In C. Day and A. Lieberman (eds) *International Handbook of Teacher and School Development.* London: Sage.

Groundwater-Smith, S., Martin, A., Hayes, M., Herrett, M., Layhe, K., Layman, A. and Saurine, J. (2006) 'What counts as evidence: mixed methods in a single case.' Paper presented at the AARE Annual Conference, Adelaide, Australia, November.

Grundy, S. (2007) 'Killing me softly: the audit culture and the death of participation.' In *Action Research and Education in Contexts of Poverty: A Tribute to the Life and Work of Professor Orlando Fals Borda* (pp. 71–82). Bogota: Universidad de la Salle.

Hargreaves, D. (1999) 'The knowledge creating school.' *British Journal of Education Studies, 47*(2), 122–144.

Hartley, D. and Whitehead, M. (2006) *Teacher Education: Globalisation, Standards and Teacher Education.* London: Taylor and Francis.

Kelly, L. and Groundwater-Smith, S. (2009) 'Revisioning the physical and on-line museum: a partnership with the Coalition Of Knowledge-Building Schools.' *Journal of Museum Education, 34*(1), 55–68.

Kemmis, S. (2009) 'Understanding professional practice: a synoptic framework.' In B. Green (ed.) *Understanding and Researching Professional Practice*. Rotterdam, Netherlands: Sense Publishers.

Mockler, N. (2001) 'Professional learning portfolios: a tool for the reflective practitioner.' Paper presented at the Australian Association for Research in Education Annual Conference, Fremantle, Australia, December.

Mockler, N. (2005) 'Trans/forming teachers: new professional learning and transformative teacher professionalism.' *Journal of In-Service Education, 31*(4), 733–746.

Mockler, N. and Groundwater-Smith, S. (2009) 'Seeking for the unwelcome truths: action learning beyond celebration.' Paper presented at the Pedagogy in Practice Conference, Newcastle, Australia, July.

Mockler, N. and Groundwater-Smith, S. (2010) 'Professional learning side by side.' In A. Campbell and S. Groundwater-Smith (eds) *Connecting Inquiry and Professional Learning in Education: Joining the Dots*. London: Routledge.

Needham, K. (2006) 'Zen and the art of school improvement: a case study of using students as researchers into their own learning.' Paper presented to the joint Collaborative Action Research Network/Practitioner Research Conference, Utrecht, Netherlands, November.

Needham, K. and Groundwater-Smith, S. (2003) 'Using student voice to inform school improvement.' Paper presented to the International Congress for School Effectiveness and Improvement, Sydney, Australia, January.

Sachs, J. (2007) 'Learning to improve or improving learning: the dilemma of teacher continuing professional development.' Keynote address presented to the International Congress for School Effectiveness and Improvement Conference, Slovenia, January.

Somekh, B. (1994) 'Inhabiting each other's castles: towards knowledge and mutual growth through collaboration.' *Educational Action Research, 2*(2), 357–381.

Wenger, E. (1998) *Communities of Practice: Learning, Meaning and Identity.* Cambridge: Cambridge University Press.

Zschokke, S. (2009) 'Web building in Araneus diadematus.' Online. Available at http://www.conservation.unibas.ch/team/zschokke/webconstruction. php?lang=en (accessed 8 September 2009).

Suggested further readings

Coalition of Knowledge-Building Schools. Online. Available at http://www. ckbschools.org (accessed 14 October 2010).

Groundwater-Smith, S. (2005) 'Learning by listening: student voice in research.' Refereed paper presented at the International Practitioner Research/CARN Conference, Utrecht, Netherlands, November.

Groundwater-Smith, S. and Mockler, N. (2002) 'Building knowledge, building professionalism.' Paper presented to the Annual Conference of the Australian Association for Research in Education, University of Queensland, Australia, December.

Groundwater-Smith, S. and Mockler, N. (2009) *Teacher Professional Learning in an Age of Compliance: Mind the Gap.* Dordrecht: Springer.

Groundwater-Smith, S. and Mockler, N. (2011) 'Sustaining professional learning networks – the Australasian challenge.' In C. Day and A. Lieberman (eds) *International Handbook of Teacher and School Development*. London: Sage.

Needham, K. (2011) 'Professional learning in an across school network: an epidemic of passion?' In N. Mockler and J. Sachs (eds) *Rethinking Educational Practice Through Reflexive Inquiry: Essays in Honour of Susan Groundwater-Smith*. Dordrecht: Springer.

Chapter 14

A fair go for students in poverty

Australia

Geoff Munns, Leonie Arthur, Margery Hertzberg, Wayne Sawyer and Katina Zammit

Introduction: teachers for a fair go

'Getting a fair go' is a saying many Australians recognize. It is commonly understood as a call for a just treatment and a value that speaks of equality for all, regardless of social and cultural background. 'Fair go' is also an equity and social principle underpinning the New South Wales Department of Education's Priority Schools Programs. As a principle, it means students from all backgrounds and circumstances have opportunities for educational success, and this success is strengthened by the pedagogies of their teachers. This chapter tells the pedagogical stories of five teachers who epitomize this principle. They teach in low socio-ecomonic status (SES) communities and have been identified for the ways they engage students in their learning and, consequently, open up critical possibilities that their classrooms will work towards more equitable student outcomes. The teachers work in different contexts, with different groups of students and across the early, middle and later years of schooling. Their classroom stories are part of a wider picture about student engagement undertaken in the *Teachers for a Fair Go* research project. This project is the latest phase of the Fair Go Project (FGP) and involved intensive case study research into the classroom pedagogies of 30 'exemplary' engaging teachers of students in poverty, exploring the causal impact of their work on the outcomes of their students. Case studies used a co-researching methodology, inviting and sanctioning teachers as equal key players in the collection and analysis of data about their classrooms.

What follows is a description of the theoretical framing around student engagement that has been developed in the FGP, and deployed as a methodological and analytical tool for the case studies of the exemplary teachers. From this framing and analysis, a number of pedagogical themes that characterize these teachers' classrooms are emerging. These are then presented and illustrated through the five teachers' pedagogical stories. The illustration recognizes that there is a wide diversity of lived experiences across and within low SES communities, and effective teachers understand this as they develop different teaching practices as locally produced solutions to the unique challenges of their context. Put another way, there are many different ways toward student engagement, and these are invariably linked with contextual issues, student responses and teacher-preferred style. Nevertheless, the research has shown there are important shared pedagogical themes among this group of exemplary teachers, and reflecting on these offers an opportunity to consider further what might make the educational difference for students who live in poverty.

The Fair Go Project's student engagement framework

The FGP is a joint undertaking between a team of researchers from the University of Western Sydney (School of Education) and Priority Schools Programs.[1] The first phase was action research employing a co-researching ethnographic methodology, which brought together university researchers, teachers and school students. The student engagement framework was developed in this phase. The second phase is the case study research described earlier, and this part of the research is the focus of this chapter.

A student engagement framework has been developed in the FGP. It was reached in two ways. The first was through utilising ideas from within the sociology of pedagogy, and the second was inductively from the research. The literature review and the action research were simultaneous processes. A more detailed discussion of the project and its theoretical framing can be found in Fair Go Team (2006) and Munns (2007). For the purpose of this chapter, a number of key ideas about student engagement within the framework are introduced and then illustrated through the work of the five teachers. The first idea about engagement is that substantive student engagement (termed *small 'e' engagement*) is multifaceted. Simply stated, this means students are engaged when there is an interplay of high cognitive, high affective and high operative components: they are thinking hard, feeling good and working to be better learners. This view of engagement is consistent with the research literature (Fredricks et al. 2004). The second idea is that engagement is influenced by the messages that students receive in classrooms. The work of Bernstein (1996) was used here. Bernstein argues that classrooms deliver powerful messages to students through their curriculum, pedagogy and assessment practices. These messages help shape individuals' perceptions of what they might do now and in the future and what they might become when they leave school. In this way, schools and classrooms operate to structure the consciousness of students. The research of the FGP has shown that classroom messages can be engaging for students, even though there has been a long history of low SES students receiving disengaging messages

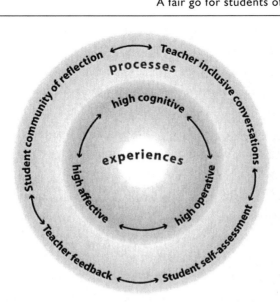

Figure 14.1 The fair go pedagogy

through the processes of curriculum, pedagogy and assessment (see, for example, Comber and Thomson 2001; Hayes 2003; Mills and Gale 2002). The pedagogy that delivers engaging messages and is promoted in the FGP is illustrated by Figure 14.1.

The engagement framework has a dual focus on the nature of the classroom learning experiences (inner circle) and the classroom processes (outer circle). The experiences are directly related to the definitions of engagement discussed earlier. Figure 14.1 shows that these experiences need to be developed so there is a balanced interplay between high cognitive, affective and operative learning experiences and classroom processes that will support their implementation. Within this balanced interplay, developing high cognitive activities would deploy elements from the intellectual quality dimension of productive pedagogies (Hayes et al. 2006). The high operative component would pay careful attention to developing students as competent and empowered learners across their entire classroom experience. High affective assumes that the teacher and students are involved in pedagogical conversations that will bring about mutually stimulating and enjoyable emotions associated with classroom work. The classroom processes (outer circle) aim to build a reflective and supportive learning community. The research is suggesting that this dual approach builds classrooms in which students are challenged and engaged and are given opportunities to become more successful learners. They feel valued within an atmosphere of sharing and reflection where their voices as learners are encouraged and respected. The Fair Go pedagogy directly targets the messages that students receive in

Table 14.1 Discourses of power and engaging messages for low SES students

Knowledge	'We can see the connection and the meaning' – reflectively constructed access to contextualized and powerful knowledge
Ability	'I am capable' – feelings of being able to achieve and a spiral of high expectations and aspirations
Control	'We do this together' – sharing of classroom time and space: interdependence, mutuality and power
Place	'It's great to be a kid from' – valued as individual and learner and feelings of belonging and ownership over learning
Voice	'We share' – environment of discussion and reflection about learning with students and teachers playing reciprocal meaningful roles

their classrooms. Table 14.1 (above) shows that these messages are organized into five 'discourses of power' – knowledge, ability, control, place and voice.

What does teaching for student engagement look like?

Researchers conducting case studies in the FGP employed the student engagement framework as a methodological and analytical tool. This allowed the research to develop a common language and helped to identify emerging themes characterising the classroom work of these teachers. In this chapter, the themes discussed and illustrated focus on the nature of the teachers' classroom experiences (inner circle). Although each of the five teachers in this chapter taught in different contexts and across different stages of schooling, the following themes were found to be common across their pedagogies and also the pedagogies of the wider group of exemplary teachers:

High Cognitive
  • Appreciating (valuing and understanding) that classroom experiences are intellectually challenging
  • Learning as priority and explicitly considered business
  • Teaching and learning as sustained and ongoing classroom conversations
High Affective
  • Authentic learning that connects and builds community
  • Teaching as a creative process producing new imaginations about learning
  • Emotional and social safety for students
High Operative
  • Links built between cognitive, affective and operative
  • Developed status for thinkers and learners that targets and minimizes student resistance
  • Thoughtful and dynamic repertoire of practices.

These emergent themes across the pedagogies of exemplary teachers help to build a picture of what might make a difference for students in poverty, and it is to this picture that the chapter now turns.

Pedagogical stories from five classrooms

Case 1 – Donna

Donna is the preschool teacher at a mid North Coast school. The children are between three and five years of age and approximately 50 per cent are Indigenous. Donna has taken time to establish strong relationships with the families so that they trust her and are happy to send their children to preschool. She understands the complexities of the local Indigenous community and is sensitive to families' realities.

Donna uses a daily diary that combines photographs and text as well as slide shows of photographs to share information and to start conversations about children's learning with families. Donna uses these occasions to build parents' skills and confidence and to encourage conversations between children and families. She also identifies children who need extra learning support and helps families to access early intervention services for their children.

Family and community involvement in the creation of the preschool's outdoor environment has helped to generate a sense of ownership and feeling of belonging in the preschool – it is a *place of emotional and social safety* for families as well as children. The physical environment is welcoming and supportive. Repetition and structure within each day promote success and provide boundaries within which the children feel safe enough to regulate their own behaviour.

The strong connections with the families and local community enable Donna to provide an *authentic learning environment that connects with and builds community*. Resources include contemporary Indigenous images and reflect children's everyday lives, enabling children to draw on their funds of knowledge in their learning. Donna builds a sense of community amongst the children. There is a shared ownership of the preschool, with inclusive language such as 'our garden'. Children have input into the rules and responsibilities in the room, including making their own symbols to depict expectations. There is a strong focus on respect for others, listening to each other and sharing ideas, and the building of relationships amongst children.

Teaching is viewed as a creative process producing new imaginations about learning. Donna provides a stimulating learning environment with a range of learning centres for children to choose from and large blocks of time that encourage in-depth investigation and relationship building. The environment is designed to *develop the children's status as thinkers and learners and to minimize student resistance*. *Intellectual challenge* is provided through open-ended experiences, where children are encouraged to problem solve and to use deeper thinking. The integration of literacy and numeracy resources in play-based experiences also encourages children to take on roles of literacy and numeracy users in meaningful ways and to value themselves as learners. Donna wants the children to take the success that they have at the preschool with them to school so that they go to school feeling confident and capable.

Donna draws on a *repertoire of practices* to support and extend children's learning. For example, she demonstrates where to start reading and how to save children's drawings from the interactive whiteboard onto the computer. At other times, she sits with children doing puzzles and uses questions and comments such as 'Do you think that piece will fit there? That piece will fit a curved side' to support a child's successful puzzle completion. She supports children to initiate interactions and join in play and social experiences with other children by pointing out what others are doing and helping children to negotiate roles. She encourages persistence and engagement by intervening when children become frustrated and start to lose interest in an experience, making comments such as, 'Let's see what else you can do here.' She joins in children's play and models problem solving by experimenting and hypothesizing and by verbalizing her thinking. At other times, she explicitly points out literacy and numeracy concepts and processes such as directionality of print and uses explicit language to describe mathematical concepts. These *sustained conversations* with individuals and small groups support and extend learning. These strategies effectively *link the cognitive, affective and operative*.

Case 2 – Sonia

Sonia teaches a year 2–4 class in a central school (Kindergarten to year 12) in far western, rural New South Wales, with a significant population of Aboriginal students. The years 2 and 3 are studying a science unit on insects and bugs. Year 4 students are researching a self-selected topic, with the activities written up in a learning matrix that demonstrates their learning and choice of assessment tasks. Sonia focuses on *classroom experiences that are intellectually challenging*. All students are involved in problem solving and building knowledge, with Sonia checking students' understandings after modeled and guided teaching. Using negotiated learning and assessment frameworks, she guides students to independent thinking and learning through questioning and affirmative statements.

Learning is a priority and is explicitly considered. For example, Sonia talks with students about respecting others in the classroom so that everyone has maximum opportunity to learn. 'You are not respecting the teacher's right to teach or the students to learn when you are "off task".' She discusses learning and what being 'on' and 'off' as a learner looks and feels like and the thoughts students have at these times.

Explicit teaching and clear demonstration of core knowledge for all lessons are employed. Students are continually asked to think, reflect, review and evaluate the central ideas being explored. There are *continuous conversations* about the learning process and content outcomes: 'What can you do? What do you need to know?' The matrices provide a point of discussion about what students still need to learn and a means for Sonia to help them learn. They also encourage students to self-regulate their learning.

Links to real-life contexts, the students' world and the local area make learning tasks and processes significant for the students. Respect is shown to her students and, in turn, students respect others in the classroom. A *community of learners* is established: 'Ivy, this is Mr G Boy (fellow student). He's going to teach you how to use the trundle wheel. Ask all the questions you want.' She acknowledges that the parents have had a bad time at school so she needs to gain their confidence so they can assist her with their child's learning. She insists that the community needs to know you care, commenting, 'It is important to keep in touch with "Pop", the elder. That way you know what is happening in the community.'

Sonia draws on students' funds of knowledge when teaching. She relates familiar terms and words to the students' experiences and knowledge as a means of explanation and extending learning. Students are invited to be learners through Sonia's discourse and reflective conversations about learning. The class sees learning as a journey: they discuss prior learning in relation to the 'new', comparing writing reports to writing 'reviews'. This was presented as a learning journey (visually created on Smartboard), as students reflected and assessed how much they knew and what they needed to know, 'seeing' what had been covered and how much was still to do.

Sonia focuses on making a difference, although this can be frustrating, making the students feel safe and making them believe in themselves. Students work in a *safe learning environment* where having fun and laughing is paramount. Sonia states: 'I talked with the kids about how they wanted to learn and gave the kids a sense of ownership and safety in their classroom environment and they thrived, loved it. It was important for the classroom to be a fun place with laughter.'

Another key message is, 'It is okay not to know, it is okay if you make a mistake.' Her language reinforces this message: 'It doesn't matter if you are wrong.' 'You guys are awesome, just fabulous.' Sonia believes that students need to know that they can succeed through persistence and building resilience.

Sonia's scaffolds provide access to meaning: building a link between existing knowledge and new understandings. Rubrics and matrices (*operative*) are used for *building knowledge (cognitive)* and *relationships (affective)* – 'thinking hard' and feeling good about themselves as learners. They assist students in choosing topics and ways to learn. Sonia's questioning techniques guide students' reflections. She believes this relinquishes the power of the teacher and helps the students to have respect for their own learning. Individual challenges for students encourage them to complete tasks successfully, *minimizing student resistance.*

Through the deployment of a *thoughtful and dynamic repertoire of practices,* including scaffolding, goal setting, reflection and self-assessment, Sonia provides calm and explicit instructions where structure is balanced with self-direction. Students know what they need to do and how to do it, with information and communications technology (ICT) integrated into tasks. Alternative achievable learning activities are set for students of different abilities, providing options for students to achieve at basic, sound, or high levels. As she reminds her students, 'You can't be less than basic but you can be higher than high.'

Case 3 – Dan

Dan teaches in a large inner suburban primary school (800 students) in Sydney. The student cohort represents over 40 cultural-linguistic groups, with the majority being Muslim and Arabic-speaking Australians. Almost 100 per cent of the students come from multilingual backgrounds.

Dan's students have a clear sense that their classroom is strongly focused on *learning as priority and explicitly considered business.* This focus has an almost relentless quality, with a high rotation of *intellectually challenging* tasks. It's hard but enjoyable work for students and the teacher. As one student puts it, 'We do learning and it's fun at the same time.' Tasks are often introduced with an element of surprise as a way of engaging students. As an example, Dan produces five different brands of tennis ball and challenges the students to devise criteria and tests to determine the best brand to purchase for particular uses by kids in their playground and community. For the next hour, balls are dropped, bounced, prodded and observed. In between, they discuss what they have been learning and consider this against syllabus outcomes. Later, Dan takes out a spray can and paints a square metre on a piece of paper on the ground in front of the students. Out in the playground, students work in teams to decide how to spray on the grass shapes that have the largest area. *Links between the cognitive, affective and operative* build in a simultaneous process of students thinking hard, enjoying their work, and learning to be collaborative and thoughtful learners.

There is *creativity* in the way Dan designs and begins learning experiences, and these are invariably *authentic* and *connect learning with the local community.* As a large science project, students test the different dishwashing detergents that their parents buy, so that more critical shopping choices can be made by the families. In a critical literacy project, students create photo-stories of their local community designed to showcase it in a positive way. Modern music soundtracks to the stories link their worlds across local, cultural and familial spaces. A student captures what this means. 'The work is like entertainment and joyful.'

While there is a great sense of adventure in Dan's pedagogy, there is also much about the way it looks and sounds that is worth considering. The *sustained and ongoing classroom conversations* build the learning community and keep students on the main game. 'Don't waste time copying questions off the board. This is quality thinking time.' 'I think you ought to think about that a bit more. What do we know? Can we trust that?' Importantly also, Dan presents himself constantly as a co-learner: 'Stop, everyone, I've just noticed something.' 'Let's work it out.' He builds inclusivity at the point of intellectual challenge for all. This is particularly important for the low academic standard students. In other situations, these students might receive a nagging, behaviour focus rather than a teacher who shares their thinking and expects success with differentiated tasks and assessment. They seem to understand that theirs is a classroom where it is possible to have *new imaginations about their learning*. 'In other classes, we just wrote stuff from the board and learnt nothing.' 'I have friends in this class and in other classes I had no friends.'

Classrooms in these kinds of communities sometimes bubble with tensions, with overt and covert resistances from dispirited students. By contrast, here is a pedagogical environment of *emotional and social safety*, consciously crafted to target the insecurities of low expectations and low-level task compliances through the *developed status for thinkers and learners*. As Dan explains, 'I believe my students relate to my classroom with positive emotions. I avoid using teacher power to regulate behaviour…. As a teacher, my worst days are always those in which I chose to focus on managing the behaviour of my students above the quality of my planning and pedagogy.'

The pedagogy in this classroom is hard work. There are no back-outs or compromises, and the high rotation of high-level tasks requires perseverance for both teacher and student. This works for all students in the end because all are involved in high-level tasks, no one gets punished and no one influences the planned pedagogy. The feeling in this classroom is that this is a long project focused on learning, where the *thoughtful and dynamic repertoire of practices* are given time. Students or problems are not there to be quickly 'solved'. 'The challenge I face at the beginning of each term is to ensure every student will be an insider, totally engaged in what they do at school. While this challenge is sometimes only measured with small successes, I always try to reflect on how I might improve my planning and pedagogy for better engagement.'

Case 4 – Sue

Sue's high school, within a South West Sydney housing estate, has 460 students representing 24 cultural and linguistic groups including Indigenous students. There is a 25 per cent mobility rate. Sue is head teacher (transition), learning support team leader and mentor for beginning teachers.

Transferring from a local primary school, Sue pioneered the innovative *Xtend* program for first-year high school students. Sue integrates English, maths, human society and its environment (HSIE), and visual arts. Students have other teachers for the remaining subjects. *Xtend* caters to learners who are identified as at risk but with the potential to perform above their peers, despite literacy, numeracy and social challenges. Many *Xtend* students fall below national benchmarks for literacy and numeracy.

Learning is the priority, and necessary administration tasks are secondary to this core business. The bell rings and students enter the classroom, choose seats and open exercise books. When at least half the class is seated, Sue begins the maths or English quiz (dependent on the subsequent lesson) and within 30 seconds all are present and involved. After three minutes, the game, which is a deliberate contextualized skills strategy, concludes. Sue introduces the body of the lesson. 'We're researching ancient Egypt and you'll need to use some of that spelling quiz vocabulary in your report.' Students regroup and begin their selected information report. Now the inextricable links *built between cognitive, affective and operative* are evident. Students have opted to work in pairs, threesomes, or individually. Most work with another person, but the autistic student works alone, sanctioned by Sue's skill in providing *emotional and social safety.* His strength is maths, so in maths Sue encourages him to work with others, validated by his peers, who call him 'the maths king'. Sue's emphasis on group work is deliberate, because focused discussion about work aids the many students still learning English and promotes an *authentic learning environment that connects and builds community.* Sue reminds the students to 'think about who you need in your group ... make sure everyone has equal work. It can be different but must be equal.' Some groups select reference books and others source-relevant websites.

Once students are settled and working, Sue picks up the roll and checks attendance. She then moves between groups to monitor progress and provide constructive feedback to ensure that students are challenging themselves to do intellectually demanding work: 'A little bit of good work is better than a lot of ordinary work.' *Appreciating that classroom experiences are intellectually challenging* is confirmed in student interview data such as, 'She's like a stalker... she's our right-hand man when we need help' and 'It's easy and it's challenging...easy because it's fun and challenging because it's hard work.'

Sustained conversations about possibilities and relevance usually occur as Sue works the room. In this lesson, some groups show their original semantic map research plan (content to be covered) to demonstrate progress. Although students work toward the same syllabus outcomes, there is choice and hence ownership and responsibility regarding how these will be achieved, thus *developing students' status as thinkers and learners, which minimizes student resistance.* At the same time, Sue's *thoughtful and dynamic repertoire of practices* ensures success, especially in the variety of ways she provides assistance. Potential resistance is aborted. For example, Sue unobtrusively selects a book, opens it to the relevant page and places it on the student's desk en route to another group. This non-focused student looks up, looks at the book, smiles and studiously attends to the task.

Teaching is viewed as a creative process producing new imaginations about learning and so the prescribed mathematics textbook drill on Egyptian numbers is reconstructed so that students need to analyse and synthesize this information to construct a game that will teach Egyptian numbers to a local year 4 primary class. Sue challenges the group using a conventional die because it does not display Egyptian numbers. Once students realize they will have to make one, Sue begins a considered conversation that deliberately uses the metalanguage (cube and net) to ensure students mathematically solve the problem.

Students work so purposefully and quietly that the automatic lighting system, sensing no one in the room, turns the lights off, which does cause laughter. And…it's lights on!

Case 5 – Eve

Eve is in her third year of teaching and teaches English/English as a Second Language (ESL) to years 7–12 in a high school of 600 students, 87 per cent of whom are from language backgrounds other than English (LBOTE) and approximately 10 per cent of whom have been in Australia for five years or less. Many students have gaps in their literacy that have an impact on their learning outcomes in all subject areas.

The *intellectual challenge* in her classroom manifests as high expectations and higher order cognitive tasks, particularly through the work of synthesising, such as synthesising contextual information about texts being studied or synthesising responses across a range of texts. Student reflection and meta-cognition are strong and highlight *teaching and learning as sustained and ongoing classroom conversations.* Conscious reflection by students on their learning is built into every unit of work, which also drives the classroom's focusing on *learning as priority business and explicitly considered business.*

In terms of *authentic learning that connects and builds community*, three areas in particular are important. The first is the principle of independence. Students are helped to take responsibility for their own learning, with Eve helping to move them in this direction. Second, the classroom is characterized by continual enquiry, questioning and discussion, which creates intellectual space for student participation. This, third, is one way in which *voice* is manifested.

When students are from traumatized refugee backgrounds, *emotional and social safety* becomes an issue, especially when, as the study of English often tries to do, connections are made between texts and students' lives. Eve sets out to give students an 'emotional connection' to every text or unit. This is more than the simple necessity of 'reading' through the lens of one's own experience; rather, it is a conscious attempt to have students affectively 'commit' to the experience of the text as part of *intellectual* engagement. In this context, student vulnerability is an issue and trust becomes important. Eve therefore works to ensure that no student's experience is allowed to become a source of anxiety. Students need only ever discuss what is comfortable for them, and this will often be done in pairs.

The developed status given to thinking and learning in itself targets and minimizes student resistance. The culture includes a stable, purposeful consistency in the ways in which the classroom operates. Students are always occupied, with no 'dead moments'. There are strong messages that 'we are here to do business and the business of the lesson is not to have confrontations over your behaviour.' Where there is resistance or disruption, students gain a strong sense that Eve has *chosen* not to dwell on this and has made a conscious decision to avoid escalation, making use of re-directing. Eve at all times shows respect for students, never diminishing them, while 'getting on with business'. All of these strategies are accompanied by a high degree of choice in the classroom, which moves the locus of control away from Eve alone.

The thoughtful and dynamic repertoire of practices by which the classroom operates as *high operative* include a great deal of scaffolding. Many examples and models are given of the work being undertaken, and order and sequence are paramount. Despite the L2 status of the students in subject English, lessons in Eve's class move very quickly. Things are not 'left to hang'. Group-work, for example, is usually a quick-in, quick-out activity. Eve takes what is complex, analyses it to create teachable parts, then resynthesizes it as the teaching goes on, so that students see the product as a complex whole, not just as the parts. All activities move toward comprehending a 'bigger picture'. The sense that 'we're in this together' is also strong in her classroom as students see that Eve is learning as well.

Engaging classroom messages and the Fair Go

The FGP believes there is much to be learned from watching and listening to teachers who are recognized for the ways that they engage students living in poverty and make a difference to the relationships these students have with education. From the outset, we wanted to co-research with teachers whose students wanted to be in their classes for the right reasons – because here were places where they could be helped to become stronger and more productive learners. We hope that the classroom stories of teachers highlighted in this chapter have shown that this process must invariably play out differently across stages of schooling, among students from a great variety of cultural backgrounds and in a diversity of community contexts. Nonetheless, the stories present for consideration a number of critical emerging themes that appear to be holding the pedagogies together. The themes resonate strongly with the 'authentic instruction' research of Newmann and Associates (1996) and the productive pedagogies movement (Hayes et al. 2006). From the FGP's perspective, the themes point to classrooms where students receive powerful messages that their learning is worthwhile and connected and that they are helped to be capable within a shared community where their voices are recognized and valued. The messages talk of classrooms where students 'get a fair go'.

Acknowledgements

We would like to acknowledge a number of educators who are committed to improved educational experiences and outcomes for low SES students and who have contributed to the ideas explored in this chapter. First, we recognize Donna Deehan (Manning Gardens Public School), Sonia Squires (Mungindi Public School), Dan Sprange (Hampden Park Public School), Sue Barrett (James Meehan High School) and Eve Mayes (Condell Park High School), who opened up their classrooms and their teaching for the research and contributed strongly to the analysis of their pedagogies. Second, we acknowledge the University of Western Sydney Fair Go Team, whose classroom research and critical participation brought forward the student engagement framework discussed in this chapter.

Notes

1 Priority Schools Programs (PSP) are aimed at improving educational outcomes for students living in the poorest communities in New South Wales. It was previously known as the Priority Schools Funding Program (PSFP) and the Disadvantaged Schools Program (DSP).

References

Bernstein, B. (1996) *Pedagogy, Symbolic Control and Identity: Theory, Research, Critique.* London: Taylor and Francis.

Comber, B. and Thomson, P. (2001) 'Just new learning environments: new metaphors and practices for learners and teachers in disadvantaged schools.' Keynote paper in Department for Education and Skills, Experiencing Change, Exchanging Experience Virtual Conference, June 25–July 13.

Fair Go Team (2006) *School Is For Me: Pathways to Student Engagement.* Sydney: Priority Schools Funding Program, New South Wales Department of Education and Training.

Fredricks, J. A., Blumenfield, P. C. and Paris, A. H. (2004) 'School engagement: potential of the concept, state of the evidence.' *Review of Educational Research*, 76(1), 59–109.

Hayes, D. (2003) 'Making learning an effect of schooling: aligning curriculum, assessment and pedagogy.' *Discourse: Studies in the Cultural Politics of Education*, *24*(2), 225–245.

Hayes, D., Mills, M., Christie, P. and Lingard, B. (2006) *Teachers and Schooling Making A Difference*. Crows Nest: Allen and Unwin.

Mills, C. and Gale, T. (2002) 'Schooling and the production of social inequalities: what can and should we be doing?' *Melbourne Studies in Education*, *43*(1), 107–125.

Munns, G. (2007) 'A sense of wonder: student engagement in low SES school communities.' *International Journal of Inclusive Education*, *11*(3), 301–315.

Newmann, F. and Associates (1996) *Authentic Achievement: Restructuring Schools for Intellectual Quality*. San Francisco: Josey Bass.

Suggested further readings

Haberman, M. (2005) *Star Teachers: The Ideology and Best Practices of Effective Teachers of Diverse Children and Youth in Poverty*. Houston, TX: The Haberman Foundation.

Hattie, J. (2008) *Visible Learning: A Synthesis of Meta-Analyses Relating to Achievement*. London: Routledge.

Loughran, J. (2010) *What Expert Teachers Do: Enhancing Professional Knowledge for Classroom Practice*. Crows Nest: Allen and Unwin.

Portelli, J. and McMahon, B. (eds) (2011) *Student Engagement in Urban Schools: Beyond Neoliberal Discourses*. Charlotte, NC: Information Age Publishers.

Thomson, P. (2002) *Schooling the Rustbelt Kids: Making the Difference in Changing Times*. Stoke-on-Trent: Trentham.

Chapter 15

Using critical mathematics to understand the conditions of our lives

United States

Eric 'Rico' Gutstein

Introduction: why did Robert Wilson[1] die?

On September 24, 2009, Robert Wilson, a 16-year-old Black male student, left Fenger High School in his Roseland community of Chicago, where he was an 11th-grader. In a fight that broke out among dozens of Fenger students who lived in two different communities, the student was hit in the head with a wood board, knocked to the ground, kicked and tragically died. Someone filmed it with a cell phone, which made it to the internet and international news. The videos, on YouTube, have been seen well more than a million times.

The other neighborhood in which Fenger students live is five miles away and includes the Altgeld Gardens public housing development, one of Chicago's oldest. Altgeld was built in 1945 for returning Black World War II veterans, for them to work in the thriving industrial stronghold of South Side Chicago. At one point, 125,000 steelworkers worked in the region. Today, however, both Altgeld and Roseland are economically devastated, overwhelmingly Black communities. The 'Gardens', almost 100 per cent Black, is the most isolated public housing development, far from many city services. Only one bus line serves it, and it can take up to an hour (including waiting time) just to get to the city's subway system. The nearest supermarket is miles away. Further, because of its proximity to industrial zones, it is surrounded by pollution. A local media report aptly summarized the situation:

> The Altgeld Gardens Phillip Murray Homes community is boxed off from the rest of Chicago – a trapped 190-acre island between highways, trash heaps, pollution and industry. It is the Far South Side – the end of the city.
>
> (Ehmke and Jablonska 2009)

Like most Chicago neighborhoods (indeed, across the United States), there was a local high school, Carver High, which opened in 1971. In 2000, it became a military high school (the first to convert in Chicago) and, although students needed to subscribe to military discipline, local youth could attend. However, in 2006, the Chicago Board of Education (appointed by the mayor) changed Carver into a selective-enrolment military academy. Local students now have to score high on standardized tests, fill out applications, and be interviewed and agree to a military code of conduct. Fenger is the other school nearest to Altgeld, and students now have to take two buses to reach it.

Chicago, a city of neighborhoods, is one of the most segregated areas in the United States and very turf-oriented. For various historical, sociopolitical, cultural and economic reasons, residents from one community are often not welcome elsewhere, even when of the same race or ethnicity. Compounding this mix is Chicago's gang history (dating back to the infamous Al Capone) and the historic disinvestment in US cities since the 1980s advent of neoliberalism, which exacerbated poverty and inequality (Demissie 2006). When the Board turned Carver into a military academy, parents knew their children would have to attend Fenger or another school outside of the neighborhood, and that this would jeopardize their children's safety. Chicago has an unfortunate history of low-income communities without sufficient resources being pitted against each other; the Altgeld parents were right in being concerned. Roseland and Altgeld students – who live in very similar communities – have been at odds for years, but closing Carver only made it much worse.

Destroying neighborhood schools: 'killing the heart of the community'

Closing Carver as a neighborhood public school was part of Mayor Daley's *Renaissance 2010* plan. Daley unveiled the plan in 2004 at a meeting of the Commercial Club of Chicago (his close allies among the financial, banking, corporate and real estate elites of the city). Renaissance 2010's goal was to close 60 to 70 neighborhood schools and open 100 new ones (overwhelmingly charter or 'contract' schools, similar to charters). Five years later, that had largely happened, as education privatization is central to the agenda (Lipman and Haines 2007). However, every time the Board proposes closing a school, parents, students, teachers, administrators, alumni and community residents resist and protest. The principal reason is, as one parent poignantly declared, 'When you close a school, you kill the heart of a community'. However, a secondary reason very important in Chicago is the danger of crossing boundaries. Chicago has the highest rate of youth homicide of any major US city for the fourth year in a row (Wren 2009). In just the first two-and-a-half months of the 2009-10 school year, 12 students have been killed and

78 shot. Parents and residents repeatedly warn at school-closing hearings and Board meetings *not* to close neighborhood schools because spiked violence will occur, but the Board consistently ignores community wisdom, which has been proven correct time after time (Brown et al. 2009).

Adding to the mix is that in summer 2009, Fenger was 'turned around'. Under Renaissance 2010, Chicago Public Schools (CPS) revamps schools in four ways: closings, consolidations, phase-outs and turnarounds. In a turnaround, CPS fires *every* teacher, administrator, counselor, security personnel, paraprofessional, classroom aid, custodial staff and kitchen worker. They may reapply, but there is no guarantee they will be re-hired. In fact, only 9 of 100 teachers who were at Fenger during the 2008-9 school year returned the next. Thus, the vast majority of teachers knew students for only three weeks when the fight broke out in which the student died. Gone were many veteran Black teachers, some who lived in the neighborhood and knew and taught students and their parents, siblings, cousins, aunts, uncles and neighbors. Gone were teachers who had built relationships with students and knew the neighborhood and how to defuse situations. Right before the student was killed, the school had reported numerous fights and rising tensions. As Deborah Lynch (2009), former president of the Chicago Teachers Union wrote, 'Those are the times when a seasoned staff can identify strategies and resources to address and prevent further problems' (2009: 13).

Further, Carver was not the only school taken from these communities. Many believe the decision to close Carver as a neighborhood school, coupled with phasing out two other local schools and turning Fenger around, have all contributed to destabilization, displacement and spiked violence in the far South Side of Chicago. This overwhelmingly Black, low-income community is hard hit by economic crises, environmental devastation, institutional racism, and policies of exclusion and marginalization.

But these factors, by themselves, do not fully explain why 'Robert Wilson' died, or why there is so much youth-on-youth violence in Chicago's poor communities of color. Though I do not wish to be reductionist, my first premise in this chapter is this: *the sooner marginalized and excluded youths understand who their real enemy is, the sooner they will stop killing each other.*

My argument is that the vast majority of youths who attend neighborhood public schools in Chicago – almost entirely economically low-income, and Black and 'Brown' (Latino, mainly Mexican, but also Puerto Rican, and Central and South American) – have a common enemy, and it is not one another. This enemy is not easy to precisely define and, although it is represented by individuals, in its essence it is systemic. It embodies systems of oppression: institutionalized and structural racism, economic exploitation, stratified labor and educational systems, gendered exclusion and sexism, environmental devastation, poverty and more – all of which are integral parts of the larger system of global capitalism. The righteous rage that many Chicago youth of color bring into the classroom is based on their position at the bottom of U.S. society. Without overwhelming the reader with data, it is enough to say that Black males in the United States born in 2001 have one chance in three of going to prison in their lifetimes, whereas White males have about one chance in 17 (Bonczar 2003). Fewer than 50 per cent of Black or Latina/o CPS high school students graduate in four years (Allensworth 2005). Black unemployment, especially for youths, is close to twice that of Whites, whereas the poverty rate for Blacks and Latinas/os is close to triple that of Whites (United for a Fair Economy 2009).

I am arguing here that there is a connection between how people experience their lives and their actions. I do not claim direct causality, or that, if students from the margins develop a political perspective on the root causes of their oppression, there will be no more youth violence. Life is far too complicated for such facile solutions. I am suggesting, however, a real relationship between students' anger, rebellion and resistance, on the one hand, and their lateral lashing out on the other. Here, I draw on Franz Fanon who studied and supported the Algerian independence movement from France in the early 1960s. In speaking of how colonized Algerians reacted to the brutality the French enacted upon them, Fanon (1963: 52, 54) wrote:

> The colonial man will first manifest this aggressiveness which has been deposited in his bones against his own people. This is the period when the niggers beat each other up, and the police and magistrates do not know which way to turn when faced with the astonishing waves of crime in North Africa…The settler keeps alive in the native an anger which he deprives of outlet; the native is trapped in the tight links of the chains of colonialism…The native's muscular tension finds outlet regularly in bloodthirsty explosions – in tribal warfare, in feuds between septs [clans], and in quarrels between individuals…While the settler or the policeman has the right the livelong day to strike the native, to insult him and to make him crawl to them, you will see the native reaching for his knife at the slightest hostile aggressive glance cast on him by another native…

My contention here is that, like the Algerian people, both Altgeld Gardens and Roseland youth's deep-seated anger is largely due to their location in society and the oppressions they experience. When a Roseland youth involved in the brawl that killed Robert told the media about why they fight with Altgeld students, 'As far as I know, they don't like us, and the way I feel, we don't like them' (Ahmed et al. 2009), he made it clear that no real reason existed for the horizontal violence that emerges in response to a 'hostile aggressive glance'. As Fanon points out, the 'tension finds outlet regularly in bloodthirsty explosions', such as that which killed Robert Wilson.

Reframing the resistance: 'If you feelin gangsta bang on the system'

This quotation hung in Patrick Camangian's English classroom in a Los Angeles public school, quite like Fenger and in a similar community. Translated in his words, this means to

> capture the importance of using students' willingness to 'bang' [fight each other] but channeling their anger towards the very social system that undermines their existence... rather than practice sub-oppression when banging on other oppressed people, let's study and work together to bang on this oppressive social system.
>
> (P. Camangian, personal communication, November 28, 2009)

Camangian attempted for his students to deeply analyze their own lives in the context of a critical English curriculum so that they could use what they learned in class to act in life and work to change the conditions that enveloped them. My orientation is that what Camangian does in his English classes can be done in mathematics classes as well. Paulo Freire (1998: 74) wrote:

> One of the basic questions that we need to look at is how to convert merely rebellious attitudes into revolutionary ones in the radical transformation of society. Merely rebellious attitudes or actions are insufficient, though they are an indispensable response to legitimate anger. It is necessary to go beyond rebellious attitudes to a more radically critical and revolutionary position.

To go beyond the anger requires understanding the root source of oppression. One cannot guarantee that students' pain, hurt and anger will automatically dissolve, but political analysis can lead students to understand that directing the anger at their own kind is misplaced. It is a task the critical teachers can undertake, both for themselves and their students. As Freire commented '...the radical [educator] wants to know about resistance to understand better the discourse of resistance, to provide pedagogical structures that will enable students to emancipate themselves' (Freire and Macedo 1987: 138).

Understanding the conditions of our lives through critical mathematics

Youth need the opportunities to be, in Freire's terms, 'subjects who meet to *name* the world in order to transform it' (1970/1998: 148), but what does that have to do with mathematics education? What connection can one possibly draw between the violence heaped upon, and enacted between, young people in marginalized urban US communities and what they do in their math classes in a highly regimented school district such as Chicago's? In response, I present my second argument: that even in generally repressive institutions – public, urban, US schools – *teachers can engage students in using critical mathematics to study the conditions of their lives.* Further, these studies can materially make a difference in students coming to realize that they and other youths living in a different neighborhood actually have enemies in common.

'Don't let them pit us against each other!'

With these words, Erika ended the PowerPoint presentation by the 21 high school seniors in the 'math and social justice' class at the Greater Lawndale/ Little Village School for Social Justice (known as 'Sojo') in Chicago. About 75 parents, relatives, friends, fellow students and community members attended this public event. Presented in late May 2009, it was the culminating project for the class in the 2008-9 school year. Students titled the presentation 'Our Issues, Our People: Math as Our Weapon', and they did it on subsequent nights in each of the two communities from which Sojo draws: South Lawndale (or Little Village, a Mexican immigrant community) and North Lawndale (a Black community).

The 'us' to whom Erika referred were the Latina/o and Black students at Sojo and in Chicago, and the United States more broadly. The school is 30 per cent Black and 70 per cent Latina/o and 98 per cent low-income. North and South Lawndale have a history of solidarity with each other going back to the 1983 election of Harold Washington, Chicago's first Black mayor. After Washington won the Democratic Party primary in Spring 1983, he faced a Republican Party challenger in the general election later that year. Chicago is a Democratic Party town – the last Republican Party mayor's term ended in 1931. When hundreds of thousands of Whites crossed party lines to vote for Washington's White challenger, the Latina/o community came out strongly for Washington and made the difference. Washington won virtually all the city's Black votes, but only 12 per cent of the White votes. However, more than half of the Latinas/os voted for him, making the difference. A key Latino activist, Rudy Lozano, crossed the bridge and organized Latinos/as to vote for Washington – Lozano was from Little Village.

However, these two communities also have a history of friction. Students in greater Lawndale historically attended Farragut High School, on the border separating North from South Lawndale. Farragut has been the site of much tension between the two neighborhoods. And since Sojo opened in 2005 as a new small school in Little Village, the Mexican community – one of four small schools in a new building (see Russo 2003) – safe passage from school for Black North Lawndale students has remained elusive, as some Latinas/os report feeling 'invaded' by Black youth. Despite efforts by students, staff and parents from all four schools on campus, along with support from some Little Village residents who decry the anti-Black violence, Black students have been harassed and even attacked as they walk after school to their bus stop to travel home to North Lawndale. Thus Erika's statement had particular meaning to our class.

That Erika finished the class presentation with that statement is not unusual given the nature of the math and social justice class or this particular social justice school. I am a mathematics educator at a local university and was part of the design team that founded the school, and I have worked with the school since it opened. In Sojo's first three years, my role was to provide professional development, support mathematics teachers and their students, and help co-teach, especially the critical mathematics projects that we developed. During the first three years, we interjected a number of relatively short social justice mathematics projects (Gutstein 2007; Sia and Gutstein 2007) into the regular course. However, as we approached the fourth year, the mathematics department and I collectively decided to have a 12th-grade class focused entirely on learning mathematics through studying students' social reality. It was my role to develop the curriculum, with students, and to teach this class and study it, with students and teachers as co-researchers (see Gutstein 2006 for similar work at the middle school level).

Students and I chose to study five units, though we did not complete them all. Sojo students take four years of math, so the math and social justice class was an option when they chose their classes in spring of their 11th grade. We met three times that semester to decide upon the units. The contexts, which they either suggested or I proposed and they accepted, mattered to them. Next, I discuss the unit on *displacement*, the longest of the year (about 14 weeks). This unit most directly helped students understand the political commonalities between the two Lawndales.

Displacement means both similar and different things to the two neighborhoods. For North Lawndale, displacement initially meant gentrification. Two 'el' lines (public above-ground subway systems) serve it; its northern boundary lies along an expressway and, with no traffic, it takes perhaps ten minutes to drive downtown. North Lawndale also has the most *greystones* (architecturally desirable, limestone-fronted buildings) in the city and, in 2006, Chicago launched the 'Historic Chicago Greystone Initiative', drawing much attention to North Lawndale, including by developers wanting to cash in on a real estate boom. Thus gentrification was very much on the agenda. This translates into displacement because when land and house values soar, long-time residents cannot afford either increased property taxes (which landlords pass on to renters) or home purchases. However, since the 2007 housing crash, foreclosures skyrocketed, adding another dimension to displacement in North Lawndale.

Displacement in Little Village, however, has a different meaning. Although also hit by a dramatic rise in foreclosures (both communities had more than triple the number in 2008 as in 2005), Little Village has not yet been marked by gentrification. Unlike North Lawndale, it is not on the train line and its housing is less attractive. However, Little Village has its own form of displacement – the specter of deportation. Estimates are that about a half-million undocumented immigrants live in Illinois, primarily around Chicago, and most are Mexican (Mehta and Ali 2003). Little Village is the largest Mexican community in Illinois, with more than 90,000 residents (US Census Bureau 2000). It is common knowledge that thousands of undocumented people live in Little Village, and I personally know many. Thus, displacement there means, for many, living in the shadows, in fear of the ICE (Immigration and Customs Enforcement agency).

The unit was far reaching and, despite the time, we could not cover all I had planned, but we did a lot. A key mathematical concept was to use *discrete dynamical systems* (DDS, a pre-calculus topic) to model real-world phenomena that change over time. Using a DDS, one can create a loan (e.g. a mortgage) amortization table and interest and principal costs for each period and the balance due at the period's end. We used DDS to explore mortgages, specifically sub-prime (high-cost) loans. We looked at adjustable-rate, interest-only, balloon and pay-option loans. Students used graphing calculators to create and analyze balance-due-over-time graphs and understand how negative amortization occurs. They became quite proficient and could answer (for example): how much one would owe after 165 months on a 30-year adjustable-rate mortgage of $150,000 that began at 5.5 per cent per year and went up 0.75 per cent at the start of years 2, 4, 6, and then remained there for the life of the loan.

Our political framework for studying sub-prime loans was to begin to understand (1) an aspect of how capitalism works, specifically how banks loan and make money, (2) predatory loans and the disproportional number of Blacks and Latinas/os receiving them, (3) the relationship of this disproportionality to the high number of foreclosures in Lawndale, (4) whether the community would remain affordable for current residents, that is, whose place is Lawndale, and (5) what we could do about the situation.

To answer whether people could stay in Lawndale, students looked at real estate price trends and median family income for each community. Using US Department of Housing and Urban Development guidelines that state a family should pay no more than 30 per cent of its income on housing (or else they incur 'hardship'), students computed whether families at the median could afford new housing in Lawndale. During the community presentation, the student group presenting on gentrification had several slides on this question. After showing a slide with a brochure for a new North Lawndale condo, they presented and explained the following slides:

Can You Afford This?

- House value: $285,000
- North Lawndale median household income: $20,253
- With a 10 per cent down payment, 90 per cent of 285,000 = $256,500
- 30-year mortgage, with a 5.25 per cent interest rate
- Monthly payment is $1,416.40.

Can You Afford This?

- Monthly payment x 12 = $17,000 for the year
- 'Hardship' means paying > 30 per cent income on housing
- Paying $17,000 per year for housing, need ~$57,000 a year
- This is roughly *3 times North Lawndale median.*

They presented similar data for Little Village and also provided a definition of gentrification, analyzed a graph on foreclosures, and posed (and addressed) the question: *why should we care?* The concluding slides for their part of the presentation were:

How Do They Get Away With It?

- These people get away with this because they only say the benefits that are convenient to the community but not the bad things that it causes in the process to the people in the community – foreclosures, prices going up, displacement.

What Can We Do?

- The people could gain knowledge
- People can organize.

Students made the entire (82-slide!) PowerPoint by themselves. To help prepare, I critiqued and posed questions, but all ideas and text were their own.

To help students begin to understand capitalism through how banks work, we analyzed what happens when a family cannot quite make their loan payments. We found that a median-income Little Village family could afford about $808 a month for housing, without hardship. Students then computed the monthly payment on a $150,000, 30-year fixed-rate loan at 6 per cent a year, about $899. They found that if a family took on this mortgage but paid only $808 per month, at the end of 30 years, they would have paid about $291,000 – but would still owe almost $92,000. I then wrote the equation on the board: $150,000 –$291,000 = $92,000.

Students could hardly believe that one could pay almost twice as much as borrowed, over 30 years, and still owe $92,000 even though I explained that this was how capitalism works and that banks consider it to be what they are due as the cost of loaning money. I told students, 'This is legal. This is how banks loan and make money.' I then repeated it, slowly, to a silent, somber classroom.

This conversation continued and was embedded in mathematical and political investigations throughout the unit (year), focused on students understanding their own lives at a deeper level. We examined why there were foreclosures in Lawndale, the reasons behind gentrification, who stood to gain, why some residents favored condo developments, who was investing in Lawndale and why. (We discovered that a transnational capital investment firm specializing in vulture capitalism, with offices on three continents, was planning on investing in a controversial Little Village development.) We asked what the future might hold and what social forces contributed to migration from Mexico to Little Village. This last question was particularly complicated because we examined the mathematics of how the North American Free Trade Agreement, as an example of neoliberal free trade policies, impacted both Lawndales but differently. For Little Village, it contributed to farmers being displaced from the Mexican countryside because of US corn subsidies to agribusiness and eventually making their way to the community without documents; for North Lawndale, it led to the loss of manufacturing jobs (Bacon 2008; Oxfam 2003; Scott 2003; US Census Bureau 2007).

My students addressed key questions and gradually made sense of displacement's complexities through integrating mathematical and political analyses. The unit's final project required them to write about what they had learned, including the relationships between the two parts of the unit – gentrification and immigration/deportation. Part of Monica's essay is below:

> Some connections that I see between these two parts of the unit are that in both communities, people are being forced out their homes. Of course, it's different situations, but similar causes. African Americans are being forced out their homes because they can't pay for their homes. The taxes go up so much that they can't afford to keep living in those communities, so they are forced to look for another place to live. For Mexican people, the problem is that they don't have jobs in Mexico because corn isn't being sold. That forces Mexicans to leave their family and homes to come to the US to look for a job. This is how the units connected. They face similar situations but different causes....What I learned about the world is that many cultures have similar situations. But sometimes we act wrong by fighting each other instead of uniting to help each other succeed....We saw in the videos so many similarities. People are being forced out of their community through gentrification.

Latinos (especially Mexicans) are being forced out their countries by not having a good paying job. Also, the house mortgages don't only affect one community, but both. They are sometimes the target of bad loans that only make banks richer! I want the people in my community to know that we are really similar with these situations. That there is more that makes us similar, less that makes us different. If we want to fight the bigger people out there, the best way is to unite. Fighting each other is not going to take us anywhere. I think this is something very important our community should know.

We need many more analyses such as this, that unity is needed to fight the 'bigger people out there', and not to let them 'pit us against each other', as Erika said. In this class, students used mathematics to *begin* to understand who the larger enemies were and to realize their common struggles. Though one mathematics class cannot necessarily stop students from putting the blame for oppression on other marginalized peoples, this class provides evidence that critical mathematics can potentially support youth – such as Robert Wilson and others – in learning about these larger issues. I conclude with words from Vero, another student, about youth violence in Lawndale. This suggests how critical mathematics can play a role:

I've learned to question how and why... Mr. Rico [my classroom name] told me that I was just giving people the mathematical answers...I went from questioning things in math to questioning things in life. Now I question everything and everyone... [I asked: Why?] Because we're taking [pause] regular math and implementing it, we use our knowledge to address other issues that affect others, people of color, low-income people, etc.

She continued:

The reason why some people act so aggressive is not because that's how we are, but because that's how we are meant to be because of what's happening to us. So like all the police and stuff, all these North Lawndale shootings, Little Village shootings, another shooting, another kid dead, or something like that, it's just that that was led by something else. It's just not, people don't just pop out with a gun and start shooting. It's because something is going on that is leading people to do certain things... it's not a way of excusing it, but it's a way of addressing the question: why?

As Paulo Freire wrote, in *Pedagogy of the Oppressed*, 'No oppressive order could permit the oppressed to begin to question: why?' (1970/1998: 67). Vero and her compatriots in this class, instead of targeting one another, were beginning to question: why? They were learning to use critical mathematics to understand the conditions of their lives and who were their real enemies, and they were developing the knowledge, skills and dispositions to change their world.

Acknowledgements

This research was partially funded by a Great Cities Institute Faculty Scholarship, the University of Illinois–Chicago. I express my appreciation to students of the math and social justice class at Sojo High School and to Anita Balasubramanian, Patty Buenrostro and Pauline Lipman for helping me conduct this research and think through the arguments.

Notes

1   Robert Wilson is a pseudonym and a metaphor for all the youths who have died in similar situations. Other students' names used in the chapter are also pseudonyms, unless their words are from a public presentation.

References

Ahmed, A., Mack, K. and Sweeney, A. (2009) 'Fenger kids tell why they fight.' *Chicago Tribune*, Online. Retrieved from http://www.chicagotribune.com/news/local/chi-fenger-safe-passage-06-oct06,0,2119252.story

Allensworth, E. (2005) *Graduation and Dropout Trends in Chicago: A Look at Cohorts of Students from 1991 to 2004.* Chicago: Consortium on Chicago School Research.

Bacon, D. (2008) *Illegal People: How Globalization Creates Migration and Criminalizes Immigration.* Boston: Beacon Press.

Bonczar, T. P. (2003) *Prevalence of Imprisonment in the US Population 1974–2001.* Washington, DC: Bureau of Justice Statistics. Online. Retrieved from http://www.ojp.usdoj.gov/bjs/pub/pdf/piusp01.pdf

Brown, J., Gutstein, E. and Lipman, P. (2009) 'Arne Duncan and the Chicago success story: myth or reality?' *Rethinking Schools, 23*(3), 10–14.

Demissie, F. (2006) 'Globalization and the remaking of Chicago.' In J. P. Koval, L. Bennett, M. I. J. Bennett, F. Demissie, R. Garner and K. Kim (eds) *The New Chicago: A Social and Cultural Analysis.* Philadelphia: Temple University Press.

Ehmke, L. and Jablonska, J. (2009) *The Desert of Altgeld Gardens.* Medill Reports Chicago, Online. Retrieved from http://news.medill.northwestern.edu/chicago/news.aspx?id=143727

Fanon, F. (1963) *The Wretched of the Earth* (trans. C. Frankington). New York: Grove Press.

Freire, P. (1970/1998) *Pedagogy of the Oppressed* (trans. M. B. Ramos). New York: Continuum.

Freire, P. (1998) *Pedagogy of Freedom: Ethics, Democracy, and Civic Courage* (trans. P. Clarke). Lanham, MD: Rowman and Littlefield.

Freire, P. and Macedo, D. (1987) *Literacy: Reading the Word and the World*. Westport, CT: Bergin and Garvey.

Gutstein, E. (2006) *Reading and Writing the World with Mathematics: Toward a Pedagogy for Social Justice*. New York: Routledge.

Gutstein, E. (2007) 'Connecting *community*, *critical*, and *classical* knowledge in teaching mathematics for social justice.' *The Montana Mathematics Enthusiast, Monograph, 1*, 109–118.

Lipman, P. and Haines, N. (2007) 'From accountability to privatization and African American exclusion: Chicago's "Renaissance 2010".' *Educational Policy, 21*(3), 471–502.

Lynch, D. (2009) '"Turnaround" – the deadliest "reform" of all.' *Substance News, XXXV*(2), 1, 13.

Mehta, C. and Ali, A. (2003) *Education for All: Chicago's Undocumented Immigrants and Their Access to Higher Education*. Chicago: University of Illinois at Chicago, Center for Urban Economic Development.

Oxfam (2003, August) 'Dumping without borders: how US agriculture policies are destroying the livelihoods of Mexican corn farmers.' Oxfam Briefing Paper. Oxford: Oxfam.

Russo, A. (2003, June) 'Constructing a new school.' *Catalyst*. Retrieved from http://www.catalyst-chicago.org/06-03/0603littlevillage.htm

Scott, R. E. (2003) *The High Price of 'Free' Trade*. EPI Briefing Paper 147. Washington, DC: Economic Policy Institute. Retrieved from http://www.epi.org/publications/entry/briefingpapers_bp147/ (accessed November 17)

Sia, J. and Gutstein, R. (2007) 'Detailed mathematics unit.' In A. Mangual and B. Picower (eds) *Revealing Racist Roots: The 3 R's for Teaching about the Jena 6*. New York: Teacher Activist Groups.

United for a Fair Economy (2009) *State of the Dream 2009 Charts*. Boston: United for a Fair Economy. Online. Retrieved from http://faireconomy.org/news/state_of_the_dream_2009_charts

US Census Bureau (2000) *Census 2000, Summary File 3*. Washington, DC: U.S. Census Bureau.

US Census Bureau (2007) 2007 ZIP Code Business Patterns (NAICS), online. Retrieved from http://censtats.census.gov/cgi-bin/zbpnaic/zbpsect.pl

Wren, A. (2009) *Medill Exclusive: Chicago Again Poised to Be Country's Most Violent City for Youth*. Medill Reports Chicago, online. Retrieved from http://news.medill.northwestern.edu/chicago/news.aspx?id=149207

Suggested further readings

Fanon, F. (1963) *The Wretched of the Earth*. New York: Grove Press.

Freire, P. (1994) *Pedagogy of Hope: Reliving Pedagogy of the Oppressed*. New York: Continuum.

Gutstein, E. (2006) *Reading and Writing the World with Mathematics: Toward a Pedagogy for Social Justice*. New York: Routledge.

Gutstein, E. and Peterson, B. (eds) (2005) *Rethinking Mathematics: Teaching Social Justice by the Numbers*. Milwaukee, WI: Rethinking Schools.

Lipman, P. (2004) *High Stakes Education: Inequality, Globalization, and Urban School Reform*. New York: Routledge.

Chapter 16

Resources for changing schools

Ideas in and for practice

Terry Wrigley, Pat Thomson and Bob Lingard

Introduction

It is usual at this stage of an edited collection to attempt to summarize, in the sense of unifying and signing off, the preceding evidence and arguments. This would be inappropriate in view of the rich and diverse experiences and innovative and critical thinking represented in earlier chapters. We prefer to see this final chapter as a response rather than a conclusion, and one that will undoubtedly open up further debate and action. We will draw out from the chapters some of the implications for changing schools in socially just ways and towards a richer and wider democratic citizenship, and point to some other important matters.

We began to conceptualize this book in light of the complex, multiple and overlapping challenges facing schools today. Some of these arise from major global crises: climate change, war, poverty, the financial crisis. Others stem from the hegemony of neoliberal political and policy frames globally and nationally, which prioritize individual choices and interests over the common good, with the flawed assumption that individuals pursuing their own self-interests will produce the good society. Other challenges facing schools are the result of accelerated cultural change, arising partly from the rapid development of information and communication technologies but also from the hybridity and stylistic dynamism of youth cultures – often cultures of overt or deflected resistance; as every teacher knows, 'kids are different nowadays'. The increased mobility of people within and between national borders compounds the cultural diversity of both of these and their impact on schools.

We have long been concerned that the dominant theories and regimes of change favoured by politicians in recent decades do not live up to the complexity and fluidity of this situation. Policies tend to simplify whereas the realities facing schools have become ever more complex. In this context, attempts to 'improve schools' that are largely focused on making them more efficient, while maintaining traditional school structures and cultures, are misguided and misleading and will not meet the needs of all individuals, communities or nations in the twenty-first century.

In particular, the pressure to improve 'outputs' without taking this complex environment seriously is intensely problematic, particularly for schools serving neighbourhoods blighted by poverty. Doing school in more or less the same way but with the pressure to increase 'effectiveness' is doomed to failure; it simply does not attend to the cultural damage and demoralisation that results from poverty and other kinds of marginalisation. It is our contention, and that of many contributors to this book, that communities weighed down by chronic unemployment or marginalisation require a particular and different school ethos, curriculum and pedagogy to counter a sense of shame and futility and for schools to live up to their promises. At the same time, despite the real hardship experienced by many, we recognize that there are significant resources of hope in all communities. Schools and teachers need to work with these in productive ways; many have been exemplified in the chapters of this book.

This is why the more radical accounts of change provided by all the chapters in this book – and many others we might have included – are so important. Though we wish to avoid the attempt to distil these diverse and complex stories and emergent theories of school change into a single model or set of guidelines, it seems important to highlight recurrent patterns of response, concepts and philosophies, and the practices taken up in these schools.

We have organized these issues into three strands for analytical purposes but recognize that they intersect in mutually enriching ways:

- Rethinking pedagogy
- Rethinking inclusion and social justice
- Rethinking school organisation and change processes.

We regard these strands as a useful basis for envisaging and theorising change, and as intellectual resources for others engaged in the complexity of individual school or larger-scale change.

Rethinking pedagogy

It should be clear from every chapter in this book that worthwhile school change is a thoroughly pedagogical matter. Organisational change, and the processes through which change is promoted, must serve pedagogical ends and be pedagogical in approach. Educational leadership needs to be thought of as pedagogy, focusing on and supporting teacher, community and student learning.

We are using the word *pedagogy* first in its Enlightenment sense of human development – helping young people to become more fully human, individually and collectively. We do not see this in any ahistorical or abstract sense but as grounded in the world as it is today, in particular places and times. We also see a role for pedagogy in enhancing individual aspirations and helping to constitute a new social imaginary, an imagined better future, locally, nationally and globally. This latter might be seen as a collective aspiration.

The change processes described in different circumstances and with a diversity of focal points in this book have in common a sense that inherited practices of schooling must change because they do not help produce human beings with the resources to live fruitful lives. What they do is advantage some and disadvantage others (Labaree 2010). The inherited ways of being teachers and 'doing school' are unconducive to social transformation, either on a local or planetary scale. All of this is, of course, within a context of compound global crises: financial meltdown, increasing poverty, wars carried out with space-age weaponry on helpless populations, and threatening environmental disaster. This does, indeed, demand a rethinking of pedagogy.

Pedagogy is bigger than methodology: it involves reflection on society, values, history, environment, learning itself, but it is empty to speak of pedagogical transformation without also addressing specific approaches to teaching and learning. We have made the point before, but it is worth repeating because it is so important: there must not be a trade-off between care and intellectually demanding pedagogies and curricula. Deep care is central to socially just pedagogies, which understand the need to scaffold from where students are at, in respectful ways, but which seek to make available the high-status knowledges valued in educational systems. Such approaches represent a commitment to epistemological inclusion. Effective pedagogies are contextualized and connnected to students' lifeworlds but seek to stretch beyond these in educative ways.

Perhaps one of the most difficult demands of pedagogy today is the need to recognize and work with the multifarious differences that students bring to school. Such pedagogies of difference come up against the debilitating pedagogies of sameness implicit in schooling systems driven (to distraction!) by high-stakes testing and test data as reductive forms of educational accountability. We need an alignment across the message systems of curriculum, pedagogy and assessment. Such alignment is more difficult to achieve today in those schooling systems where the evaluation message system through high-stakes testing and reductive systems of accountability drives both curriculum and pedagogy. We are convinced that aligning evaluation with the higher-order purposes of schooling and demanding pedagogies will in the long run achieve higher standards and better outcomes for all. Schools and teachers collectively need to be involved in political work aimed at achieving better policy frameworks and richer and more intelligent forms of educational accountability. This would require schools and the communities they serve to develop a broad statement of their purposes and appropriate ways of recognising good outcomes against these purposes. Such outcome statements do not necessarily require numbers but might consist of productive narratives of a school's broad achievements.

Establishing connectedness and building on concerns

The search for 'relevance' is not in itself sufficient, nor is the proposal that learning be made more 'experiential', as both can mean an uncritical assimilation to the status quo. We prefer 'connectedness' to 'relevance' because it indicates both a respect for students' knowledges and interests and the need to scaffold learners into other knowledge forms, genres and media from which disadvantaged students should never be excluded. Repeatedly, these chapters point towards an enhanced kind of learning environment, a real learning community.

Such environments produce high-quality cognitive development, education for citizenship, and authentic engagement and motivation – knowledge that is more than a drizzle of inert facts and mind-numbing worksheets. They produce learning, which is simultaneously grounded and critical (Chapters 4 and 8). Going beyond the progressive tenet that learners should have opportunities to pursue their own interests, many chapters place a focus on young people's *concerns* (e.g. Chapters 3, 7, 8, 9 and 10).

While recognising that some local communities can be far from democratic and inclusive, as can be some global networks, it is crucial for teachers to work with these zones of connection to help students develop thoughtful and well-considered responses. In some cases, this involves real-world problem solving (Chapters 7 and 9) and, in others, the school may provide an 'offline' environment for simulated participation (Chapters 4 or 10) with or without the use of information and communication technology (ICT). School activities can provide opportunities for enhancing connections, such as dramatic play, photography, or building a garden with the help of parents (all in Chapter 14). In other cases, standard school subjects are revitalized by deploying established academic knowledge in the interest of critical citizenship (Chapters 2 and 15, among others).

Being explicit about whose knowledge counts

In their various ways, the authors in this book raise the questions: Whose knowledge? Where does it go? And in whose interests does it work? They speak of a collective construction of knowledges grounded in the learners' lifeworlds and rooted in place and identity. This suggests that teachers must focus on the question, Who are the young people in my class? and help learners question why their lives are as they are, what they might do if it is not fair, and how they can change it, individually and collectively.

The terms 'funds of knowledge' (Moll and Greenberg 1990) and 'virtual school bag' (Thomson 2002) point to the importance of understanding community-based, popular, and extended cultural knowledges and youth cultures as assets that are normally discounted, instead mobilising and converting them into 'symbolic capital' (Bourdieu 2004; see also Moore

2008) which can be drawn upon in work and further and higher education (Chapter 15). This proposition runs directly counter to standard educational processes whereby working-class culture is excluded and mis-recognized, where Indigenous knowledges are denied, where cultural differences are elided and only professional and higher class cultures and knowledges are ratified and become 'cultural, social and symbolic capital' that advantages some and disadvantages others (Bourdieu 2004).

Giving recognition

Without such recognition, it is difficult to see how schools can provide a route to economic success for disadvantaged young people. This means that at least some of the curriculum should be student-led (Chapters 3, 8, 9 and 11). It means changing the patterns of language use in classrooms to become more dialogic; for learners to use their own vernaculars as well as the formal academic language of the country, and ask their own questions rather than being limited to three-word answers to closed, rhetorical or test questions (Barnes 1971). Learning should be marked by substantive conversations that respect young people's capacities for intellectual knowledge-creating work.

This notion of conversations about learning is taken up in Chapter 14 with a double effect. Such conversations provide important support to students growing up in poverty, confirming that they are indeed capable of successful learning in response to cognitive challenges; they also develop a metacognitive awareness of what good learning looks like, so that students do not mistake copying notes for learning or assume that quantity is quality. The teacher's role is to 'produce new imaginations' about learning.

The problem with the habit of assigning low-level exercises to lower-attaining students, who are often also from poor and marginalized communities, is not just the 'low expectations' often referred to in school improvement literature, it is the manifest lack of respect for the learners. The important issue is how to connect higher cognitive challenges to learners' experiences in a context of emotional support and affirmation.

A sense of place

Many of the chapters concern themselves with place-based learning. This use of context is not simply decorative or motivational; it is the foundation for cognition and reflective action. It has a strong affective and aesthetic dimension too (Chapters 8, 10 and 11), and the exploration and direct appreciation of local environments is a necessary means towards gaining a sense of planet Earth. In addition to first-hand visual experience, Chapter 10 suggests imaginative visualisations, thought experiments and tactile rituals, whereas the students in Chapter 9 benefit from computer-mediated access to distant continents, in tandem with young people from other schools.

Regaining control of time

It is important to defend the time it takes for young people to come close to real-world environments, which is too easily lost where there is pressure to hurry to the next item on a syllabus. Standard patterns of learning alienate from learners a sense of ownership over classroom activities; the teacher or the timetable decides on each activity and when it must finish and the product be handed over. In England, attempts have even been made by government agencies to standardize to the minute how each lesson should be divided up, under the illusion that learning will accelerate. Such approaches, besides impoverishing schooling, are also disrespectful of teachers.

Many chapters in this book demonstrate the importance of allowing learners more control over activities, with a more extended timeframe for research, creative projects leading to an exhibition (Chapters 3 and 4), or by building a nursery curriculum upon children's experiences and reactions in a 'slow-learning' rhythm (Chapter 11). Deep conceptual learning takes time – this is slow learning. Other chapters describe the benefit of pupils working with the same teacher for a longer section of the day or week (Chapter 8), of breaking with the regular timetable for a block of two to three days on a theme requiring interdisciplinary learning (Chapter 8), and of the different sense of pace when students engage with adults and outside agencies to solve a problem (Chapter 9). Chapter 10 shows how narrative can be used as a thread to develop a richer flow of experience and ideas.

Open architectures

To give back more control to the learners while maintaining a shared structure and building a learning community, many teachers have moved beyond the individual lesson as their primary planning unit and are working with more open architectures of curriculum organisation literally and metaphorically. Chapters 4, 8 and 9 describe the use of Storyline, a form of thematic work based on the outline of a narrative. Chapter 10 explains the benefits of a storythread for environmental learning. Other chapters illustrate the uses of project method based on an agreed problem or issue, or the advantages of engaging pupils in a real-world problem (Chapters 2, 4, 7, 8 and 9).

Critical and creative learning

Critical thinking is promoted in many different ways. Problem solving is central to the transformation of mathematics, used as a tool for critical understanding of injustice, as outlined in Chapter 15. Children learn the importance of philosophical questioning in Chapter 2. Local actions in Chapter 8 enable young people to raise critical questions about issues facing humanity.

But criticality is not enough if we wish to develop a spirit of hope in young people. In Chapter 11 children collaborate with creative artists to gain an experience of aesthetic creativity. The arts are unduly neglected in efficiency-driven curricula but give the combined satisfaction of personal expression, presentation to an audience, and the unity of 'head, heart and hands'.

Being clear about outcomes

There are many ways of framing learning so that it has a convincing outcome – involving some use value rather than simply the exchange value of marks, grades and test scores (Chapters 4, 8, 9, 10 and 14 provide rich examples). A sense of motivation arises, after a problem-solving and design process, from generating a product or presenting to an audience. This was envisaged a century ago by Dewey and has been well developed in recent decades in more progressive education systems. This also takes pedagogy in a different direction to the functionalism of vocationalist curricula. While recognizing the importance (and the motivation for older adolescents) of acquiring saleable skills, we should resist the increasing pressure to define education mainly in terms of production of human capital and enhanced productivity (Ball 2008; Rizvi and Lingard 2010).

Working with the disciplines

The formal knowledge deriving from academic disciplines provides learners with the linguistic or conceptual tools to name and frame their experiences in new ways and potentially opening up educational opportunities. Bringing disciplinary knowledge together with the life experiences of learners was strongly advocated by Dewey (1938); he saw experience and curriculum coming together to produce 'real' learning, rather than being kept as two polar and irreconcilable opposites. This accords with Vygotsky's (1978) social constructivist theory that language and other symbolic systems – our cultural inheritance – work as tools for understanding. It also relates to a 'critical realist' recognition (Bhaskar 1975) that the surfaces of phenomena may not of themselves reveal the deep structures and 'laws' of reality.

A particularly strong example of this dynamic is described in Chapter 15, where drawing on funds of knowledge involves taking phenomena from everyday life and making them critical. This pedagogy is in the Freirian tradition of re-presenting to learners aspects of their daily lives and helping learners to examine and analyse them in ways that reveal causal relations of injustice (Freire 1972a, 1972b). Thus social relations and school knowledges come together to help students understand and deconstruct their everyday lives. Here we see mathematics rooted in power relationships in the community and the pedagogical strengths of drawing knowledge from the students' lifeworlds and from their global awareness, shining the light of mathematical knowledge onto it to help learners make critical sense of their world and set about changing it.

It must also be emphasized that many of the schools represented in this book not only work with traditional disciplines but draw upon a broad repertoire of approaches to assist students in the process of knowledge building and (in the words of Chapter 10) produce 'new imaginations about learning'. These include generic techniques such as concept mapping and metacognitive reflection (Chapter 14), the deployment of ICT as a tool of global social connection (Chapter 9) and the development of new architectures of interdisciplinary learning (philosophy for children, project method, Storyline, storythread, and media production and real-world problem solving) (Chapters 2, 3, 4, 9 and 10, among others).

Rethinking inclusion and social justice

The 14 'case study' chapters of this book clearly represent a wide variety of local contexts, school systems, national cultures and political environments. The schools have different histories, starting points and trajectories for change. Some represent a response to high levels of poverty and marginalisation, whereas others are situated in more settled environments. All are built on an understanding that the inherited traditions of school-based education are socially, culturally and pedagogically inadequate because they are mismatched to the identities, cultures and needs of those they purport to serve. This has been exacerbated in recent decades by global commercial processes that have thoroughly transformed youth cultures and identities while at the same time pressuring schools and governments to accommodate to the standards incorporated in international tests. Such a situation presents a complex problem of inclusion for educators and institutions.

It is beyond doubt that poverty and marginalisation impact on levels of achievement and that substantially higher resources are needed to enable schools in more troubled neighbourhoods to respond to social distress and disruptive relationships. At the same time, raising aspirations is a political question: the collective decision to provide an engaging and fruitful education in neighbourhoods and communities, which the economic and political system has *made* disadvantaged, requires a conscious rejection of deficit thinking about students and their families and a joint commitment to working with them towards a better future. This is a politico-pedagogical challenge within and beyond the physical boundaries of the school. Thus, we are working with a deeper and broader construct of social justice than that now dominant in many schooling systems, which basically reconstitutes and reduces social justice to closing the performance gap on high-stakes, standardized tests.

School ethos

It is our contention that inclusion, adequately defined, is a central issue for all schools. With Slee (2011), we would acknowledge, however, that we need to spend more time on working against overt exclusions in schools than spending inordinate amounts of time defining inclusion. All schools include students experiencing physical or behavioural difficulties or emotional traumas. Schools are patterned according to often tacit assumptions about 'ability' or 'intelligence' and their bases, assumptions that can be deeply prejudicial. The major divisions in society according to 'race' (including language needs), ethnicity (cultural differences), gender (along with sexuality), disabilities and social class (exacerbated in many places by extensive poverty), with associated patterns of prejudice and discrimination, are reflected to different degrees in schools. A lack of commitment concerning these issues simply strengthens prejudicial attitudes and habits and ensures exclusion for many students. Even beyond this, however, we would argue the need to reflect and debate the extent to which young people in general, with their rich identities and cultures, are genuinely included in the school as community.

A strategic German conference in the mid-1990s, 'Future of education – school of the future' (Bildungskommission NRW 1995), agreed the following statement of aspiration:

> *School is a Home for Learning*
> * a place where everybody is welcome, where learners and teachers are accepted in their individuality and difference
> * a place where people are allowed time to grow up, to take care of one another and be treated with respect
> * a place whose rooms invite you to stay, offer you the chance to learn and stimulate you to learn and show initiative
> * a place where diversions and mistakes are allowed but where evaluation in the form of feedback gives you a sense of direction
> * a place for intensive work and where it feels good to learn
> * a place where learning is infectious.

Unless the ethos of a school is inclusive in such ways to all of its members, the attempt to include particular groups of students will be conflictual and frustrating. Conversely, schools that do not reach out to students with particular needs or talents are less likely to overcome traditional rigid behavioural patterns and expectations and will be experienced as alienating by many of today's young people.

Inclusion involves both respect for and attention to the needs of all students. 'Inclusion' can never be limited to the assimilation of 'different' individuals into a preexisting structure or set of norms; the structure and norms of traditional schooling need rethinking to reach out to the diversity of students who are expected to inhabit schools for ten or more years of their lives.

Polis

The concept of 'polis' (explicit in Chapter 3) underpins all the contributions to this book. Schools contribute to the formation of a polis in three ways: by operating as democratic communities; by teaching students about histories, philosophies and practices of democracies; and by supporting democratic actions at neighbourhood, national and even global scales. This central ideal provides strategic direction to the change process, the transformation of internal policies, practices, relationships and ethos and the way the school connects to its environment, and its curricular as well as pedagogical development (Chapters 3, 7, 8, 10, 14 and 15, among others).

Going beyond a more rudimentary emphasis on 'student/pupil voice', contributors emphasize agency, participation, community and identity among learners, teachers and families. The learners' citizenship is respected and is a driving force for change and political engagement. Recurrent themes are concern for the environment (Chapters 7, 8 and 10) and the recovery of dignity and well-being in marginalized cultures and communities (Chapters 2, 6, 7 and 15, and others).

This is not to suggest abandoning adult responsibility for the internal ordering of the school or an idealization of young people that overlooks degrees of immaturity or the habits and attitudes produced by their experiences of life. Clearly teachers cannot ignore the impact of consumerism or demeaning ideologies such as racism, sexism, disableism, or homophobia, which are often internalized by young people as low self-worth and result in pessimism about their intellectual capabilities and potential (e.g. Chapters 2 and 6).

School should be a space where limiting ideologies and internalized prejudices can be discussed and challenged, and where habits of a *caring* political engagement can be cultivated. The cultivation of an orderly educative community, the school as a 'safe village' for growing up, is the material foundation for the school's intellectual endeavours and its students' confrontations with the world's problems. Conversely, serious intellectual engagements, such as that nurtured through Philosophy for Children (Chapter 2), promote attitudes of mutual care based on critical reflection and a questioning disposition.

Anti-deficit, anti-pathologizing discourses

The strong boundary between traditional schools and their geographical neighbourhoods is limiting for all schools, as it hinders the partnership between teachers and parents and reduces opportunities for school learning to build upon family- and community-based learning. It is particularly problematic in impoverished neighbourhoods, where the teacher's isolation from students' families and vernacular lifeworlds creates a professional learning gap, which is all too easily filled by pathologizing generalisations. Even in the most troubled environments, teachers can develop a deep understanding of their students, with all their complexities, contradictions, hopes and fears.

Research demonstrates that the vast majority of parents and families are greatly concerned about the future of the next generation and understand the importance of education for increasing life chances, even if this does not translate into unqualified support for schooling (Chapters 6 and 14) or the capacity to support young people in school. Most families are caring and hopeful for their children's futures, even if they are struggling financially and emotionally.

Where there has been a long history of racial oppression (Chapter 6) or decades of unemployment (Chapter 13), parents themselves may need to be reasssured that their children do have ability, that they can succeed at school. The teachers in such schools insist on a perspective of 'complex hope' involving 'an optimism of the will that recognises the historical and structural difficulties that have to be overcome' (Grace 1994: 57).

Working with differentiation and aspirations

Another related and important issue is that of what is sometimes called *differentiation*: the manner in which schools respond to achievement differences in a class or in the student population. The schools represented in this book have found ways of responding to diverse needs and talents without stigmatising, dividing or ranking into hierarchies of 'ability' (which, of course, often amount to different prior experiences linked closely to parental education and occupational status). As Mike Rose (2005) has recently argued, the notion of ability has been defined to equate to particular kinds of book work, whereas the intelligences embedded in practical and manual work have been discounted. Many of the chapters in this book show that there is no necessary division between hand and head and that education that uses a range of approaches does indeed allow many more young people to be successful.

Ironically, in England in recent years, teachers have been called upon both to 'raise expectations' and to increase the division of learners into 'ability groups'. There is considerable evidence in these chapters (e.g. Chapters 5, 6, 7 and 14) that raising expectations should be seen as a political and not just a technical issue; high expectations are collectively co-constructed as an act of resistance, a defiance of the limits assumed by a divided economy and society and its ideologies. However, also in England, some groups of teachers and schools have resisted these constraints and have been able to demonstrate that 'learning without limits' (Hart et al. 2004) is not only feasible but results in a higher achievement. The same is true of aspirations, as Appadurai (2004) has cogently argued: they are collective cultural capacities and 'form part of wider ethical and metaphysical ideas which derive from larger cultural norms' (p. 67). The school's task involves working with the community's aspirations and indeed challenging and raising them (Chapter 12).

Thus, in several of these chapters dealing with schools serving impoverished or marginalized communities, a necessary attention to core skills ('the basics') goes hand in hand with high intellectual challenges (e.g. Chapters 2 and 8) so that school tasks are educationally meaningful.

Rethinking school organisation and change processes

There is a substantial international literature, and especially in English-speaking countries, on school change (variously termed 'school improvement', 'school reform', 'school leadership'). Much of this shares the important conclusion that sustainable and meaningful change requires the full professional participation of teachers and other staff, gradually extended to recognize the rights of students and parents. The maxim 'You can't mandate what matters' (popularized by Fullan 1993, but derived from McLaughlin 1990) sums up this position in respect of education policy and leadership work in schools. There is broad agreement on the importance of staff development, collaboration in strategic planning, revising plans as you go, ongoing evaluation, support for developments in pedagogies, and so on. However, much of the generic emphasis on process fails to take hold of the social and cultural situations in which schools must operate. Nor, for the most part, does such an emphasis connect with other knowledge and theory of education around curriculum, pedagogy, inclusion, school ethos and community links.

More problematic is much of the literature on *leadership* that, despite its recent extensions towards 'distributed leadership', 'teacher leadership' and now 'pupil leadership', frequently suffers from a lack of political and pedagogical direction. Leadership, in its vernacular sense, surely involves recognizing the perils of the place in which you find yourselves and having some sense of where you could move to and how you might get there. The leadership manifest in the contributions to this book reflects this richer, vernacular sense of 'leadership' that is expressed through collaboratively developed statements of the common purposes of specific schools, augmenting or even resisting system-mandated demands. Such leadership develops intellectual resources at the school site to mediate the worst of systemic pressures.

A focus on learning is, of course, central to meaningful school change, and the transformation of learning and teaching lies at the heart of the change processes illustrated in every chapter of this book. However, learning does not take place in a vacuum; facilitating more successful and meaningful learning entails thinking about school structures, questions of power, the ways in which educators are able to reflect upon current practices, and how schools relate to broader systems of public policy, management and evaluation.

Many of the changes described in this book have taken place despite official discouragement or indifference; others with varying degrees of support. Whether changes are initiated on a local or a systems level, whether they start with two or three individual teachers within a school or with the attempt to reform a national curriculum, the concept of *critical mass* is of vital importance. Innovative educators have to work together in whatever niche they can find to demonstrate the possibility and worth of doing things differently.

The word *vision* has become a cliché by now in the literature on school management and leadership, yet it is often used in hollowed-out ways. Such hollowing out is linked to broader politics today, which are subsumed by the mundane managing of the everyday in managerialist and incrementalist ways, lacking any aspirational and new social imaginary about a better future. As John Berger (2007: 36) has asked, 'How to continue without a plausible vision of the future? Why have we lost any view of what is beyond as life-time?' At the heart of the development process of all of the schools and networks represented in this book is a real sense of political, environmental, cultural and social vision: a sense that schools must be different because the world must be different, and a recognition that schools can and must contribute to this. Schools both help create and manifest aspirations about a better future; they help construct and express such a social imaginary.

The commitment to 'doing justice' is, indeed, a central driving force behind deep and sustainable school change. This kind of change arises when educators feel the contradiction between the patterns of their daily actions (methodologies, rituals and so on) and the needs both of their students and the world at large. There is a tension between the residues of a past based on exploitative power relations and a just and sustainable future. They feel a contrast between the traditional expectations and mores of schooling and their sense of what their students could become. And, of course, schools serve both collective 'public good' purposes and individual purposes associated with the advancement of some and not of others. Leadership in schools continually works with and against the tensions inherent in these competing purposes. This is a very real challenge for educational leadership.

The following paragraphs are not exhaustive but seek to draw together some important threads to elucidate the processes of change described in various chapters, as a resource from which others may learn.

Using educational theory

The theories developed by educators in the past, themselves engaged in a struggle to make education more meaningful, productive and progressive, are a vital resource for changing schools today. A central lesson, in addition to the importance of conditions that aid cooperative design and reflection, is that these processes are strongly related to educational and social theory. (See for example references to Sizer, Chapter 2; Dewey and the European reform tradition, Chapter 3; Piaget and Vygotsky, Chapter 4; and so on.)

The school teachers, sometimes with university partners, see themselves as knowledge builders, in some cases writing and publishing for a wider readership. They are research- and practice-informed and research- and practice-informing. The Bielefeld Laboratory School (Chapter 3) provides a particularly strong example of academic partnership, with its arrangements for part-time release from teaching to raise planning and evaluation to the level of research. Lillian de Lissa (Chapter 11) provides another important kind of connection in its creative partnerships with artists and performers. Thus, the schools written about in this book can be seen to be producing theory and practising it.

Deep questioning is integral to school culture

In all these schools, processes are at work for building a solid, foundational and shared sense of educational purposes. As a step towards reinventing Buranda State School (Chapter 2), the teachers had to discuss why schools exist and reached the understanding encapsulated by 'Every single child, as good as they can be'. Similarly, these teachers also had to reflect and discuss what their personal teaching philosophies were. This is the foundation for shared leadership, which means far more than processes of administrative delegation. Professional community and teacher collaboration must be constructed around an agreed philosophy of schooling.

Using teamwork

Of the utmost importance, we believe, are teams of staff who can collaboratively design the curriculum and teaching approaches besides evaluating the benefits and drawbacks of change processes and outcomes. Whilst structures vary across the schools in this book, many are characterized by collaborative design and evaluation in coherent teams, but linked strongly to whole-school gatherings and representative groups and with a strong sense of the direction and aspirations of the school as a whole, including community involvement.

Ringstabekk School (Chapter 4, and see also Chapter 9) is uniquely well placed, as it builds upon a standard structural feature of Norwegian 'youth schools' (13- to 16-year-olds) that a team of teachers should work mainly or entirely with a particular year group. Given that teachers are each qualified to teach two or three subjects, a team of five or six teachers is able to cover the curriculum, provide learning support where needed, provide pastoral care and guidance, and maintain strong contacts with parents. Relationships are close and relatively trouble-free, and the team is to a great extent self-managing, with the power to alter the use of time, to organize fieldwork visits and all-day special events at two weeks' notice. In effect, each year level is a school-within-a-school.

Networks

Also important is participation in wider networks of educational reform, which can now stretch across the globe through internet contacts. Networks may be formally established (see especially Chapter 13) or consist of many informal relationships brought about by frequent visits (Chapter 3 and others). They may be built on the principle of researching and sharing their own practice (Chapter 14) or be grounded in an already existing network, such as the Brazilian social movement referenced in Chapter 7. In all these circumstances, however, it is clear that practical breakthroughs arise through intellectual struggle and critical reflection, not by association alone.

An important condition is the flexibility that comes from recognizing that each participant school has its own path of development. This is the 'thisness' of each school (Thomson 2002). Equally important, however, are the sharing and development of a pedagogical and social vision.

Use of time/space

A number of chapters raise questions about the organisation and use of time. The norm in secondary schools in many countries has been that students should move every hour (or less) to a different subject specialist. Some schools represented here have developed alternative and more flexible patterns in the use of space, time and expertise that are more conducive to engaged and sustainable learning. Many such alternatives are based on reducing the number of classes taught by each teacher and, conversely, the number of teachers whom each student encounters (see Sizer 1985). An extended contact between students and at least some of their teachers facilitates greater responsiveness to the particular circumstances of students.

We also reflect that 'slow learner' has been a frequent euphemism for 'limited in ability', whereby students who are seen as lacking academic ability, narrowly measured, are slowed down still further through the use of atomized worksheets and tedious repetitive exercises. Yet, slow learning, by analogy to slow cooking, can be a virtue, providing a depth of understanding of exemplary content (Chapter 4), whereas fast-paced lessons merely skim the surface. The slower pace of deep conceptual learning stands in stark contrast to the rapid curriculum coverage often demanded by systemic curriculum and testing demands.

School–community relationships

Though schools in disadvantaged areas need a greater coherence and mutual understanding between staff and parents, they can be doubly disadvantaged by instability of both the local population and the school staff. Policies based on market competition and on 'naming and shaming' not only make it more difficult to recruit well-qualified and willing teachers but demoralize and stigmatize existing staff, encouraging their early flight to 'easier' schools. In such a context, it is particularly important to identify key individuals with a power to link the school to the wider community (Chapter 11). Involving parents with great frequency as audiences and receivers of their children's schoolwork motivates young learners but also parents for whom bringing up their children may be both extremely difficult but, at the same time, their only satisfaction in life.

Dealing with the wider environment and accountability

It would be disingenuous to pretend that all education regimes are equally conducive to positive change but, equally – though this is parlous – some schools do prove capable of negotiating the contradictions in their environment. In a high-surveillance system, of course, the risks remain high that a school which is treading a new path will not have time to show results before someone blows a whistle and demands that they follow the 'normal rules' (Hargreaves 2003).

The relationship between innovative schools and the surrounding school system inevitably throws up political dilemmas. These are often marked by discursive ambiguity, as when innovative teachers use a popular term such as *standards* or *expectations* but with a different accentuation (Volosinov 1986; Chapter 12, for example).

Supporting public education systems

One particularly contentious issue in some countries is the argument that privatized school management, including schools run by profit-making businesses, will resolve problems that public systems of governance are incapable of. Many of the chapters in this book show clearly that radical change can and does occur in public school systems, especially when supported by additional concessions, resources and encouragement. The Bielefeld Laboratory School (Chapter 3) has a singular governance structure connecting its development processes both to the university and to regional government while ensuring that the centre of gravity and responsibility for its students reside firmly in the school. Paradoxically, the Social Justice School featured in Chapter 15, a charter school in the United States, established its independence through political action in resistance to the conservative breakup and business takeover of the Chicago public school system in order to retain and develop its strong community roots (see Lipman 2004; Lipman and Haines 2007). It is no easy matter, however, in a high-surveillance system to secure a sufficient degree of independence over curriculum, pedagogy and assessment. We note the stance of the Movement of Landless Workers (Chapter 7), which both insists on public funding of education and equally insists on maintaining maximum autonomy in school ethos and curriculum, including teacher education.

Making philosophy practical

In his book *The Challenge and Burden of Historical Time*, socialist philosopher István Mészáros (2008) argues that global capitalism's sense of time is built upon a sense of 'exploitable labour time'; there is an insatiable drive to achieve greater profitability through more intensive and extensive production, regardless of human need, with a consequent loss of historical time consciousness. It is no accident that neoliberal ideologists espouse slogans such as the 'natural order' of the here and now, the 'end of history', and 'there is no alternative'.

> The apologists of capital did – and continue to do – everything they could in order to obliterate people's awareness of historical time, in the interest of eternalizing their system.
>
> (Mészáros 2008: 21)

By contrast:

> Only those who have a vital interest in the institution of a positively sustainable social order, and thus in securing the survival of humanity, can really appreciate the importance of historical time at this critical juncture of social development. ... The time of the oppressed and the exploited, with its vital dimension of the future, cannot be obliterated. It has its own logic of unfolding, as the irrepressible historical time of our age of make or break. Only the total destruction of humanity could put an end to it.
>
> (Mészáros 2008: 22)

In many ways, this dichotomy is mirrored in paradigms of school change. The hegemonic version, espoused by many governments around the world, is based on a straightforward drive to improve test scores through intensifying learning processes. It is marked by measures such as 'time on task' (regardless of the in/significance of the task) and the demand to raise test scores, whether or not the tests are valid or reliable. There is a diminishing sense of the longer, slower timescale of personal development, let alone of collective historical time and human aspirations.

A different sense of learning time is suggested in the schools and networks featured in this book, schooling as a time for critical reflection on the world. Critical thinking is not a 'skill' to be taught fundamentally as a set of techniques – though they exist and can be drawn upon – but a perspective and attitude of challenge to a world that is deeply unjust, dangerous and destructive. Schools have always provided a 'space apart' from reality; the Greek root of the word *school* was synonymous with *leisure* as opposed to work (available, of course, only to a privileged minority). At the same time, in different forms at different points in history, forms of school have emerged as a place apart that facilitates moral engagement with the real world – which enables participants to see beyond the day-to-day, reach to the heart of the matter, and envisage new and better ways of living. This was true, in different ways, of Socrates' discussion circles in ancient Greece, the centres of learning of the Islamic world, the great medieval universities, and of the schools set up by reformers such as Owen, Pestalozzi, Montessori, Dewey and Freire.

There has been an important political debate in recent decades about whether, and how much, schools can make a difference. This has generally been understood in rather simple quantitative terms, with statistical attempts to apportion gains in test scores to socio-economic background and school or classroom effectiveness. The subtitle of our book goes beyond this, to speak of the difference education can make to the world. The educators who have generously written chapters for this book clearly believe that schools not only can make a world of difference to individual learners but must make a significant difference to the world they inherit – that teachers have a role to play in developing young citizens' powers to make the world a better place.

The literatures about schools 'making a difference' often work around a binary, emphasising either that schools can make almost *no* difference until social inequalities in the broader society are overcome or that schools and teachers can make *a major* difference irrespective of these contexts of inequality. Our position sits across this binary (Lingard et al. 2008). Educational change committed to equality and a better world requires political commitments to overcoming inequality and redistributive funding to schools serving poor communities. Today, schools and policy also need to engage in a politics of recognition, working with, valuing and acknowledging differences; this is a real challenge at the systemic level, as bureaucratic and managerialist systems tend to universalize and essentialize schools and school populations in their imperatives and exhortations to schools and teachers.

We certainly need reform of schooling practices and government policies. But schools can make a difference even under restrictive contemporary policies, as many chapters in this book illustrate. Following Bourdieu, we would suggest that there is a reproductive logic in the practices and forms of schooling supported by default structures, habits and norms. Many wonderful examples of schools and teachers in this book have illustrated how that logic *can* and *must* be challenged. Complex individual and collective, educational and broader political movements are required to achieve the kinds of change required in society, schooling systems, schools and educational practices to achieve that long revolution towards a better world. As Martin Luther King observed, 'The arc of the moral universe is long but it bends towards justice.'

This project is impossible without philosophical thinking, in terms of reflection and debate among students but also around questions of school change. Though the words *vision, mission* and *values* have frequently been trivialized in the school improvement literature, the level of reflection that they signify is indispensable before and during any worthwhile process of educational change.

Philosophy involves a grappling with meanings, the meanings of words and actions, the significance of everyday cultural phenomena that we often simply take for granted, the meaning of life. It does not necessarily require a distinct or difficult vocabulary and can be made accessible (as we see from many examples in this book) even for the very young. Equally, all teachers are capable of reflecting on the significance of their school culture – the meaning, orientation and impact of everyday behaviours, rituals, discourses and relationships – in the wider context of a philosophical reflection about the state of the world. This cannot replace a process of grappling with the details of classroom methodology or school organization, but without it even the most meticulously planned changes in lesson plans and school timetables will turn out to be insignificant rearrangements of inherited modes of schooling.

Paulo Freire remains a shining example of philosophy made practical in educational reform. His early work as a teacher of adult literacy working with desperately poor peasants and agricultural labourers in North-East Brazil shows how discussion about basic words – home, work, landowner, hunger, city – becomes a process of problematization, of teasing out the threads of power that run through everyday habits and encounters. However, one does not have to read many pages of *Pedagogy of the Oppressed* (Freire 1972a), for example, to realize the extent to which philosophical reflection, about learning and about society, underpins and drives forward detailed planning of the curriculum and teaching. This philosophical reflection is not resolved once and for all, but must engage with changing realities. Characteristically, on his return to Brazil from exile after the military dictatorship, Freire urged those who wished to follow and promote his methods to 'rethink Paulo Freire' for new times.

Schooling is only a part of education, but it is highly significant as a site either for the domestication of each new generation or for launching them on a path of discovery and potential liberation. It can serve either to reproduce ideologies or to provide the resources and habits to question and move beyond them. School structures and cultures and patterns of classroom language and learning can either reinforce social inequality or challenge it.

In recent years, school change has predominantly been geared towards serving the needs of the economy more efficiently. As Stephen Ball (2008: 11–12) has argued:

> The social and economic purposes of education have been collapsed into a single, overriding emphasis on policy making for economic competitiveness and an increasing neglect or sidelining (other than in rhetoric) of the social purposes of education.

But for all of us who are concerned about the scale of crushing poverty in our own country or city and across the planet; for those of us who struggled to prevent the launching of wars that we predicted would be mayhem; for the millions of educators and billions of young people who live with a heightened sense of the fragility of planet Earth and its ecology – education involves more than this. Alongside the powerful resources afforded by new technologies, *changing schools* is an urgent challenge and a significant contribution to (though never a substitute for) the struggle to imagine and create a better future.

The schools represented in this book are not only committed to this struggle, but also serve to demonstrate its potentials, possibilities and benefits. Their example gives us all a sense of optimism and hope for a more just, and truly educational, future.

References

Appadurai, A. (2004) 'The capacity to aspire: culture and the terms of recognition.' In V. Rao and M. Walton (eds) *Culture and Public Action*. Stanford: Stanford University Press.

Ball, S. (2008) *The Education Debate*. Bristol: Policy Press.

Barnes, D. (1971) 'Language in the secondary classroom.' In D. Barnes, J. Britton and H. Rosen (eds) *Language, the Learner and the School*. Harmondsworth: Penguin.

Berger, J. (2007) *Hold Everything Dear: Dispatches on Survival and Resistance*. London: Verso.

Bhaskar, R. (1975) *A Realist Theory of Science*. Leeds: Leeds Books (republished 1997 London: Verso).

Bildungskommission NRW (1995) *Zukunft der Bildung – Schule der Zukunft* [Future of education – education of the future]. Denkschrift der Kommission 'Zukunft der Bildung – Schule der Zukunft' beim Ministerpräsidenten des Landes Nordrhein-Westfalen, Neuwied.

Bourdieu, P. (2004) 'The forms of capital.' In S. Ball (ed.) *The Routledge Falmer Reader in Sociology of Education*. London: Routledge .

Dewey, J. (1938) *Experience and Education*. New York: Collier Books.

Freire, P. (1972a) *Pedagogy of the Oppressed*. Harmondsworth: Penguin.

Freire, P. (1972b) *Cultural Action for Freedom*. Harmondsworth: Penguin.

Fullan, M. (1993) *Change Forces*. London: Falmer.

Grace, G. (1994) *Education and the City: Theory, History and Contemporary Practice*. London: Routledge and Kegan Paul.

Hargreaves, A. (2003) *Teaching in the Knowledge Society: Education in the Age of Insecurity*. New York: Teachers College Press.

Hart, S., Dixon, A., Drummond, M. and McIntyre, D. (2004) *Learning without Limits*. Maidenhead: Open University Press.

Labaree, D. (2010) *Someone Has to Fail: The Zero-Sum Game of Public Schooling*. Cambridge, MA: Harvard University Press.

Lingard, B., Nixon, J. and Ranson, S. (2008) 'Remaking education for a globalized world: policy and pedagogic possibilities.' In B. Lingard, J. Nixon and S. Ranson (eds) *Transforming Learning in Schools and Communities*. London: Continuum.

Lipman, P. (2004) *High Stakes Education: Education, Inequality, Globalization and Urban School Reform*. New York: Routledge.

Lipman, P. and Haines, N. (2007) 'From education accountability to privatization and African American exclusion – Chicago public schools' renaissance 2010.' *Educational Policy*, 21, 471–502.

McLaughlin, M. (1990) 'The Rand change agent study revisited.' *Educational Researcher*, 5, 11–16.

Mészáros, I. (2008) *The Challenge and Burden of Historical Time: Socialism in the Twenty-First Century*. New York: Monthly Review Press.

Moll, L. and Greenberg, J. (1990) 'Creating zones of possibilities: combining social contexts for instruction.' In L. Moll (ed.) *Vygotsky and Education*. Cambridge, MA: Harvard University Press.

Moore, R. (2008) 'Capital.' In M. Grenfell (ed.) *Pierre Bourdieu: Key Concepts*. Durham: Acumen.

Rizvi, F. and Lingard, B. (2010) *Globalizing Education Policy*. London: Routledge.

Rose, M. (2005) *The Mind at Work: Valuing the Intelligence of the American Worker*. New York: Penguin.

Sizer, T. R. (1985) *Horace's Compromise: The Dilemma of the American High School*. Boston: Houghton Mifflin.

Slee, R. (2011) *The Irregular School*. London: Routledge.

Thomson, P. (2002) *Schooling the Rustbelt Kids: Making the Difference in Changing Times*. Crows Nest: Allen and Unwin.

Volosinov, V. (1986) *Marxism and the Philosophy of Language*. Cambridge, MA: Harvard University Press.

Vygotsky, L. (1978) *Mind in Society: The Development of Higher Psychological Processes*. Cambridge, MA: Harvard University Press.

Index